News in Their Pockets

STUDIES IN MOBILE COMMUNICATION

Studies in Mobile Communication focuses on the social consequences of mobile communication in society.

Series Editors
Rich Ling, *Nanyang Technological University, Singapore*
Gerard Goggin, *University of Sydney, Australia*
Leopoldina Fortunati, *Università di Udine, Italy*

Haunting Hands: Mobile Practices and Loss
Kathleen M. Cumiskey and Larissa Hjorth

A Village Goes Mobile: Telephony, Mediation, and Social Change in Rural India
Sirpa Tenhunen

Negotiating Control: Organizations and Mobile Communication
Keri K. Stephens

Cultural Economies of Locative Media
Rowan Wilken

Transcendent Parenting: Raising Children in the Mobile Age
Sun Sun Lim

Shifting Dynamics of Contention in the Digital Age:
Mobile Communication and Politics in China
Jun Liu

News in Their Pockets: A Cross-City Comparative Study of Mobile News
Consumption in Asia
Ran Wei and Ven-hwei Lo

NEWS IN THEIR POCKETS

A Cross-City Comparative Study of Mobile News Consumption in Asia

Ran Wei and Ven-hwei Lo

Ran Wei is Professor at the School of Journalism and Communication, Chinese University of Hong Kong, and Distinguished Professor Emeritus at the University of South Carolina, U.S.A.

Ven-hwei Lo is Visiting Professor in the Department of Journalism, College of Communication, at Hong Kong Baptist University.

OXFORD
UNIVERSITY PRESS

OXFORD
UNIVERSITY PRESS

Oxford University Press is a department of the University of Oxford. It furthers
the University's objective of excellence in research, scholarship, and education
by publishing worldwide. Oxford is a registered trade mark of Oxford University
Press in the UK and certain other countries.

Published in the United States of America by Oxford University Press
198 Madison Avenue, New York, NY 10016, United States of America.

Library of Congress Cataloging-in-Publication Data
Names: Wei, Ran, 1962– author. | Lo, Ven-hwei, author.
Title: News in their pockets : a cross-city comparative study of mobile
news consumption in Asia / Ran Wei and Ven-hwei Lo.
Description: New York, NY : Oxford University Press, [2021] |
Series: Studies in mobile communication |
Includes bibliographical references and index.
Identifiers: LCCN 2020042608 | ISBN 9780197523728 (hardback) |
ISBN 9780197523735 (paperback) | ISBN 9780197523742 |
ISBN 9780197523766 | ISBN 9780197523759 (epub)
Subjects: LCSH: Journalism—Technological innovations. |
Cell phones and college students—East Asia. | College students as consumers—
East Asia. | News audiences—East Asia. | Smartphones—Social aspects—East Asia.
Classification: LCC PN5360 .W45 2021 | DDC 079.5—dc23
LC record available at https://lccn.loc.gov/2020042608

DOI: 10.1093/oso/9780197523728.001.0001

9 8 7 6 5 4 3 2 1

Paperback printed by Marquis, Canada
Hardback printed by Bridgeport National Bindery, Inc., United States of America

To our families with love for their unwavering support

CONTENTS

ACKNOWLEDGMENTS

This book is special to us in two significant ways: First, it is the cumulation of over two decades of research in mobile communications dating back to the 1990s. The most popular mobile technology for personal communication at that time was the pager, a predecessor of the ubiquitous mobile phone. The study of using pagers to access news expanded my research horizons in the emerging mobile media. Second, the book is a milestone of our collaboration that has run for more than 20 years. Dr. Lo is a guru in statistics, while writing is my strong suit. We make a perfect team for collaboration. Between us, we have coauthored three books and 35 journal articles, including several impactful studies on the mobile phone. Our previous works laid the solid foundation for this book. As the junior collaborator, I have learned so much from Dr. Lo over our long period of collaboration. For his generosity, mentoring, and good taste in wine, I'm forever grateful.

In my academic career spanning three decades, I have also had the good fortune to work with an international coterie of brilliant scholars in Asia and America who share my interest in mobile communication, such as Drs. Xiaoge Xu at Ningbo-Nottingham University, Katherine Yi-ning Chen at National Chengchi University in Taipei, Edson Tandoc of Nanyang Technological University in Singapore, and Guoliang Zhang from Shanghai Jiao Tong University in China. In many ways, this book is derived from and built upon our previous studies that include coauthored articles published in *New Media & Society* (2014), *Journalism Studies* (2020), and *Communication & Society* (2014), as well as several papers presented at annual conferences of the International Communication Association (ICA, in 2012 in Phoenix, Arizona; 2019 in Washington, DC) and the International Telecommunication Society (ITS, in 2019 in Bangkok, Thailand). Directly or indirectly, our collaborators in these publications contributed to this book. We're particularly grateful to Dr. Katherine Yi-ning Chen, who contributed to Chapter 3 on motives of mobile phone use, and Drs. Edson

Tandoc and Guoliang Zhang, who contributed to Chapter 6 about media credibility. They also generously helped coordinate the focus groups in Taipei, Singapore, and Shanghai. Their gracious assistance and collegiality are duly acknowledged.

Our thanks go next to Rich Ling and his editorial committee, who oversee the Oxford University Press mobile communication serials, and the two anonymous reviewers, who offered constructive suggestions on our proposal. We are grateful to a number of former colleagues of mine at the University of South Carolina for their enthusiastic support of the initial idea—Drs. Keith Kenny, Kenneth Campbell, Augie Grant, and Jane O'Boyle, and Profs. Scott Farrand, Doug Fisher, and Ernie Wiggins. We're particularly thankful to Mr. Bruce Burton, a former newspaper editor, who read the drafts and offered critical but highly constructive comments to improve each chapter. We also wish to thank the following assistants at the Chinese University of Hong Kong: Darron Chan organized a focus group under a stressful situation; Leo Liu and Yi Jing Jing helped with the tedious but essential tasks of verifying sources, checking references, and formatting tables and figures.

Writing a book is a major undertaking and requires commitment. Without sacrifices (like precious time at tennis courts) and the support and love from our families, we would not have been able to complete this project in 12 months. During these disruptive and testing times, we are especially grateful for being able to stay in touch closely with members of our families virtually, defying the barriers of time, distance, and even a global pandemic. They are our personal cheerleaders (greetings like "Are you done with your book?" sound like a lovely cheer). To them, we dedicate this book!

This book originates from the curiosity about pagers as a mass medium, a marginal idea at that time, and is completed at a time when smartphones serve as a lifeline for millions of users around the world during the height of the COVID-19 pandemic. We thank the editors at Oxford University Press for their professionalism during a public health crisis and their assistance in the publishing process.

CHAPTER 1
News Gone Mobile

THE MOBILE REVOLUTION AND NEWS ON THE GO

Picture Taipei in 2018, where a 21-year-old girl by the name of Jennifer, a political communication student at a Taipei university, wants to learn about current events. Though there is a newspaper on the table in her parents' living room, she opts to turn to ET Today (a popular news aggregator site) on her smartphone instead; she reads the full accounts and forwards it to a fellow student in her seminar class to suggest bringing it up for a class discussion. Then, on that very same smartphone, she opens up Twitter to see that her professor also had tweeted his thoughts on the news. By the time she arrived at her seminar class, she had read the news, discussed it with a peer, and had first-hand knowledge of her teacher's perspective.

Just a little over 2,000 miles southwest of Taipei, Debbie, a female journalism student in Singapore, starts off her day by reading only the headlines of the paper that her family subscribes to in order to keep up with the world. For a deep read and follow-up on the news, she and her peers in school rely on mobile news sites like the *Straits Times* (the leading English paper in Singapore), apps like Reddit, the Facebook news feed, and Google News throughout their busy day in college.

Inspired by the stories of Jennifer and Debbie, and similar experiences of our college students in Asia staying informed via the always-on smartphone, this book examines trends and patterns of accessing and consuming news via the mobile phone among Asia's young generations of Y (aka millennials or digital natives) and Z (aka centennials or the mobile-first digital natives), who are self-taught sophisticated users of mobile phone and devices. We're curious about their motives and experiences of

News in Their Pockets. Ran Wei and Ven-hwei Lo, Oxford University Press (2021). © Oxford University Press.
DOI: 10.1093/oso/9780197523728.003.0001

reading news on the mobile phone they carry with them 24/7. More importantly, it addresses the high stakes in consumption of mobile news in terms of whether it has the potential to fill the void left by declining traditional media and serving as a democratic function in turning Asia's civic-minded young people into active citizens.

It is a globally acknowledged trend that consuming news on the fastest-diffused communication technology in human history—the mobile phone—constitutes a key aspect of the ongoing *mobile revolution* (i.e., the wireless telecommunication technology as an engine of economic growth and infrastructure expansion that is changing the lives of millions worldwide). However, the phenomenon of using the mobile phone as a device to receive news began only in the early 1990s in Finland, when news was first delivered to 2G phones as texting in SMS (short message service). Shortly after the launch of the 3G network and the debut of smartphones (e.g., IBM's Simon Personal Communicator) in 1992, news that reached mobile screens expanded into on-demand news pushed by news organizations to subscribers. Following the launches of the iPhone in 2007 and iPad in 2010, respectively, the mobile phone converged with the Internet. The always-on broadband connectivity, availability of social media platforms, and development of mobile news apps enabled users to access news 24/7 on their phones or smart devices (Kopomaa, 2000; Pestin, 2011; Weiss, 2013; Wolf & Schnauber, 2015). Soon enough, the mobile phone has morphed into an information and communication hub for users on the go.

At the dawn of 5G networks, as the mobile phone continues to saturate the world's populations, consumption of news that is convenient, quick, brief, and in real time via the mobile phone has gone mainstream (Poindexter, 2016). A report issued by Knight Foundation (2016) found that nearly the entire population of U.S. adult mobile phone users (89% of 144 million) consumed news on their mobile devices. In the six-year period between 2013 and 2019, the percentage of Americans who used mobile phones and smart devices to access news doubled to 57% from 28% (*Reuters Institute Digital News Report*, 2019).

To respond to the rise of the mobile phone as gateways to consume news content and take advantage of the mobile opportunities, news organizations around the world have pursued a *mobile-first strategy* (i.e., designing a news site first for the mobile screen and then adapting it to larger screens like the PC; see Hill & Bradshaw, 2018) in creating and delivering digital news content. The popular practice to deliver news includes mobile versions of websites, news delivered on social networking sites (e.g., Twitter updates), news blogs or bloggers via mobile phones, tagging, and news apps such as CNN and BuzzFeed. As Poindexter (2016) pointed out, the trend of mobile-first news consumption has upended the news media industries in forcing them to respond to the screen shift from PC to mobile. By the end of 2011, more than half of newspapers with a sizable circulation in the United States had built a mobile presence.

THE EVER-EVOLVING MOBILE NEWS

It is hard to believe that all of this started only in 1993 when Nokia introduced the first phone (the Nokia 2010) that popularized texting SMS of up to 160 characters (Gayomali, 2012). The technology was quickly employed to send news alerts to subscribers (Westlund, 2013). News in SMS texting relied on radio telegraph (e.g., sending messages by radio waves), the same category of wireless technology used in an earlier personal communication device—the pager. In addition to paging personal messages, pager system operators provided subscribers with news updates, headlines of breaking events, and weather and traffic conditions, thus turning the pager into a mobile outlet to disseminate news (Leung & Wei, 1999a).

In 2000, news services in the form of SMS were launched in Finland. It was considered the debut of mobile news (Cellphones Nowadays Blog, 2012). Other operators followed suit in offering news via mobile phones as part of the mobile data service. Table 1.1 provides a timeline of key events and developmental stages of mobile news, from which it can be argued that two key technologies aided the earliest generation of news packaged and delivered to mobile phone subscribers on 2G networks: SMS and push. Headlines were aggregated from news media and pushed to subscribers in SMS and MMS (Multimedia Message Service).

Substantial progress in news service to mobile phone users took place during the 3G (third generation of wireless telecommunications technology) era in the new millennium.[1] 3G networks offered faster speed in data transfer and mobile broadband service (e.g., mobile Internet and Wi-Fi hot spots). It was in the 3G era that third-party content providers and traditional news media organizations experienced substantial growth of mobile data service, in which news sites—for example, CNN Mobile—were pushed to subscribers. In 2014, the *Women's Daily of China* launched a mobile version of its print paper, setting the trend of mobile news publishing known as "*Shouji Bao*" (paper in MMS for the mobile phone) in China.

Meanwhile, news videos were added to mobile data service (Wolf & Hohlfeld, 2012) to enrich the presentation of news. But as Westlund (2010) noted, the speed and cost of loading pictures and videos limited the usage of mobile news sites at a time when 3G networks were unreliable and short

Table 1.1 TIMELINE OF MOBILE NEWS EVOLUTION WORLDWIDE

2G and the early 2000s: Push technology and news alerts

- In 1984, Matti Makkonen, a Finish engineer, advanced the idea of sending texting messages known as SMS over the cellular network.
- In 1997, push technology, a service that pushes digital information to a message receiver from a server through push notifications, debuted (Lasica, 1997). Media organizations the San Jose Mercury News, CNN Interactive, and ESPNET adopted the technology to send personalized news to subscribers.
- Push news services were adopted in non-Western countries, such as Brazil, China, Kenya, and Uganda (Westlund, 2013).
- In 2000, news service in SMS to subscribers was launched in Finland.

3G in the late 2000s: Mobile devices emerged as a primary means of accessing news

- In 2007, Apple's iPhone was introduced in the United States, starting the shift from PC to mobile devices for news consumption.
- News organizations in the West sought to make mobile news delivery more user-friendly, by including QR technology or providing flat-rate subscription (R. Wei, Lo, Xu, Chen, & Zhang, 2014; Westlund, 2008).
- The advent of Wi-Fi-enabled smartphones with touch screen led to the fast growth in consumption of news-related content and services (Westlund, 2013). Consumers were able to access news content with mobile browsers, such as Safari.
- 3G technologies and smartphones led to news content presented in "interactive and individualized multimedia" for the mobile screen (Van Eimeren & Frees, 2006, p. 408).
- Legacy news media started developing their own mobile apps to provide news on a mobile operation system (either Apple's IOS or Google's Android), such as BBC News and CNN. Stand-alone mobile news apps such as Reddit and Bussfeed gained popularity.

4G in the 2010s: The golden years of mobile phone and devices

- In 2019, *Nikkei* (Japan Economic Daily) accelerated its "digital first" strategy. The paper started to publish stories first online, before sending them for print.
- Mobile-first strategy gained momentum (Hill & Bradshaw, 2018). Webster (2011) characterized the mobile-first industry transition as shifting from a "push" to "pull" model.
- By 2011, 62% of American daily newspapers having more than 25,000 circulations owned a mobile application, and 44% of Swedish newspapers had a mobile news site. Mobile apps were widely offered by legacy news media in most countries, such as China, India, and Australia.
- Meanwhile, mobile phone users also access news via popular social media platforms such as Facebook and Twitter, making social networking sites (SNSs) their primary news sources (Shim, You, Lee, & Go, 2015).

of wide deployment; adoption of non-iPhone types of smartphones was slow. Technically, early models of smartphones relied on tiny pixelated screens. Due to such technological limitations, the mobile web for news featured hyperlinking with no imbedded tools for sharing or commenting. As Dimmick, Feaster, and Hoplamazian (2011) observed, consuming news on the mobile phone using numerical pads amounts to nothing more than a marginal phenomenon in the early 2000s.

Then, the debut of iPhone in 2007 changed everything. Though it was not the first smartphone, it was a game changer. The iPhone was one of its kind with a touch screen and adapted 3G networking technologies and mobile hotspot (Wi-Fi) capability. Its operating system was equipped with a full HTML web browser; the touch screen made swiping and scrolling the new ways to navigate, replacing the clumsy buttoning method. In addition, the availability of the full QWERTY keyboard enabled users to text and e-mail on the phone just as on a PC. Table 1.2 highlights both barriers and growth factors to mobile news.

Thanks to the popularity of the iPhone, and proliferation of other, less expensive but fully capable smartphones such as Samsung and LG, and the deployment of the next generation of network technology—4G (LTE—long-term evolution)—in 2009, news delivered to the mobile phone has diversified from text messaging (e.g., SMS, MMS) and e-mail in the first decade of the 21st century to QR code, video clips, mobile versions of websites, trending news on social media, podcasts, and mobile news apps in the second decade. News apps such as AP Mobile on IOS and Android have emerged as a platform for accessing news, further changing the way digital news is accessed and consumed.

In summary, while the news went mobile in the 3G era, news accessed from the mobile phone has gone mainstream in the 4G era. By 2016, more people accessed and consumed news from their mobile phones and digital devices than they did from desktop computers, according to a Reuters Institute report (Newman, Fletcher, Kalogeropoulos, Levy, & Nielsen, 2017). The Pew Research Center (2014) highlighted this trend in its *State of the News Media* report: "News is a part of the explosion of social media and mobile devices, and in a way that could offer opportunity to reach more people with news than ever before."

The 4G era has ushered in a golden age of the mobile phone—equipped with 24/7 broad-band, the phone has become slicker and smarter; smartphone screen sizes have become bigger to facilitate video viewing on the go (e.g., the iPhone 7 Plus display is 57% larger than the 2007 original iPhone); apps developed specifically for mobile phones continue to grow.

Table 1.2 FACILITATORS AND BARRIERS OF MOBILE NEWS CONSUMPTION

Facilitators	Barriers
• Improved network connectivity such as Wi-Fi hot spots	• In the early 2000s, prior to 3G networks, the content on mobile web browsers was typically text with limiting visuals to avoid long page loading and high costs of data
• Location-based services: Mobile news outlets can cater news content to a user's specific geographic location	• Buttoning as the method of navigation
• High-choice platforms: Mobile phone users can install and use news apps based on their needs and interests	• Poor connection speeds on wireless networks resulted in long news page loading time
• Sense of agency: Users are allowed to interact with the news by posting comments or sharing it	• Small screen size affects reading time and comfort
• Changes of reading and news consumption habits: Young generations (aka digital natives) prefer to read short articles with inviting visuals	• High cost of subscription to mobile data package
• Multimedia materials provision	• SMS and MMS were the main forms of news
• Smartphones with large screen size were transformed from a talking device and a mini-computer into a media-rich platform for disseminating news, information, and entertainment	• Few interactive features imbedded in mobile news

Sources: Shim et al. (2015); Verkasalo, López-Nicolás, Molina-Castillo, and Bouwman (2010); Dunaway et al. (2018); Westlund (2013).

The smartphone in one's pocket has become a daily necessity for millions of its users who depend on it for information and social interaction.

Accordingly, audiences are exposed to news more than at any other time due to readily accessible multiple forms and diverse platforms such as mobile push notifications, mobile news sites, news posted on social media, and news apps. In addition to being quick and easily accessible on the go, mobile news delivered on 4G networks represents Internet-like networked and interactive communication, providing users with opportunities to interact with news organizations and journalists. For example, mobile users can not only seek news but also follow news on social media sites such as Twitter. In a short span of 10 years, the mobile phone has transformed the ways in which millions of people access and interact with the news (Nel & Westlund, 2012).

At a time of declining news consumption, journalism is in flux, if not crisis (Spyridou, Matsiola, Veglis, Kalliris, & Dimoulas, 2013). Mobile news seems to fill the void, making smartphones the new face of digital news. As Wolf and Schnauber (2015) noted, with the rapid adoption of Internet-powered mobile devices, "a new medium for digital journalism has entered the field" (p. 1).

RISING CONSUMPTION IN ASIA

Similar to the rising trend in accessing and consuming news on the mobile phone in Europe and the United States, Asian countries are also at the forefront of consuming mobile news. In 2014, Japan, one of the first countries in Asia that offered Internet access via mobile phones, saw 15% of its population using mobile phones as the gateway for accessing news. The rapid deployment of the 3G and 4G networks in countries such as China and India have helped them narrow the digital gap with the West in Internet penetration (Poushter, 2017). In fact, mobile Internet provides the right technology and right tools in the world's most populous region to extend Internet connection to hundreds of millions of Chinese and Indians who would otherwise have no means to go online.

Japan, Korea, and Hong Kong, to name a few, are leaders in Asia's mobile revolution (Abonen, 2008). As summarized in Table 1.3, the mobile phone adoption rate topped 100% in Asia's leading cities such as Hong Kong and Singapore, which means a large number of users in those cities owned more than one phone. China's Internet survey agency, CNNIC (2019), reported that the number of people accessing the Internet using mobile phones had reached 847 million in China as of December 2019, accounting for 99.1% of all Internet users in the country. Only a decade ago, the share of mobile Internet users was below 40%. Owning a smartphone and going online are synonymous in China and India.

In the world's largest mobile phone populations totaling nearly 3 billion subscribers in 2018, millions of users in Asia rely on the smartphone as an information hub to access and consume news, driving digital news consumption in the region. According to an industry report (CNNIC, 2019), 87% of Chinese Internet users accessed news from the mobile phone, and 70% relied on social media platforms for acquiring news. Newman, Fletcher, Kalogeropoulos, Levy, and Nielsen (2018) at Reuters Institute for the Study of Journalism reported that the smartphone has also become the most common means for people in Taiwan to consume news; the percentage of mobile news seekers was 20% higher than that of those who

Table 1.3 PENETRATION RATES OF SMARTPHONES IN ASIA'S FOUR LEADING
CITIES: SHANGHAI, HONG KONG, SINGAPORE, AND TAIPEI

Cities	Total mobile population and rate	Smartphone users	% of smartphone users in population
Shanghai	Mobile subscribers totaled 39.87 million in 2020 at the rate 156%.[a]	35.2 million smartphone users in 2020 in Shanghai[e]	88.28% among mobile populations in 2020
Hong Kong	Mobile subscriber rate was well over 200% among its 7.5 million residents in 2019.[b]	4.9 million of smartphone users in 2019[f]	67.56%
Singapore	95% of the population used mobile phones in Singapore and 91% used smartphones in 2018.[c]	In 2017, the number of smartphone users in Singapore was estimated to reach 4.27 million.[g]	91% of people used a smartphone in 2018.[i]
Taipei	85.2% of youth have a mobile phone; 95.5% of them use a smartphone.[d]	17.2 million used smartphones in Taiwan in 2016. In 2020, the number of smartphone users was predicted to top 18.8 million.[h]	81.73% of the population in 2020

Sources: [a] MIIT (2020). [b] OFCA (2019). [c] Digital Marketing Blog (2018). [d] Focus Taiwan (2018). [e] MIIT (2020). [f] OFCA (2019). [g] Statista (2019). [h] Statista (2016). [i] Statista (2019).

accessed news from a PC. Similarly, more than 70% surveyed smartphone users in Hong Kong said they used the phone to consume news.

Table 1.4 lists the rising trends in mobile news consumption in Asia's leading cities, where almost all smartphone users accessed news for consumption, ranging from 75% in Taiwan to 96% in Hong Kong. Additionally, Asian mobile news consumers use various social media platforms for reading news, including the popular all-in-one mobile apps WeChat and Line. In addition to reading news, they also share and comment on news accessed via their phones. Consumption of mobile news thus spans the boundary between public information and personal space.

OUR FOCUS: THE AUDIENCE PERSPECTIVE

A number of issues arise from the popularity of mobile news consumption in Asia's most mobile cities. From an audience's perspective, our study

Table 1.4 CONSUMPTION OF NEWS ON MOBILE PHONES IN THE FOUR
ASIAN CITIES

Cities	Size of mobile news users	Mobile news consumption[f]
Shanghai	500 million Chinese read news on their mobile devices, accounting for over 70% of the nation's users.[a]	75% of WeChat users used it for news.[g] Two-thirds of Chinese adults spend 40 minutes a day reading news on the mobile app WeChat.[a]
Hong Kong	In 2018, over 96% of people used smartphones to go online every day, among which 71% used smartphones to read news.[b] In 2018, 68% of surveyed users used the mobile phone to consume news.[c]	Facebook for news, 52%; WhatsApp for news, 41%; YouTube for news, 33% 51% shared news on social media, messaging, or e-mail; 23% left comments via social media or web sites.
Singapore	In 2018, 91% of people used smartphones; among those people, 34% checked news updated on their phones.[d] Over 76% accessed news via the smartphone.[c]	Facebook for news, 48%; WhatsApp for news, 41%; YouTube for news 27% 41% shared news on social media, messaging, or e-mail; 17% left comments via social media or web sites.
Taipei	In 2018, 75% of people in Taiwan used mobile phones for news reading.[e] 76% of 1,005 respondents accessed news via the smartphone.[c]	Line for news, 57%; Facebook for news, 54%; YouTube for news, 43% 42% shared news on social media, messaging, or e-mail; 23% left comments via social media or web sites.

Sources: [a] China Daily (2017). [b] Go-Global (2014). [c] Newman, Fletcher, Kalogeropoulos, and Nielsen (2019). [d] Today (2020). [e] Newman et al. (2019). [f] Newman et al. (2019). [g] Chinanews (2019).

examining how news accessed from the mobile phone is consumed is guided by these broad research questions:

1. Why do Asian college students use the mobile phone to keep up with news? What factors motivate them to choose their mobile phones as the preferred gateway to access news?
2. As young people shy away from reading newspapers or watching TV news to stay informed, will mobile news fill the void? Will mobile news help them develop new patterns of consumption such as engagement with news?

3. How do they evaluate the credibility and appeal of news content they consume via the mobile phone?
4. Most important of all, will mobile news fulfill a democratic function in shaping Asia's civic-minded young generations into citizens? That is, does consuming mobile news make any difference in terms of acquiring political knowledge from the news? What are the promises and what are the inhibiting factors?

In this book, we define mobile news as hard news, especially "the political and related news that journalists believe citizens need to perform their democratic duties" (Gans, 2003, p. 28)—that is, news as a public good that is both objectively important and created and delivered to mobile phones by traditional news organizations or professional journalists. Mobile news also includes news forwarded and shared on social media and messaging platforms from those traditional sources and news sites. In other words, we examine user behavior toward the mobile phone as a gateway for consuming news disseminated by legacy media organizations. The format and types of mobile news that we examine include texting in SMS, Web 1.0 technologies (e.g., e-mail alerts, MMS, links, mobile version of news sites), and Web 2.0 technologies such as blogs, mobile micromessaging apps (WeChat, Twitter, Line), and news apps for the mobile screen.

Our definition of mobile news as disseminated from traditional media outlets for mobile phones is informed by several trends. First, Asians are increasingly consuming traditional news media via popular social and mobile platforms (Newman, Fletcher, Kalogeropoulos, & Nielsen, 2019; Sidlow, 2008). Second, mobile phones have become domesticated in the young users' everyday lives as the foremost source of information over other, more conventional sources such as television news and newspapers (Sidlow, 2008). Third, traditional journalists provide the majority of trusted news content consumed through digital media (Mitchelstein & Boczkowski, 2010). Fourth, news accessible from the mobile phone bears some resemblance to digital news for the web.

Why a focus on news? Why a study of mobile news? And why now?

We decided the focus based on two considerations: (1) the important link of hard news (e.g., reports about politics, world events, and business) to citizenship and democracy and (2) the role of communication technology in disseminating news in Asia, where the world's largest mobile population resides.

First, news is defined in the traditional sense of what is important in the public domain that is created by professional journalists employed by news organizations. As M. Mitchell, Gottfried, Barthel, and Shearer (2016) argued, "news remains an important part of public life" in the era of flourishing digital media (p. 3). Reading and viewing news represent a kind of civic behavior, a prerequisite for participation in political and public affairs. Taking advantage of mobility and the widely deployed 3G/4G networks, mobile phone users are able to access news on the go; the mobile phone in general and the smartphone in particular make it possible to increase news consumption even though news consumption worldwide is in decline (Barthel, 2019). In addition, past research shows that people who are interested in political news tend to spend more time reading and viewing news via the mobile phone than do people who are not (Martin, 2015; Zhang & Ha, 2016).

Media scholars (Schudson, 1998) suggested that consuming news to gain public knowledge functions as a training ground for civic obligations and citizen behavior in the political process. Consuming news is considered key to fulfilling democratic citizenship (Dunaway, Searles, Sui, & Paul, 2018). According to the American sociologist Herbert Gans (2003), "the democratic process can only be truly meaningful if these citizens are informed," and "being informed is considered beneficial to citizens' participation in the political and democratic process" (p. 1). Thus, consuming news is a critical link among journalism, informed citizenry, and democracy (Schudson, 1998). To become engaged in the political process, audiences need to use the public information and civic facts learned from news. Past research has shown that knowledge gained from news and interest in politics are both antecedents and predictors of political participation.

We agree with the assessment of Dunaway et al. (2018) that the next important frontier of technological change with far-reaching democratic consequences is "mobile" (p. 108). In an environment of mobility and easy access, how do mobile phone users consume news, and what are the processes and effects of mobile news consumption? In this book, we focus on the contextual and temporal factors that shape consumption of mobile news as a different form of digital news. We aim to examine the patterns of mobile news consumption—how young Asian mobile phone users seek, consume, evaluate, and engage with news—as well as the learning effect of consuming news accessed from the mobile phone.

Consumption of mobile news is becoming increasingly widespread worldwide; however, the process by which users consume news from the mobile phone to fulfill their citizenship role is unclear. Will mobile news provide the opportunities for engaged consumption and acquisition of political knowledge? In the context of Asian societies such as Taiwan that is experimenting with the Western ideal of democracy or those (e.g., Hong Kong) aspiring to become a viable democracy, making sense of an informed citizenship is particularly meaningful. The young generations in Asia grew up with the Internet and expect free flow and exchange of information. We believe that understanding the processes and effects of their mobile news consumption behavior enlightens the understanding of rapid social change in Asia.

Second, Westlund (2013) suggested that mobile news holds the future of digital journalism. As the summary in Table 1.3 indicates, more than two-thirds of mobile phone users in Asia's leading cities consume news from their phones; this share is comparable to that of the United States and European countries. But empirical studies on using the mobile phone and devices as gateways to access and consume news in Asia are few and far between, falling behind the rapid increase in 4G-supported data services and rising tide of consumption of news on mobile phones. The time to fill the gap is now—hence the immediate relevance of our study on the increasing consumption of mobile news in Asia.

Moreover, past research of mobile news tends to be fragmented and piecemeal, looking at one aspect (adoption or perception) or use (consumption and displacement effect) over a single, limited period, typically with a one-shot design. Using two waves of survey data, we attempt a comparative approach to examine the process and effects of mobile news in four of Asia's leading cities with different social political systems. With survey data from two time periods and a cross-societal (e.g., four Asian cities) design, our research adds new theoretical insights to the growing mobile communication literature.

SCOPE OF INQUIRY

The rapid adoption of smartphones has created a new type of news consumer who prefers the phone and tablets over laptops and desktops to acquire and consume news content (Westlund, 2013). Barthel (2019) describes them as a new type of news consumer. The scope of our study, therefore, is defined as an inquiry into consumption of mobile news among young adults in Asia. That is, we seek to examine user motivations and behaviors of approaching the mobile phone as a gateway to consume news disseminated by legacy media. We are particularly interested in exploring the process and effects of mobile news consumption with the aim to further the understanding of the mobile phone as an emerging medium that has become central to the way young people consume and experience news (R. Wei, 2020; Zhang & Ha, 2016).

A study of how young Asian mobile phone users consume news will help understand their disposition for civic duties and political participation. The technological advantages of mobile news include being interactive, personalized, multimedia, and highly portable (Ha et al., 2018), which make keeping up with the news as a civic obligation much easier. Moreover, consuming news from the mobile phone represents types of active and participatory forms of media use that resemble the characteristics of the engaged social media news consumer (Hermida, Fletcher, Korell, & Logan, 2012). Accordingly, if actively consuming news on mobile phones differs from passively receiving it, does it make any difference in what users learn from the news content? Our book explores trends and patterns of mobile news consumption among young people of college age in the emerging mobile sphere (Rheigold, 2006; R. Wei, Huang, & Zheng, 2018), especially in addressing the implications of news consumption for their connections to civic political culture.

In his book titled *The City in Your Pocket*, Timo Kopomaa (2000) envisioned the mobility of information on pocket-sized devices as the hallmark of postindustrial society. The ubiquitous mobile screens afford users an information hub and a personal, intimate space for social interaction. In a sort of parallel to Kopomaa's book, *News in Their Pockets* as the title of this book means the always-on mobile phone as a gateway to access digital news and the connector to various social media platforms to engage with the news; it also means an emerging paradigm of consumption of news accessible to mobile phone users anywhere, anytime. In its essence, *News in Their Pockets* exemplifies the everyday social practices of consuming a novel form of personalized news on the go.

SIGNIFICANCE OF THE STUDY

But, you may ask—as do we—so what? Leading scholars in new media studies (Dutton & Peltu, 1996; Lievrouw & Livingstone, 2002; Lin & Atkin, 2014; Rice, 1984) argue that the history of communication technology, and telecommunications technology in particular (Ellison, 2004; Lubrano, 1997), is basically a history of social change often in unpredictable ways under the influence of various socio-political forces and technological innovations. This leads to the question—what role do technological advances in mobile telephony play vis-à-vis socio-political factors in influencing how young Asian mobile phone users consume news and public information about current affairs? Specifically, will the mobile phone that brings personal freedom to millions of users in Asia also be what Pool (1983, p. 5) called "technologies of freedom"[2] in disseminating news?

The mobile phone seems to possess the attributes of technologies of freedom: dispersed, decentralized, easily accessible, and inexpensive. The technological attributes (e.g., inherent technological features) or affordances (e.g., affording users various action possibilities) of the mobile phone highlight mobility, personalization, and interactivity (Vishwanath, 2016). In this sense, consuming news anywhere and anytime from the ubiquitous mobile phone (i.e., Internet-enabled smartphones) supported by a decentralized network (i.e., distributed networks over cells) empowers users to access and engage in news in previously rare contexts. The mobile phone in the pockets of its users qualifies as a promising technology of freedom to access and consume news and public information.

On the other hand, consumption of news via the mobile phone always takes place in the broader socio-political context, which may shape the consumption. The social shaping of technology perspective (MacKenzie & Wajcman, 1985; Williams & Edge, 1996) emphasizes the role of a range of social and political factors that filter technology. As Dutton (2013) argued, "the real predictor of new media is not media technologies, but the broad social-political and cultural conditions" (p. 11). It seems to us that consumption of mobile news heightens the tension between "technologies of freedom" and state control of digital media in hierarchical societies with an authoritarian tradition. For example, early references to the outbreaks of COVID-19 in Wuhan, China, appeared on the popular mobile messaging app WeChat. However, they did not last long. In circumstances like this, the precise nature of the dynamics of technologies versus social conditions of news consumption is open to empirical investigation systematically.

It seems to us that Asia presents a preferred site to test the promise of the mobile phone as a "technology of freedom" because it has the largest number of mobile phone users in the world. There are comparable numbers of users who live in free and democratic Asian countries and contrast with those who reside in hierarchical societies with a long authoritarian tradition. Hence, our ultimate goal is to examine the interplay between an empowering communication technology and constraining social systems in the context of mobile news consumption, shedding light on the great technology-versus-society debate.

In short, consuming news on mobile phones by millions of users around the world is relatively recent; scholars still view it as "a young phenomenon" (Wolf & Schnauber, 2015, p. 5). We consider mobile news as an analytical focus to understand the complex relationship between communication technology of freedom and social control. Using data collected from two waves of surveys and a cross-societal design, our findings will shed light on the promise and peril of digital news delivered to the mobile screen.

THE ORGANIZATION OF THE BOOK

The book consists of nine chapters. Chapter 1 introduces trends in mobile news, focus, scope, and significance of the study. Chapter 2 establishes the analytical framework and methodology. Chapters 3 through 7 report the key findings about the five dependent variables: motives of mobile news consumption; patterns of mobile news consumption; engagement with news consumed on the mobile phone; the perceptions and evaluations of mobile news; and knowledge gained from mobile news consumption. Chapter 8 presents structural equation models (SEMs) to illustrate the processes and effects of mobile news consumption. Chapter 9 draws conclusions from the key findings as theoretical insights.

This book provides empirical analysis of the evolution in news production and dissemination, at a time when mobile technology empowers citizens of every nation with more information about local and global events. What has been developed as a communication tool in Western democracies for private chat may have turned into a technology of worldwide influence and global citizenry thanks to the use of mobile phones as a gateway to consume news.

CHAPTER 2

Motivation, Perception, and Engagement

MOBILE NEWS: WHAT IS IT?

To say defining the concept of mobile news is a challenge is an understatement. Indeed, whether mobile news is a definable concept is debatable, largely due to rapid technological advances in wireless networks, upgrades of smartphones, and an endless supply of new apps for Internet-powered smartphones.[1] Given the heterogeneity of devices, content, and platforms for distributing and consuming news, one can even argue what is NOT mobile news ever since Apple's iPhone swept the world. Cutting-edge mobile communication technology (e.g., smartphones, tablets, e-readers, wireless computers, and wearables) is the new phase of the Internet. Sawhney (2009) called it "mobile environments of the Internet" (p. 105). News accessed from the mobile phone is also considered the new face of digital media that generates massive and various sorts of news content and public information (E. Thorson, Shoenberger, Karaliova, Kim, & Fidler, 2015).

We view mobile news as a multidimensional construct, which is technologically rooted in personal communication devices such as pagers and the 2G GSM (Global System for Mobile Communication) mobile phone. In this sense, mobile news can be narrowly defined as aggregated news in texting form, like SMS (short message service) and MMS (Multimedia Message Service), that is fast and accessible on a personal communication device to subscribers. Born out of convenience, its origin is not as glamorous as other forms of media for mass communication technology such as the television or the telephone that preceded it. However, in a short span of less

News in Their Pockets. Ran Wei and Ven-hwei Lo, Oxford University Press (2021). © Oxford University Press.
DOI: 10.1093/oso/9780197523728.003.0002

than 20 years, the mobile phone evolved from an interpersonal communication device to "a quasi-mass communication medium" (He, 2008, p. 185; Westlund, 2008).

As outlined in Chapter 1, advances in mobile network technology from 2G to 3G in the 1990s and to 4G in the 2000s accelerated the development of the mobile phone from a device for telecommunication in the 1990s, to a quasi–mass communication medium in the early 2000s, to an informational gateway or media platform to browse the web in the 2010s. The smartphone provides users with a web experience that integrates game-changing features such as a keyboard on a touch screen; it changed the way users access and consume news (R. Wei, 2020; Westlund, 2010, 2013). As the diffusion of the smartphone has deepened, the screen has further shifted away from PC laptops to mobile devices. Abonen (2008) characterized the mobile phone as the seventh mass media.[2] As such, the informational and media functions of mobile phones assume greater importance (E. Thorson et al., 2015; R. Wei, 2008). Meanwhile, the scope of news created and delivered to smartphones has broadened—the mobile phone is considered as bona fide media for consuming news without the boundaries of time and space (Chan-Olmsted, Rim, & Zerba, 2013). Mobile news has evolved further from aggregating content from newspapers and news wires, to reproduction of digital content of web versions with embedded links, to a mobile sphere of user-originated content (R. Wei, 2016).

Paul Levinson (2004) upgraded the status of mobile phones by redefining them as "media-in-motion." His definition underscores a key aspect of the mobile phone—it is always carried by its users, who turn it into a gateway or platform to access and consume news. In other words, the mobile phone affords its users with portability, mobility, always-on connectivity, interactivity, and multimediality (Schrock, 2015; Vishwanath, 2016). Portability allows users to carry their Internet-powered phone in their pockets all the time, which expands consumption of news from fixed locations to broader contexts such as on transits, in waiting areas, and any place away from home. Use of the ubiquitous mobile phone to access news is particularly common as an "in-between" opportunity to catch up with the latest news and updates on social media sites. The mobile phone thus extends the reach of news to a large number of users who are not necessarily news junkies. The news-as-on-demand model (Westlund, 2013) of mobile news provides users with choices to read, listen, or view the news in the forms of texting, apps, or mobile news sites. Communication via the always-on mobile phone crosses the boundaries between private and public communication (J. Katz & Aakhus, 2001); it brings down the divide among interpersonal, small group, and mass communication (Campbell &

Ling, 2008), as well as the clear division between media use and nonuse (Zhou, 2019). Rice and Hogan (2007) called the nonstop use of the mobile phone as "continual conversation" (p. 20) and as a ritual of being perpetually connected.

More importantly, interactivity (the degree to which users can interact with news content) as another key affordance of Internet-enabled smartphones provides instant social connectivity and personalized interaction. In the context of using the mobile phone as a gateway for accessing news, interactivity means hypertextuality—the ability to connect within sites of disparate webpages through clicking on a tagged word, phrase, graphic image, or video link (Chung, Nam, & Stefanone, 2012). Interactivity also means users have tools such as hyperlinks to interact with news by posting their comments or sharing the news (e.g., clicking, forwarding, recommending, and commenting).

"Mobile first" in digital news publishing represents the most recent development of mobile news—designing news for the mobile screen to respond to the trend of more traffic coming from mobile rather than desktop devices (Poindexter, 2016). Mobile news consumers can go straight to apps tailored for the phone and homepages by keying in the URL, ushering in a new phase of consuming news via the mobile phone.

Therefore, by virtue of the advances in mobile phones and upgrades in mobile network technology, the globally popular mobile phone has evolved from a talking device into a mass media channel, which Campbell characterizes as "a resource that allows people to construct and participate in the abstract domain of social experience" (Miconi & Serra, 2019, p. 3453). As such, similar to previous new media, the ubiquitous mobile phone has started to play a larger role in influencing the culture and political life of society (Martin, 2015; R. Wei, 2020).

In summary, the concept of news via the mobile phone, which was narrowly defined as a device to access news fast, has broadened as an emerging media platform for engaged consumption of news and a potential technology of freedom. Nevertheless, the processes and effects of consuming mobile news are less understood. Systematic research is particularly needed for documenting, describing, comparing, and explaining emerging patterns of mobile news consumption among different segments of users in different societies. Media scholars (Peters, 2012; Westlund, 2008) plea to further theorize the concept of mobile news. Against this backdrop of evolving mobile news and responding to the urgent need for a thorough understanding of mobile news, our study focuses on the processes and consequences of consuming mobile news.

A FRAMEWORK FOR ANALYZING MOBILE NEWS CONSUMPTION

Our approach to achieve a full understanding of consuming news via the mobile phone is to integrate the motives, processes, and consequences of consuming mobile news into a framework for analysis. The foundation of our framework is informed by an extensive review of the literature and our own previous studies, which include sociological theories of news, mass communication theory of media use, uses and gratifications (U&G) theory, interactivity theories, credibility and perceptions of news, sociological theory of technology, and political socialization theory, among others.

In this study, we divided consumption of mobile news into five discrete aspects, which gives us the five dependent variables of this study— motivations, consumption, engaged consumption, perceptions, and knowledge acquired from mobile news. The framework is depicted in Figure 2.1; it allows us to address three broad questions about mobile news consumption among the young generations: *why* (motivational factors), *how* (the consuming process and experience), and *what are the consequences* (outcomes/effects of consumption)?

MOTIVATIONS, CONSUMPTION, ENGAGED CONSUMPTION, PERCEPTIONS, AND KNOWLEDGE
Motivational Factors

Using the mobile phone seems natural for the young generations, who grew up at a time when the mobile phone had been widely diffused worldwide. However, employing the mobile phone as a gateway to access news is not. In fact, news consumption requires varying degrees of motivation or cognitive reasoning about expected rewards from the behavior. In other words, consumption of news as what is important domestically and

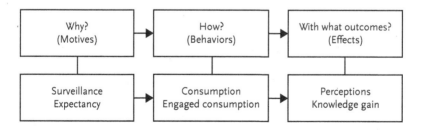

Figure 2.1 Analytical Framework of Mobile News Consumption
Credit: Ran Wei and Ven-hwei Lo

internationally requires an internal drive. Scholarship on this topic (Chen, Lo, Wei, Xu, & Zhang, 2014a; Shim, You, Lee, & Go, 2015; R. Wei & Lo, 2015) indicates that this is particularly true among young people who have not formed the habit of news consumption. X. Li (2013) found that personal initiative was a stronger predictor of using the mobile phone to seek news than was innovativeness.

Therefore, to establish the set of psychological motivations that provide this drive and a sense of consuming news as a civic obligation that influences consumption behavior, the process of mobile news consumption should be understood through examining young people's underlying needs, wants, and expectancies that turn into motivations for actual news consumption.

The U&G approach to media use views media selection as an active "cognitive orientation" that prompts media users to seek information about what is going on in the world at large (Blumler, 1979, p. 17). According to E. Katz, Blumler, and Gurevitch (1973), U&G is concerned with the social and psychological origins of needs, which generate expectations from the mass media, which then lead to selective use of media, resulting in the needs being gratified. Past research of mobile news (Incollingo, 2018; Joo & Sang, 2013; Poindexter, 2016; R. Wei & Lo, 2015) informs us that motives for use of traditional media such as newspapers are applicable in explaining the behavior of mobile news consumption. Applying the "motivational news use" approach (E. Katz et al., 1973; Shoemaker, 1996) enables us to explore how young people view news accessible from the mobile phone as an opportunity to meet their informational needs, which in turn prompts them to read and view the news while they could use their phones to do many other things—listen to music, play games, or simply chat. In this sense, we define *motivation as intentional use of the mobile phone for accessing news to satisfy a range of social and informational needs*. Gratifications sought from mobile phone use will serve as a set of motivational factors that foster consumption of news via the mobile phone.

Furthermore, past research (Schrock, 2015; Vishwanath, 2016) suggested some major affordances[3] of mobile media such as portability, availability, personalization, interactivity, and multimediality. To mobile phone users, what do these affordances mean? We propose that their appraisals of mobile affordances as unique features can be understood through the expectancy-value perspective of media choice (Fishbein & Ajzen, 1976). The value-expectancy theory (Babrow, 1989) addresses a range of perceived benefits obtained from selecting media to use and the distinct values and benefits entailed by the selection. LaRose and Eastin (2004) refined the approach with the concept of expectancies revolving around media motives and uses.

For instance, information expectancy illustrates an individual's selection of media, traditional or digital, for the expected reward of learning more about a topic (Flanagin & Metzger, 2000).

Therefore, the expectancy value approach complements the U&G theory by enabling us to include user appraisals of news accessed via the mobile phone, or what Shao (2009) called "usability attributes," as the second set of motivational factors. We anticipate that these two sets of motivational factors (i.e., gratifications of mobile phone use and expectancies of mobile news) will predict consumption of mobile news, engaged consumption, perceptions of mobile news, and learning from mobile news.

Consuming Mobile News

News accessed from the mobile phone represents the fastest growing segment of digital news (Westlund, 2013). Use of the mobile phone as an emerging medium for news, however, differs categorically from use of traditional news media: First, users are active seekers, not passive receivers, of news content. Second, users own the phone, and thus are empowered to personalize news content and choose ways in which they wish to access news. Consuming news accessed from the mobile phone is thus defined in our study as *the behavior of seeking news via the ubiquitous mobile phone in various digital forms* (e.g., SMS, mobile websites, apps tailored for mobile, and mobile social media platforms) *to build an informational diet for personal use.*

Our definition implies consumption of news by choice that is driven by motives, needs, expectancies, and past experiences. The greater the motivation, the more mobile news will be consumed. Similarly, advances in mobile network technology and upgrades of smartphones will result in increased consumption of mobile news. Users of Internet-powered smartphones supported by 4G networks will likely consume more news accessed from the phone.

On the other hand, gender has been considered a major social factor that affects adoption and use of communication technology and mobile phone usage (Leung & Wei, 1999b; Rakow, 1992; R. Wei & Lo, 2006). Females were found to favor using the Internet and the mobile phone to communicate with family and close friends, whereas males used the phone for information seeking to accomplish tasks (Jackson, Ervin, & Gardner, 2001; Watten, Kleiven, Fostervold, Fauske, & Volden, 2008). In addition, past research shows significant differences in knowledge scores between men and women, with men tending to have higher scores. Dow (2009) found a consistent 10-point gender gap in measured political knowledge in the United States. Studies conducted in Europe and Asia (Banducci & Semetko, 2002;

Lo, 1994) also indicate that men were more knowledgeable about politics than their female counterparts.

Given the deep-rooted gender gap in consumption of hard news and in knowledge acquired from the news (Burns, Schlozman, & Verba, 2001; Delli Carpini & Keeter, 1996, 2000; Wolak & McDevitt, 2011), we anticipate that gender will matter in affecting mobile news consumption as well as influencing the consequence of consuming the news. Gender, therefore, is considered as a key social differentiator in our subsequent analyses.

Engagement with Mobile News

Considering smartphones supported by 3G/4G networks are essentially pocket-size computers with broadband capability, news consumption via smartphones provides users not only the access but also the opportunity to engage with the news, which leads to a new dimension of mobile news consumption that goes beyond reading. A study of Chyi and Chadha (2012) reported that mobile news consumers discussed news in online forums with other people, left comments to news organizations, personalized their own searchable news archives, and accessed updated news at a time and place of their choice. Thus, examining how users engage with mobile news provides us with an exciting opportunity to understand and theorize about the smartphone as a unique medium for consuming news.

The scope of engagement in the digital media environment is broad, encompassing cognitive, affective, and behavioral dimensions (Ksiazek, Peer, & Lessard, 2016). Livingstone and Markham (2008) defined news engagement as people's cognitive, social, habitual, and motivational engagement with the news media. Ha et al. (2018) operationalized news engagement as efforts made by users to obtain and utilize news content. Informed by the typology of interactivity proposed by Ksiazek et al. (2016), which highlights user-to-user and user-to-content interactivities, we define user engagement with news accessed from the mobile phone as *interactivities with the news and other users by following mobile news and sharing the news*. Similar to the behavior of mobile news consumption, engaged consumption will likely be affected by gender and advances in mobile technology.

Perceptions of Mobile News

News created and delivered to the mobile phone, which is limited by its screen size, tends to be disconnected and fragmented compared to online news for the PC. Fake news circulated on social media platforms also spreads to mobile screens. Consuming mobile news thus seems to be a risky business, requiring users to sift, evaluate, and scrutinize what they read or view for being true, objective, and visually appealing. As such, we focus on examining user perceptions of the quality of mobile news—its credibility, in particular.

Informed by the literature (Flanagin & Metzger, 2007; Gunther, 1992), we explored quality of mobile news as a property that is judged by users, who formed the perception through their experience of consuming such news. Perceptions of mobile news are defined as *subjective evaluations about the quality of news content consumed on the mobile phone.* Considering that credibility is crucial to news media (Meyer, 1988), we focus on how users make credibility judgments of mobile news. We anticipate that user experience with mobile news and reliance on the phone in their pockets for news will play a role in impacting the perceptions.

Learning from the News

Living at a time of mobile phone saturation in societies and unprecedented access to news via the phone, the pressing question is not just why and how users access news content. To us, the most pressing questions to address are: Does mobile news matter? Does consuming such news make any difference?

We seek to address these questions by measuring user learning from news accessed from the mobile phone. Any effect to be observed from consuming mobile news should be a result of motivated consumption, cognitive engagement, and positive evaluation, rather than mindless scrolling of the mobile screen or random browsing of fleeting headlines on the phone. Thus, acquiring political knowledge is designed as the last of the five dependent variables, which serves as the benchmark criterion variable to gauge consequences of consuming news accessed from the mobile phone. Following the convention in political communication research (e.g., Hoffman, 2019), we define *political knowledge as holding correct information about current affairs.*

Treating effects of consuming mobile news as the last dependent variable in our framework is also rooted in scholarship (Kleinberg & Lau, 2019; Prior, 2007; R. Yu, 2019) that views news media as indispensable outlets to acquire political knowledge, which in turn promotes civic participation in the political process.

More importantly, as Greenfield (2018) argued, technology cannot be understood "in isolation" and its effects on society cannot "be determined in advance" (p. 312). Therefore, we include a few macro predictors at the larger social, cultural, and technical system levels that play an important role in shaping the five studied dependent variables and accounting for the individual-level differences in patterns of mobile news consumption and effects of consumption. Figure 2.2 depicts the expanded analytical framework with added societal-level factors that shape the consumption.

As shown in Figure 2.2, consumption of mobile news at the macro level is subject to the influences of technology, culture, and political systems of a given society in which mobile news is created and distributed for consumption. These broad societal influences either shape the consumption or provide the context in which the consumption takes place (C. Wei & Kolko, 2005). Specifically, applying Grant's (2018) "Umbrella Perspective on Communication Technology" (p. 5), we view smartphones supported by advanced mobile networks (3G/4G) as "enabling factors" (i.e., system-level factors that make an application possible), such as deploying the next generation of a mobile network and upgrades of smartphones. The opposite of enabling factors are "limiting factors" (i.e., system-level factors that create barriers to the adoption, use, or impacts of a technology). We consider lacking press freedom and restricted information accessibility as such limiting factors in a socio-political system.

However, as Zhu, Lo, Weaver, Chen, and Wu (1997) argued, "societal influences are a constant in single society study; and cannot be observed within a single society" (p. 84). Exploring the societal factors at the macro level that shape mobile news consumption behavior merits nothing less

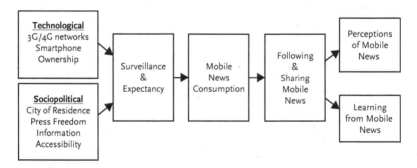

Figure 2.2 Factors That Shape Mobile News Consumption, Engagement, Perceptions, and Learning from Mobile News
Credit: Ran Wei and Ven-hwei Lo

than a comparative analysis. In addition, international and comparative studies on new media are still scarce (Leung, Lee, Lo, Xiong, & Wu, 2009). Based on these two considerations, we selected four of Asia's leading cities in mobile telephony—Hong Kong, Shanghai, Singapore, and Taiwan—for cross-societal comparative analyses.[4] These mega cities are among the most technologically, economically, culturally, and politically influential cities in the Chinese-speaking part of Asia.

Technologically, at least as far as mobile telephony is concerned, the four selected Asian cities are about equally advanced. They adopted and built the same worldwide standardized mobile communication technologies— 3G and 4G. The penetration rates of 3G/4G-supported smartphones are also comparable, reaching saturation thanks to the upgrades in network infrastructure, expanding mobile data services, and competitive pricing in subscriptions to the service. As shown in Table 2.1, Hong Kong leads with an adoption rate of 160%; Singapore came second at 143%, followed by Taipei (116%) and Shanghai (109.6%), making them Asia's most mobile cities.

In terms of mobile network infrastructure and technological upgrades, Table 2.1 highlights the comparable number of mobile network service providers and their similar mobile services to subscribers in the four cities. It is worth noting that mobile data services, including mobile news and mobile Internet, were all provided by these service providers. It can be argued that the mobile technologies in the pockets of millions of users in Hong Kong, Singapore, Shanghai, and Taipei are highly comparable; they are supported by comparable packages of mobile data and messaging service plans.

Hofstede (1991) defined culture as the "collective programming of the mind which distinguishes the members of one group or category of people from another" (p. 5). Culturally, the four cities are all dominated by Chinese or ethnic Chinese as the dominant majority. Belonging to societies characteristic of the so-called Confucian Asia (Skoric, Zhu, & Pang, 2016), residents in these cities share a strong Confucian culture, which respects social hierarchy and political authorities, privileges education, and gives priority to the family, community, and the world at large over the individual. According to Hofstede's (n.d.) cultural index of nations, the four Asian cities all score high in Hofstede's power distance index (Taipei at 80, Shanghai at 74, Hong Kong at 68, and Singapore at 58; see Table 2.2) in terms of acceptance of hierarchy and centralization of power. This means that a collectivist culture prevails across the four cities and residents are disposed psychologically to be more group oriented, harmony conscious, and connection focused. Therefore, the shared culture among the four cities

Table 2.1 A COMPARISON OF MOBILE NETWORK OPERATORS IN THE FOUR STUDIED CITIES IN ASIA

	Shanghai	Hong Kong	Taipei	Singapore
Population (in millions, 2018)	24.24	7.5	2.674	5.64
GDP in 2018	$494 billion	$362 billion	$586 billion (Taiwan)	$364 billion
GDP ranking in the world	#1 in China	#36	#21 (Taiwan)	#35
Internet penetration[a]	53.9%[b]	89.3%	92.6%	88.4%
Mobile phone penetration	109.6%[b]	160%[c]	116%[e]	143%[d]
Mobile networks	3G	3G	3G	3G
Year of updating to 3G	2009	2004	2007	2009
Networks	4G (LTE)	4G (LTE)	4G (LTE)	4G (LTE)
Year of updating to 4G	2013	2012	2014	2012
Number of network operators	3	7	4	3
Types of ownership	State	Mixed	Private	Private

Range and Type of Mobile Data Services

	Shanghai	Hong Kong	Taipei	Singapore
Mobile news services	Yes	Yes	Yes	Yes
Online SMS	Yes	Yes	Yes	Yes
Online user portal	Yes	Yes	Yes	Yes
Bundled service (phone and Internet)	Yes	Yes	Yes	Yes
Internet Messenger Live (IM)	Yes	Yes	Yes	Yes
Mobile TV service	Yes	Yes	Yes	Yes
Mobile payment	Yes	Yes	Yes	Yes
Mobile games	Yes	Yes	Yes	Yes
Mobile music	Yes	Yes	Yes	Yes
Broadband for mobile	Yes	Yes	Yes	Yes
Wi-Fi hot spot	Yes	Yes	Yes	Yes

Sources: [a] World Internet Stats (2020). [b] Shanghai Statistics Bureau (2010). [c] Hong Kong Telecoms (2010). [d] Singapore Telecoms (2010). [e] Taiwan Mobile Market (2010).

provides the basis for our comparison of their responses to news created and delivered to the mobile phone.

On the other hand, the four cities located in East and Southeast Asia differ markedly on a number of social and political dimensions, such as political systems, government types, press systems, and civic liberties.[5] They have developed different political systems with different types of

Table 2.2 POLITICAL SYSTEMS, CULTURAL DIMENSIONS, PRESS FREEDOM, AND CIVIC LIBERTIES IN SHANGHAI, HONG KONG, SINGAPORE, AND TAIWAN

Cultural-Political Dimensions	Shanghai	Hong Kong	Taipei	Singapore
Confucianism	Chinese	Chinese	Chinese	Ethnic Chinese dominated
Power distance*	74	68	80	58
Individualism*	20	25	20	17
Government type/ political system	Communist Party–led state	Executive limited democracy	Semipresidential republic	Parliamentary democracy
Political rights and civil liberties[a]	Not free	Partly free	Free	Partly free
Press role in society	State apparatus and party organ	Fourth estate/ commercial	Fourth estate	Supporting the government
Status of press freedom[a*]	Not free	Partly free	Free	Not free
Press freedom ranking in the world[a*]	176	70	42	151

*Represents data for China as a country.
Sources: [a] Freedom House (2019).

government, including a viable democracy (Taipei), a limited democracy (Singapore), a nondemocratic but free system (Hong Kong), and authoritarian rule (Shanghai). Therefore, the four selected cities represent four different archetypical political systems along the democratic-authoritarian spectrum in contemporary Asia. The differences in those aspects at the societal level are summarized in Table 2.2, which highlights the cross-societal similarities and differences among Hong Kong, Shanghai, Singapore, and Taipei. As a result of these different political systems, political rights, civil liberties, and press systems in the four cities differ substantially.

PRESS FREEDOM IN SHANGHAI, HONG KONG, SINGAPORE, AND TAIPEI

Against this large and multifarious socio-political backdrop, press freedom as a particular difference across the four cities stands out. Press freedom in the four cities is categorized by Freedom House (2019) as "not free," "partially free," and "free." We believe that level of press freedom as the context of mobile news consumption will condition the behavior of consuming such news.

McQuail (2000) defined press freedom as "independence" for protected free and open public expression of ideas and information (p. 144). Other scholars (e.g., An & Kwak, 2017) noted that the concept has multiple dimensions, including pluralism in structure, independence from the government, legislative protection, and transparency in journalistic practice. At the operational level, Freedom House (2004) defined it as "the legal environment for the media, political pressures that influence reporting, and economic factors that affect access to information."

In its most recent global survey of media independence, Freedom House (2019) ranked Taiwan as 42nd among a total of 180 countries or territories in the world, making its press one of the freest in Asia; the rankings of Hong Kong, Singapore, and Shanghai were lower, as the 70th, the 151st, and the 176th, respectively.[6] The different rankings of press freedom in Hong Kong, Shanghai, Singapore, and Taipei are tied to their own historical circumstances, social and political contexts, and media traditions.

Shanghai

Under the rule of the Chinese Communist Party, China's current media system mixes party organs with media outlets appealing to the mass market (Zhao, 1998). News media in Shanghai has enjoyed fast growth. Following the state-owned enterprise model, newspapers and broadcasting services operate under five different conglomerates, such as the Shanghai Press Group, which owns three of the largest mass-circulated dailies. The Shanghai Cultural Broadcasting & Film Group monopolizes TV networks, cable TV services, and satellite TV. These monopolistic media groups are owned and controlled by the Shanghai municipal government. Not surprisingly, their goals are to propagate official party lines and promote policies of the municipal government.

In the era of Web 2.0, these media groups also established their presence in a range of digital media, such as website and social media platforms (e.g., Weibo and WeChat) and mobile media channels. To some extent, the digital media, especially the "media-like" microblog site known as Weibo, are oriented toward the grassroots (Li & Zhang, 2018) and are less regulated than the official media. However, the media outlets in Shanghai, traditional or digital, are caught in the tension between state control of information and the public trying to find unfiltered, trustworthy sources (M. Li, 2018).

Hong Kong

Hong Kong was a former British colony, which established itself as Asia's media center thanks to the tradition of a vibrant and free press. After 1997, Hong Kong was unified with China as a special administrative region; Hong Kong has largely enjoyed autonomy under the scheme of "one country, two systems." The Basic Law (Chapter III) explicitly protects various fundamental rights of 7.5 million Hong Kong residents, including freedom of speech and freedom of the press. As China's political influence over Hong Kong has increased since the 1997 handover, concerns over the rapidly declining press freedom have been raised. As F. L. Lee (2018) observed, the tug of war between political pressure from the Beijing government and freedom of Hong Kong's press continues.

Nevertheless, the former British colony structurally retains a pluralistic media system, in which private and public broadcasters coexist. In the press sector, mainstream for-profit commercial newspapers dominate the market. The government-run newspapers published by the mainland have their presence in Hong Kong largely as niche media.

Singapore

Singapore represents a parliamentary democracy. Since its separation from Malaysia to become an independent and sovereign state with ethnic Chinese as the majority in 1965, the ruling party—People's Action Party—has dominated the country's politics for decades. It promotes the Confucian traditions of respect for authority and importance of family and emphasizes community and nation in political life over individual freedoms and civil rights (Dalton & Ong, 2003). Under these circumstances, the mission of media in Singapore, traditional and digital, is to support nation building rather than serve as a watchdog on the government or political parties (Skoric & Poor, 2013). Prior research (Tandoc & Duffy, 2016) has indicated something paradoxical—citizens of Singapore expect professional journalists to be both supportive and critical of the government.

Taipei

Taipei is the capital city of one of Asia's most vibrant democracies. After ending the authoritarian rule and tight control of the media under martial law in 1988, press freedom and civil liberties improved significantly on the island. Taiwan has received one of the top rankings in press freedom. As one of Asia's most free presses, the media condition in Taiwan is considered comparable to Western countries. It is now known for its robust media system with a full spectrum of ideological stances ranging from the pro-Democratic Progressive Party-led coalition, which holds a pro-independence ideology, to the pro-KMT party, which favors the status quo in relations with mainland China. In between these two large camps of partisan media, various religious and commercial news organizations coexist. However, the media on the island suffers political polarization because of rising sensationalism in journalism.

To sum up, previous study showed that the political system is a powerful societal factor affecting individuals in society (Zhu et al., 1997). Our past studies (R. Wei et al., 2014; R. Wei, Lo, Chen, Tandoc, & Zhang, 2020) show that the level of press freedom as a hallmark of a society's political system played a role in influencing news seeking from mobile phones. Mobile news seeking tended to be higher in politically illiberal societies than in free and democratic ones. We anticipate the degree of press freedom to be a strong societal influence that accounts for differences in consuming mobile news.

INFORMATION ACCESSIBILITY

Another macro-level societal variable that is relevant to our study is accessibility of information in a society. As McQuail (2000) argued, the degree of freedom of citizens to access media content is an integral component of press freedom in addition to the degree of freedom enjoyed by the news media. In the context of our study, information accessibly concerns the extent to which Asians can freely gain full access to a wide range of news created and delivered to the mobile phone.

Major differences exist in the four studied Asian cities in terms of information resource, diversity, access, and infrastructure. In Hong Kong and Singapore, for instance, with state-of-the-art information infrastructure, all kinds of digital information flow freely, and services are delivered in bilingual or multilingual media to serve different ethnic populations. The citizens in these two of Asia's most mobile cities tend to be global in outlook.

In such an environment, digital access to all sorts of news media, domestic and foreign, is uncontrolled; residents are generally well informed about domestic affairs and international events regardless of their personal interest in political or international news.

On the other hand, the flow of information is controlled in Shanghai. The environment for information dissemination lacks diversity (for instance, no online access to foreign newspapers) and is limited to officially approved media channels only. Under such an environment, the digital media outlets may be rich, but information flow is restricted and with limited diversity. To stay informed of hard news, especially reports in the foreign press, citizens living in such an environment need to be motivated by a higher level of personal interest (Iyengar et al., 2010; Trilling & Schoenbach, 2013).

Operationally, to build an information environment accessibility index, we use five key indices as markers, which differentiate the four Asian cities into separate categories of information accessibility. They include the global outlook from the development and competitiveness of a city on a global scale (e.g., Frankel, 2010), the state of development in information and communication technology (e.g., Kamba & Mansor, 2010; Kauffman & Techatassanasoontorn, 2010; Zhang & Zheng, 2009), Internet accessibility, degrees of personal freedom (e.g., Vásquez & Porčnik, 2018), and linguistic diversity.

Global Competitiveness

Based on Kearney's (2019) global city competitiveness, which measures the vibrancy of cities in the world that stand out as global hubs along dimensions of human capital, policy, and futuristic technology pathway, we included measures of global competitiveness of the four cities in this study. In the 2018 rankings of global cities, Singapore, which led in the ranking, was considered the most global city in Asia, followed by Hong Kong, Shanghai, and Taipei. Table 2.3 shows the details of each city.

Information and Communication Technology Development Index

Issued annually by the International Telecommunications Union (ITU), the measure included such diffusion indicators as telephone per 100 people, mobile phone rate, Internet rate, and access in a country. In the most recent Information and Communication Technology (ITC) report, Hong Kong received the highest ranking among the four cities as No. 6. With a

Table 2.3 INFORMATION ACCESSIBILITY IN SHANGHAI, HONG KONG, TAIWAN, AND SINGAPORE

	Shanghai	Hong Kong	Taipei	Singapore
Global city competitiveness ranking[a]	28	7	46	4
Freedom of expression[b]	5.35 (personal freedom), ranked #135 for China	8.58 (personal freedom), ranked #3	9.04 (personal freedom), ranked #10	7.48 (personal freedom), ranked #25
ICT Development Index rankings[c]	80	6	14	18
Internet accessibility	Widely available but restricted access	Widely available and unrestricted access	Widely available and unrestricted access	Widely available and unrestricted access
Official languages: bilingual or multilingual	Chinese	Chinese (Mandarin and Cantonese) and English	Chinese	English, Chinese, Malay, and Tamil
Information accessibility[d]	Low (1)	High (4)	Medium (3)	High (4)

Sources: [a] Kearney (2019). [b] Vásquez and Porcnik (2018). [c] International Telecommunications Union (2017). [d] The index was created by the sum of the indices of a, b, and c.

ranking of No. 14, Taiwan was the second most technologically advanced city, followed closely by Singapore with a ranking of No. 18. China received the lowest ranking as No. 18.[7]

Access to the Internet

Though ITC infrastructure increases access to the Internet, access to on-line content or websites can be limited by government control in Asia. It is common that access to targeted websites or digital content is blocked by authorities. For example, the Internet penetration rate in China has reached 65.5%, and Wi-fi is also widely available across the country. However, deploying a technological mechanism known as the Great Firewall, Chinese authorities blocked about 10% of websites, including Google, Facebook, and international media outlets such as the *New York Times* and *Financial Times*. These websites are off limits to millions of Chinese Internet users.

In comparison, access to the Internet is free and unrestricted in the other three Asian cities.

Accordingly, differences in access to the Internet among the four studied cities are included as another dimension of information accessibility. Taiwan, Hong Kong, and Singapore are rated as having free access to the Internet, while Shanghai is rated as with restricted access.

Personal Freedoms

The Human Freedom Index measures countries by levels of personal and civic freedoms. The components of the personal freedom index include movement, religion, assemble, expression, and information access (Vásquez & Porčnik, 2018). In the 2018 index, with a score of 5.35 (ranging from 0 to 10), China was ranked at the bottom. The report noted that China imposed taboo topics known as "Seven Don't Speaks" (七不讲) in public communication or discussions on digital media outlets.[8] Taiwan scored 9.04, while Hong Kong scored 8.58. Singapore's score was 7.48, right in the middle among the four cities.

Diversity of Official Languages

Finally, in terms of number of official languages used to distribute news and public information, with four official languages, Singapore is noted for being the most diverse, and Hong Kong, which is bilingual, is the second. In comparison, Taipei and Shanghai have a single official language.

With all five indices being considered, Singapore was rated as the most global and information accessible city, followed by Hong Kong, two of Asia's most international cities. Taiwan was the third, and Shanghai was the fourth. Given those differences at the societal level, we anticipate that the degree of information accessibility will be another societal influence that accounts for differences in consuming mobile news in these four cities.

In summary, the key to comparative analyses of mobile news consumption is to hold some aspects of societies to be compared constant and to focus on exploring the major societal differences that affect consumption. The similarities and differences of the four studied Asian cities are presented in Table 2.4. We anticipate that differences in consuming mobile news among the users living in the four Asian cities, if any, will be attributed to different political and press systems, level of press freedom, and degree of information accessibility.

Table 2.4 SIMILARITIES AND DIFFERENCES AMONG THE FOUR ASIAN CITIES

	Shanghai	Hong Kong	Singapore	Taiwan
Similarities				
Culture: Confucianism	Similar	Similar	Similar	Similar
Ranking in ICT Development Index	Similar	Similar	Comparable	Similar
3G/4G infrastructure	Advanced GSM/LTE	Advanced GSM/LTE	Advanced GSM/LTE	Advanced GMS/LTE
Adoption of smartphones	High	High	High	High
Differences				
Political systems	Authoritarian one-party rule	Limited democracy	One-party-dominated representative democracy	Viable democracy
Press systems	State apparatus	Free and market driven	Support the state and nation building	Free and diverse
Press freedom	Not free	Free	Partial	free
Personal freedoms	Not free	Free	Partial free	free
Information accessibility	Low	High	Highest	Medium high

Our expectation is based on past research. As Verclas and Mechael (2008) pointed out, in "not free" countries, people tend to turn to the Internet and mobile phones to "read about themselves in foreign uncensored media" (p. 6). Pestin (2011) argued that these people tend to rely more on the mobile phone for accessing news because their mobile phone is also their Internet and their access to the web and social media. In this study, we will explore if and how the socio-political context may constrain or reduce the benefits and advantages in consuming news brought by 4G and smartphones.

THE DYNAMIC INTERPLAY BETWEEN TECHNOLOGY AND SOCIETY

In addition to selection of cities for cross-societal comparison, time is another dimension of our comparative analysis of mobile news consumption. According to McQuail (2000), the "nature of relation between media and society depends on circumstance of time and place" (p. 11). To trace the rapid changes in mobile technology and how the technological advances affect consumption of mobile news, we pursued a cross-time analysis of data collected respectively from the 3G era (2010–2011) and 4G era (2017–2018). It is in the 4G era that mobile technology's unique and growing advantage in terms of always-on connectivity and high accessibility might be critical in differentiating mobile news usage from traditional news consumption (Westlund, 2010). We anticipate that advances in mobile technology will contribute to greater access, increased consumption, and engagement with mobile news across the two periods.

Concurrently, news consumption is increasingly under socio-political influences in Asian societies. In the 4G era, authorities in China and Singapore have started to fill the policy gap by imposing varying degrees of control in terms of imposing new laws or censorship of news content created and distributed on the mobile phone, and ideological control over the mobile communications.

Accordingly, consuming mobile news involves a new technology that promises freedom in the four Asian cities with varying degrees of increasing political constraints. Under these circumstances, we seek to compare technological trends versus societal factors in influencing the processes and effects of mobile news consumption. As Figure 2.3 illustrates, technology and society interact in influencing the consumption of mobile news. Technology has the potential to bring positive impacts on society as a force of its own, but society provides the context that shapes the diffusion and use of technology. We expect that societal influences or increased constraints imposed by the political systems in the four Asian cities will

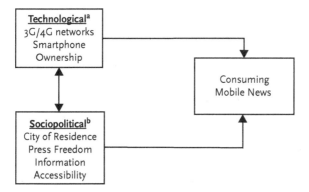

Figure 2.3 The Interplay between Technological Factors and Socio-political Forces in Shaping Mobile News Consumption in Asia

[a] Technology = having impacts on society.

[b] Society = providing the context that shapes the diffusion and use of technology.

Credit: Ran Wei and Ven-hwei Lo

have a significant and stronger impact on mobile news consumption than mobile technology.

METHODOLOGY AND DATA

Population of Study

College students in the four studied Asian cities were our population of study. They respectively belonged to Generation Y (aka millennials, born between 1984 and 1996, who are the first generation of digital natives) and Generation Z (aka centennials, born after 1997, who are the first mobile generation of digital natives) in our two waves of survey. Our decision was based on three considerations.

First, consuming news on mobile phones is particularly popular among youth (Wolf & Schnauber, 2015). As Poindexter (2016) and others (Westlund, 2013) have acknowledged, the deepening diffusion of mobile phones and smart devices created a new type of news consumer, who chooses smartphones and tablets over PC (e.g., laptops and desktops) to access and consume news. They also tend to skip traditional news media for news.

Second, young people at college age are mobile phone savvy. Scholars (Donald, Anderson, & Spry, 2010) have noted that youth in Asia have embraced the mobile phone in all aspects of their lives, using it 24/7. The mobile phone is probably the most influential medium among young people in Asia (R. Wei & Lo, 2006). This is particularly true with the college students who live away from home; they rely solely on their phone to stay connected and to stay informed.

Third, those in the age group of 18 to 24 are the principal consumers of mobile news. Accessing news 24/7 from the mobile phone is popular among young people (e.g., about 70% in Taiwan, 68% on smartphones in Hong Kong; see Chan, 2015). According to Chan-Olmsted et al. (2013), young mobile news consumers tend to follow breaking news, subscribe to several news platforms at once, value news and information utility, and pay great attention to portal news sites. Additionally, they are more likely to share news with those in their personal circles. Thus, mobile news users mix online news-consuming habits with their social media preferences in consuming mobile news.

In short, college students as a demographic group represent a key adult cohort of Asia's mobile phone users (Donald et al., 2010). It seems to us that for young people who mature into citizens, knowing what is important domestically and internationally from news is a critical part of their political socialization and growing experience. The details of sampling procedures and sampling profiles are provided in Appendix A.

Surveys

Survey was the main research method for data collection. To trace the rapid changes in mobile communication technology and how the technological changes affect consumption of news accessed from the mobile phone, we conducted two waves of parallel surveys respectively in 2010–2011 and 2017–2018.

During the span of eight years, the technology in mobile networks advanced from 3G to 4G, turning the mobile phone into a smart pocket-size information and communication hub. Smartphones supported by 3G networks provide users with a mobile web experience integrated with messaging features and a keyboard on a touch screen. In the 4G era, during the golden decade of the mobile phone in the 2010s, the broadband was expanded to smartphones with faster speeds; the always-on connectivity affords users with "ubiquitous computing" on the go. Apps developed specifically for mobile phones continue to grow in quantity and type. See Appendix A for measures and scales.

Focus Groups

In addition to the two waves of survey, a total of six focus groups were conducted in the four studied cities to gain insights into the thoughts and decision-making of Asian college students concerning mobile news consumption. Participants were from the same population of college students, but they were not respondents in any of the surveys.

Prior to the fieldwork of surveys, two focus groups used college students as the participants in Singapore in April 2016 and Taiwan in June 2016 to collect insights into their motives, likes and dislikes, and habitual use of smartphones. Their comments and thoughts were used to revise the questionnaire. Following the completion of the second survey, four more focus groups were organized to collect qualitative data on the motives, uses, and evaluations of mobile news, and the focus group discussions were used to corroborate the survey results. The details of the focus groups appear in Appendix B.

CHAPTER 3

Motivations

Beyond Access

CONSUMING NEWS WITH A PURPOSE

Although news is increasingly accessible to wider audiences thanks to the
ubiquity of mobile phones and digital devices, the behavior of news consumption is rarely random. Rather, the literature (Chan, 2015; Chen, Lo,
Wei, Xu, & Zhang, 2014b) suggests that users' consumption of news, hard
news in particular, is deeply rooted in their informational needs, civic interest, and gratifications sought from mobile phone use. Media scholars
characterized purpose-driven use of news media as motivational news use
(Shoemaker, 1996). According to an American Press Institute report (2015),
millennials acquire news via the smartphone and mobile social media sites
to satisfy a mix of civic motivations, practical problem-solving needs, and
social goals, such as discussing news with friends.

As we argued in Chapter 2, consuming and engaging with mobile news
requires motivation to seek, follow, evaluate, and process news content as
it is created and delivered via the mobile phone. This is especially true for
the young generations of millennials (i.e., Gen Yers) and centennials (i.e.,
Gen Zers), who have not yet formed the habit of news consumption. In
the context of choosing media for seeking news, motivation means a type
of reasoned action based on one's needs or an "impetus" to action (Deci &
Ryan, 1985, p. 3), or purpose-driven, intentional use of media for information seeking (Sundar & Limperos, 2013).

News in Their Pockets. Ran Wei and Ven-hwei Lo, Oxford University Press (2021). © Oxford University Press.
DOI: 10.1093/oso/9780197523728.003.0003

To analyze the purposes of mobile news consumption, we were guided by two motivational theories: (1) uses and gratifications (U&G) of the mobile phone (Dimmick, Sikand, & Patterson, 1994; Leung & Wei, 2000) and (2) expectancies of news (Eastin, Cicchirillo, & Mabry, 2015; R. Wei, Lo, Xu, Chen, & Zhang, 2014). The U&G theory (E. Katz, Blumler, & Gruvivich, 1973; Ruggiero, 2000) views selection of media for consumption as rooted in users' social and psychological needs, which can be gratified by the selected media, leading to intentional media use. The approach has been applied productively in mobile phone use, identifying a range of salient motivations for using the mobile phone such as sociability, relaxation, accessibility, information seeking, and utility (Leung & Wei, 2000; R. Wei, 2008; R. Wei & Lo, 2006; Weiss, 2013; L. Zhang & Pentina, 2012). Flavián and Gurrea (2006) found five motivating factors of consuming news websites: updating issues, specific information seeking, searching for updated news, leisure/entertainment, and habitual use. Incollingo (2018) reported five gratifications sought from mobile news sites: surveillance, amusement, pleasure, convenience, and discussions of news with others.

More importantly, the U&G theory is a useful analytical tool not only in addressing users' needs and motives for employing media but also in predicting consequences of the employment (LaRose & Eastin, 2004). The literature is rich with evidence that gratifications of the mobile phone predict diverse uses of the mobile phone. Instrumental motives explained the use of the mobile phone for news seeking (R. Wei, 2008). Chinese users' motive to escape state surveillance from mobile phone use was a positive predictor of reading news accessed via their mobile phone (R. Wei & Lo, 2015).

Accordingly, the U&G theory provides us with an active audience approach to explain how users' motivations of mobile phone use shape their behavior of consuming news via the phone. We would examine what drives Asian college students to read or view hard news via the mobile phone and then ascertain the presence of civic motivation such as surveillance. Uncovering the underlying motivations for consuming news accessed from the mobile phone lays the groundwork for the ensuing chapters' examination of patterns of consumption, engagement, and knowledge gain from consumption of mobile news.

Similarly, the expectancy value approach (Fishbein & Ajzen, 1976) considers features of media as motivations that drive media use with empirical support. Footed in theory of reasoned action (Fishbein, 1979) concerning the relationship between attitudes and behavior, the expectancy value approach attempts to determine the mental calculations that take place in attitude development that leads to behavior. The cognitive reasoning is based on assessments of beliefs and values about the given choice and the probability of that value to materialize (i.e., expectancy). The higher the probability, the greater the intention is to take action. Chan-Olmsted, Rim, and Zerba (2013) found that the more young adults believed mobile news content as advantageous, the higher their likelihood of adopting mobile news. Park, Kim, and Lee (2010) analyzed consumer preferences for using mobile phones for informational content in mobile-saturated South Korea; they reported that touch screen and full web browsers were motivational factors. Users' belief in the value of pagers as a news source predicted news consumption via the pager (Leung & Wei, 1999a).

Therefore, value expectancies of mobile news as a unique form of digital news will be another set of motivational factors. We anticipate that expectancies associated with mobile news will complement gratifications in explaining mobile news consumption behavior, evaluations, and learning effect. They promise to generate more insights into the motivational reasoning concerning mobile news consumption.

In summary, our book aims to understand why and how Asian college students consume and engage with news accessed from their mobile phones in what Schrøder (2019) called "a high-choice media environment across multiple devices and platforms" (p. 1). In exploring civic motives about consuming the news via the mobile phone, as a bridging chapter, Chapter 3 links Asian college students' civic interest as manifested in consumption of mobile news to their cognitive reasoning of why, and then subsequent consumption of news.

FINDINGS

Motivations of Using the Mobile Phone

For the tech-savvy millennials and centennials, what do they want from using the mobile phone that they carry with them 24/7? How does the mobile phone help them become hardwired for news? What do they expect to be rewarded from news that is readily accessible on their phones? To shed light on these questions, we analyzed data from the two waves of surveys, which tapped their motivations of mobile phone use and expectancies of mobile news.

The first wave of surveys conducted in 2010–2011 used a set of nine items to measure how the mobile phone was viewed as helpful in gratifying the respondents' various needs. Principal component analysis of the nine items with varimax rotation led to a three-factor solution, accounting for

Table 3.1 PRINCIPAL COMPONENT ANALYSIS OF MOTIVATIONAL ITEMS
WITH VARIMAX ROTATION (2010-2011 SURVEYS)

Uses and Gratifications Items	Factor 1	Factor 2	Factor 3
The mobile phone is helpful			
Surveillance			
To get news	.87	.20	.11
To get information about products and services	.92	.18	.07
To get entertainment information	.90	.21	.09
Entertainment			
To relieve boredom	.18	.87	.15
To relax	.16	.83	.18
To pass time	.24	.85	.07
Sociability			
To stay in touch with friends you have no time to meet	.10	.20	.84
To stay in touch with friends who live far away	.07	.13	.88
To stay in touch with your family	.07	.05	.76
Cronbach's alpha	.91	.86	.79
Variance explained (%)	28.46	25.95	23.64

Notes: Scales for uses and gratifications items ranged from 1 (strongly disagree) to 5 (strongly agree). $N = 3,538$.

78.05% of the variance. As Table 3.1 shows, the first factor consisted of three items that focused on the motivation for using the mobile phone to get news, to get information about products and services, and to get entertainment information. Because it reflects a civic motivation in using mobile phones to secure information about what's important (Beaudoin & Thorson, 2004; Shoemaker, 1996), the factor was named "surveillance motivation" ($M = 2.93$, $SD = 1.01$, $\alpha = .91$).

The second factor, named as "entertainment," contained three items that reflected the motivation for using the mobile phone to relieve boredom, to relax, or simply to pass time ($M = 3.41$, $SD = .95$, $\alpha = .86$). The third factor, called "sociability," consisted of another three items: to stay in touch with friends "you" have no time to meet, to stay in touch with friends who live far away, and to stay in touch with family ($M = 4.00$, $SD = .70$, $\alpha = .79$).

In the second wave of surveys completed in 2017–2018, principal component analysis of the same set of nine items with varimax rotation also identified three factors accounting for 73.85% of the variance. As shown in Table 3.2, the first factor, "entertainment," consisted of the three items

Table 3.2 PRINCIPAL COMPONENT ANALYSIS OF MOTIVATIONAL ITEMS WITH VARIMAX ROTATION (2017–2018 SURVEYS)

Uses and Gratifications Items	Factor 1	Factor 2	Factor 3
The mobile phone is helpful			
Entertainment			
To relieve boredom	.86	.18	.18
To relax	.84	.17	.11
To pass time	.79	.28	.13
Surveillance			
To get news	.20	.77	.23
To get information about products and services	.17	.87	.17
To get entertainment information	.27	.82	.14
Sociability			
To stay in touch with friends you have no time to meet	.19	.12	.86
To stay in touch with friends who live far away	.06	.16	.86
To stay in touch with your family	.06	.20	.70
Cronbach's alpha	.83	.84	.78
Variance explained (%)	25.08	25.03	23.74

Notes: Scales for uses and gratifications items ranged from 1 (strongly disagree) to 5 (strongly agree). $N = 2,988$.

that reflected the motivation for using the mobile phone for fun in terms of relieving boredom, relaxation, and filling some downtime ($M = 3.96$, $SD = .82$, $\alpha = .83$). The second factor, "surveillance," contained three items that reflected the motivation for using mobile phone to get news and information ($M = 3.95$, $SD = .76$, $\alpha = .84$). The third factor, "sociability," consisted of three items that reflected the motivation for using the mobile phone to stay in touch with friends and family through calling or texting ($M = 4.09$, $SD = .70$, $\alpha = .78$).

Taken together, these factor analyses of data collected from the two waves of surveys indicate that Asian college students tend to use the mobile phone to fulfill three basic informational and communicative needs: surveillance, sociability, and entertainment. Moreover, the structure of the three motivational factors was stable across the two periods of survey that spanned eight years, with each factor showing sufficient reliability. Consistent with the literature (Leung & Wei, 1999a; Ling, 2008; R. Wei, 2008), these results underscored the importance of using the mobile phone for social interaction, fun and relaxation, and information facilitation among the surveyed college students in Hong Kong, Shanghai, Taipei, and Singapore.

Surveillance, the need to search for information about the world at large, was a consistent factor of mobile phone use, revealing a civic motivation, whereas sociability was the most-sought gratification among college students in the four Asian cities. This result is understandable. It suggests that in the context of living on campus, students view the mobile phone as sort of what Wenner (1982) called "interpersonal utility," or what Bantz (1982) termed a "social resource" (e.g., something to talk about).

Participants in our focus group discussions in the four studied cities lend their perspectives to support these findings. They speak about what having a mobile phone means and explain in their own words why they consider themselves hardwired for news. A 22-year-old male student in Taipei described that missing his phone while on the go is close to something like a nightmare. He said, "I would go home right away to search for it; otherwise, I will have a bad day." His schoolmate added, "I like to use mobile apps for news such as KOL (a news site known for investigative reporting in Taiwan); the 'Around the World in 24 Hours' published on DQ (a news aggregator and mobile social platform) is awesome. I no longer bother to read newspapers or watch newscast on TV."

A 23-year-old female student in Shanghai who started using a mobile phone in the fifth grade and had her first smartphone in her freshmen year in college explains how her daily life is intertwined with her phone. She said:

> The phone is critical to me, without it, my life may just come to a halt. I use it for mobile pay on shopping trips; I stay in touch with people I cannot meet by texting or mobile apps like WeChat or QQ. If I were silent on those apps for a few days, people in my circle might think I'm a missing person or something.

A second-year female student aged 20 in Hong Kong, who had the habit of accessing news on her phone since her first year in college, said, "With a smartphone, I could have ready access to news provided by various news organizations, even when I am walking on the street."

Considering that their lives centered around the always-on smartphone, it is worth noting that surveillance is a consistent motivation for mobile phone use, underscoring the value of the mobile phone as a pocket-size informational gateway for Asian college students to fulfill their informational need so as to meet their civic goal. Thus, surveillance motivation provides the ground for examining motivational news use or intentional use of media for news, which differs categorically from random or accidental use of the news (R. Yu, 2019).

Additional student perspectives confirm this notion. To a 23-year-old female student in Shanghai, the mobile phone in her pocket meant "a quick way to stay in the know about what's going on in the world." When asked why she read news via her mobile phone, a female student in Singapore responded, "Yeah, like whenever you are bored. I won't use laptop but will scroll through my phone when I am waiting for bus or on the MRT to view the news since there is no Wi-Fi." Her schoolmate added, "I do it definitely on the phone. I only use laptop for work, and I use my phone to visit news site. You will have a lot of free time on the public transport. Use phone will be easier to read news."

A second-year female student also aged 20 in Hong Kong mentioned accessibility at no cost and convenience as reasons she chose to read news on her phone. She said, "It's always accessible to diverse content. I could access news articles from different media organizations with a few clicks, instead of buying piles of newspapers or switching from channel to channel, all for free. Now, I do not need to sit in front of a television or flipping through the pile of newspaper to read the news."

Changes Over Time in Motivations for Using the Mobile Phone

Furthermore, as Table 3.3 shows, respondents surveyed in the 2017–2018 period were likely to consider the three motivations for using the mobile phone as more important than those surveyed in the 2010–2011 period. This rising trend coincided with the network upgrade from 3G to 4G, indicating the deepening dependency of Asian college students on the mobile phone to

Table 3.3 CHANGES IN MOTIVATIONS OF MOBILE PHONE USE ACROSS TWO WAVES OF SURVEYS

Sample	2010–2011 (N = 3,538)	2017–2018 (N = 2,988)	t Value
Surveillance	2.93 (1.01)	3.95 (.76)	46.36***
Entertainment	3.41 (.95)	3.96 (.82)	25.06***
Sociability	4.00 (.70)	4.09 (.70)	5.14***

Notes: The 5-point scale for motivations ranged from 1 (strongly disagree) to 5 (strongly agree). Figures in parentheses are standard deviations.
***$p < .001$.

meet their communicative and informational needs. The three motivations reveal the underlying reasons college students in Asia view the mobile phone as an all-in-one media choice that is essential to socialize, to entertain, and to stay informed. They also illuminate the question of how the mobile phone as an information facilitator fits into their busy lives in college.

Results of a series of independent t-tests show that respondents assigned greater importance of using the mobile phone for sociability (t = 5.14, p < .001), entertainment (t = 25.06, p < .001), and surveillance (t = 46.36, p < .001) in the 2017–2018 surveys than in the 2010–2011 surveys. It seems that the more that the Internet-enabled mobile phone became an indispensable convergent media in the lives of surveyed Asian college students, the greater their motivation to use the phone to gratify their needs for socialization, entertainment, and information. We anticipate that these motivations, surveillance in particularly, will serve as an internal drive for consuming and engaging with mobile news.

Gender Differences in Motivations of Mobile Phone Use

The surveys found significant differences between male and female respondents in their motivations for mobile phone use. Data from the 2010–2011 surveys in Table 3.4 show that males (M = 2.98, SD = 1.06) were more likely than females (M = 2.90, SD = .98) to view surveillance as an important motivation for using the mobile phone (t = 2.43, p < .05). On the other hand, females were more likely than males to consider sociability (t = –5.89, p < .001) and entertainment (t = –8.17, p < .001) as important motivations behind uses of the mobile phone.

The results are consistent with the telephony literature (Dimmick et al., 1994; Leung & Wei, 1999a; Moyal, 1992; Rakow, 1992). Female users

Table 3.4 GENDER DIFFERENCES IN MOTIVATIONS OF USING MOBILE PHONE (2010–2011 SURVEYS)

Motives/Sample	Male	Female	*t* Value
Surveillance	2.98 (1.06)	2.90 (.98)	2.43*
Entertainment	3.30 (.98)	3.49 (.92)	–5.89***
Sociability	3.89 (.75)	4.09 (.65)	–8.17***

Notes: The 5-point scale for motivations ranged from 1 (strongly disagree) to 5 (strongly agree). Figures in parentheses are standard deviations.
***p < .001, *p < .05.

Table 3.5 GENDER DIFFERENCES IN MOTIVATIONS OF USING MOBILE PHONE (2017–2018 SURVEYS)

Motives/Sample	Male	Female	t Value
Surveillance	3.89 (.79)	4.00 (.72)	−4.03***
Entertainment	3.89 (.86)	4.02 (.77)	−4.18***
Sociability	4.00 (.72)	4.16 (.67)	−6.05***

Notes: The 5-point scale for motivations ranged from 1 (strongly disagree) to 5 (strongly agree). Figures in parentheses are standard deviations.
***$p < .001$.

considered the mobile phone as a social tool primarily for interpersonal communication, whereas male users regarded it as a device for instrumental purposes. Such results also fit well with Bales and Parsons's (2014) characterization of women as "expressive" and men as "instrumental" (p. 151) in the context of mobile communication.

Gender differences persisted in the data of the 2017–2018 surveys. However, the gender gap was reversed. As shown in Table 3.5, females were more likely than their male counterparts to perceive the mobile phone as helpful to meet all three needs. This particular result suggests that female college students have become more motivated to use the mobile phone for social and instrumental purposes, including staying informed, while male college students slacked off.

More accounts from focus group discussants reveal the differences between male and female college students. A female student in Shanghai explained her motive for seeking news using her mobile phone this way: "I read news randomly; but when people around me talk about some news events, I feel that I got to catch up with the news."

Two male second-year students aged 20 in Hong Kong said they started reading news on their phones when they were in their first year of middle school back in 2013. However, a male student in Hong Kong said, "at the age of 13, I already started using smartphone and downloaded various apps for consuming news."

A female student in Singapore said, "Yeah. Mobile news is definitely more immediate. News on social media is a much more accessible source." Another female student at her school added, "It is what Facebook does to make news more personal." Their male schoolmate, who routinely consumed news on news sites of established news organizations, said, "We usually visit news from the site itself. Based on previous search history, they personalize, and they will push more relevant articles to you."

Table 3.6 MOTIVATIONS OF MOBILE PHONE USE IN SHANGHAI, HONG KONG, TAIPEI, AND SINGAPORE (2010–2011 SURVEYS)

Motivations	Shanghai	Hong Kong	Taipei	Singapore	Total	F Value
Surveillance	3.30 (.89)	2.73 (.96)	2.52 (.95)	3.27 (.98)	2.93 (1.01)	162.66***
Entertainment	3.41 (1.00)	3.39 (.91)	3.23 (.97)	3.62 (.87)	3.41 (.95)	32.99***
Sociability	4.07 (.80)	3.84 (.68)	4.03 (.70)	4.02 (.70)	4.00 (.70)	13.83***

Notes: The 5-point scale for motivations ranged from 1 (strongly disagree) to 5 (strongly agree). Figures in parentheses are standard deviations.
***$p < .001$.

Cross-City Differences in Motivations

Next, we analyzed the data to examine differences in motivations of mobile phone use across the four selected cities. In Table 3.6, ANOVA tests revealed significant differences among the respondents in the four cities in both waves of surveys. In the 2010–2011 surveys, Shanghai respondents were more likely than their counterparts in other cities to ascribe greater importance to the motivations of surveillance and sociability. Taipei respondents, on the other hand, were least likely to consider surveillance as well as entertainment as important in mobile phone use. Furthermore, among the four samples, Singaporean respondents were more likely to consider entertainment as an important motive for using the mobile phone, while Hong Kong respondents were least likely to mention sociability as a major motivation for using the mobile phone.

In the 2017–2018 surveys, the cross-city differences also existed, but the patterns changed. As shown in Table 3.7, Singaporean respondents were more likely to consider surveillance as an important motive for using the mobile phone. Taipei respondents were more likely to ascribe greater

Table 3.7 MOTIVATIONS OF MOBILE PHONE USE IN SHANGHAI, HONG KONG, TAIPEI, AND SINGAPORE (2017–2018 SURVEYS)

Motivations	Shanghai	Hong Kong	Taipei	Singapore	Total	F Value
Surveillance	4.00 (.70)	3.64 (.84)	4.11 (.66)	4.05 (.76)	3.95 (.76)	58.91***
Entertainment	3.88 (.81)	3.76 (.94)	4.10 (.68)	4.08 (.78)	3.96 (.82)	30.97***
Sociability	4.13 (.65)	3.84 (.76)	4.17 (.62)	4.21 (.70)	4.09 (.70)	43.11***

Notes: The 5-point scale for motivations ranged from 1 (strongly disagree) to 5 (strongly agree). Figures in parentheses are standard deviations.
***$p < .001$.

importance to the motivations of surveillance as well as entertainment than respondents in the other three cities. Hong Kong respondents were least likely to attach importance to the three motivational factors of mobile phone use. Hong Kong college students were the first in Asia, if not the world, to embrace the mobile phone in the 1990s (Leung & Wei, 2000). It seems that in the first decade of the 2000s, new generations of college students in Hong Kong viewed the mobile phone as nothing out of the extraordinary; or rather, the phone has been imbedded so deeply into their lives that they did not think about why they use it anymore.

Regarding this shifting pattern, participants from the focus groups offered their different perspectives on consuming news via their mobile phones. A 22-year-old female student in Taipei said she relied on her mobile phone to stay informed in her busy college life: "With the phone in my pocket," she said, "I never miss any breaking news or a message that's important to know." Her schoolmate agreed. She said, "Unlike carrying a laptop or watching news on TV, you need to find somewhere to sit down for reading or watching the news."

"Accessing news quick and easy is the edge of the mobile phone": According to a first-year male student in Hong Kong, high accessibility to diverse content draws him to the phone for reading news. He said, "I like browsing news from various media outlets. Compared to traditional ways of news consumption like watching TV and listening to radio, using smartphone allows me to read news from different media at the same time."

Expectancies of Mobile News

The reasons people consume media can also be understood from their expectancies (Eastin et al., 2015). Footed in the expectancy-value framework (Rayburn & Palmgreen, 1984), media expectancy refers to expected gains from media consumption based on users' value assessment of the given media. Arguably, appraisal of mobile news in terms of its attributes represents a different approach as well as a higher level of motivational reasoning.

Accordingly, Asian college students' expectancies of mobile news were analyzed as the second level of motivational factors that drive consumption of mobile news.

Specifically, respondents in the two waves of surveys were asked to rate the importance of a set of eight attributes of mobile news. As shown in Tables 3.8 and 3.9, principal component analysis of these eight items with varimax rotation led to a two-factor solution, accounting

Table 3.8 PRINCIPAL COMPONENT ANALYSIS OF EXPECTANCIES OF MOBILE NEWS WITH VARIMAX ROTATION (2010–2011 SURVEYS)

Expectancies	Factor 1	Factor 2
Interactiveness		
To allow me to rate news	.90	.25
To allow me to correct factual errors	.89	.27
To allow me to comment on news	.88	.29
To allow me to share news online	.86	.34
Personal Value		
To provide useful news	.33	.87
To report the latest information	.32	.86
To be relevant to my schoolwork or interest	.30	.84
To be important to me personally	.16	.77
Cronbach's alpha	.90	.95
Variance explained (%)	43.15	39.16

Note: Scales for expectancy value items ranged from 1 (not important) to 5 (very important).

Table 3.9 PRINCIPAL COMPONENT ANALYSIS OF EXPECTANCIES OF MOBILE NEWS WITH VARIMAX ROTATION (2017–2018 SURVEYS)

Expectancies	Factor 1	Factor 2
Interactiveness		
To allow me to rate news	.86	.10
To allow me to correct factual errors	.84	.17
To allow me to comment on news	.87	.13
To allow me to share news online	.77	.27
Personal Value		
To provide useful news	.14	.89
To report the latest information	.15	.85
To be relevant to my schoolwork or interest	.16	.75
To be important to me personally	.19	.77
Cronbach's alpha	.85	.88
Variance explained (%)	36.00	35.00

Note: Scales for expectancy value items ranged from 1 (not important) to 5 (very important).

respectively for 82.31% of the variance for the first wave of surveys in 2010–2011 and 71.0% of the variance for the second wave of surveys in 2017–2018.

The responses uncovered two expectancies of mobile news that stand out as usability attributes characteristic of such news: The first expectancy, which had four items (43.15% of the explained variance in the first round of surveys and 36.0% of the explained variance in the second round), was "Interactiveness of Mobile News" ($M = 236$, $SD = 1.05$, $\alpha = .90$ for the first period of surveys; $M = 3.15$, $SD = .96$, $\alpha = .85$ for the second). Similar to what Beaudoin and Thorson (2004) called "anticipated interaction," it reveals the anticipated expectation that news accessed from the mobile phone can be useful for conversations with others.

The label of the second expectancy, which consisted of another four items (39.16% of explained variance in the first wave of surveys and 35.0% of the explained variance in the second wave) was "Personal Value of Mobile News" ($M = 2.92$, $SD = 1.07$, $\alpha = .95$ for the first set of surveys; $M = 3.80$, $SD = .75$, $\alpha = .88$ for the second set) because it underscores the expectation of mobile news as practical information that they can use in managing the routines of their daily lives.

To our focus group participants in the four Asian cities, news accessed from their mobile phones means a number of things. A male student aged 24 in Shanghai said, "I like news on my phone for being fast and convenient with breaking news, especially when it beats other news outlets. The content is rich in information, something I can discuss with others." On this expectancy, his schoolmate in Shanghai added, "That's why I like mobile news. It's sharable whenever you feel like sharing it with someone." A second-year male student in Hong Kong said something similar. "With a click on the link or with a screen shot," he said, "I can share the news with other people."

In short, from the user's perspective, they believed that news created and distributed to the mobile screen offers a unique opportunity to secure news as social resources in interactions with others and news that benefits them personally. That is, in judging the quantity, value, and importance of news in their pockets, Asian college students valued inactiveness and utility as distinctive usability attributes of such news.

Changes Over Time in Expectancies of Mobile News

Respondents surveyed in the 2017–2018 period tended to be more likely to regard the two expectancies of mobile news as more important than were

Table 3.10 CHANGES IN EXPECTANCIES OF MOBILE NEWS IN THE TWO
PERIODS OF SURVEY

Expectancies/Sample	2010–2011 (N = 3,538)	2017–2018 (N = 2,988)	t Value
Interactiveness	2.36 (1.05)	3.15 (.96)	32.00***
Personal value	2.96 (1.07)	3.80 (.75)	36.63***

Notes: The 5-point scale for expectancy ranged from 1 (not important at all) to 5 (extremely important).
Figures in parentheses are standard deviations.
***p < .001.

participants in the 2010–2011 period. The changes over time proved significant based on results of a series of independent t-tests.

As Table 3.10 shows, respondents in the 2017–2018 period were more likely to ascribe greater importance to both interactiveness (t = 32.00, p < .001) and personal value of mobile news (t = 36.63, p < .001) than were those in the 2010–2011 surveys. These changes indicate that as the mobile phone became smarter and bigger in screen size, and news delivered to the mobile screen became increasingly diverse in terms of headlines, alerts, links, posts, and tweets 24/7, the respondents expected mobile news to be interactive, relevant, and usable. To them, the informational utility of mobile news would lead to reward.

Gender Differences in Expectancies of Mobile News

Moreover, in the first wave of surveys, significant differences were found between male and female respondents in their expectancies of mobile news. As exhibited in Table 3.11, male respondents in the 2010–2011 surveys were more likely than their female peers to see interactiveness of

Table 3.11 GENDER DIFFERENCES IN EXPECTANCIES OF MOBILE NEWS
IN THE 2010–2011 SURVEYS

Expectancies/Gender	Male	Female	t Value
Interactiveness	2.47 (1.07)	2.28 (1.02)	5.36***
Personal value	3.02 (1.10)	2.92 (1.05)	2.70**

Notes: The 5-point scale for expectancy ranged from 1 (not important at all) to 5 (extremely important).
Figures in parentheses are standard deviations.
**p < .01, ***p < .001.

Table 3.12 GENDER DIFFERENCES IN EXPECTANCIES OF MOBILE NEWS
IN THE 2017–2018 SURVEYS

Expectancies/Gender	Male	Female	t Value
Interactiveness	3.19 (1.01)	3.13 (.93)	1.62
Personal value	3.76 (.79)	3.84 (.71)	−2.94**

Notes: The 5-point scale for expectancy ranged from 1 (not important at all) to 5 (extremely important).
Figures in parentheses are standard deviations.
**$p < .01$.

mobile news ($t = 5.36$, $p < .001$) and personal value ($t = 2.70$, $p < .01$) as more valuable.

However, gender differences in expectancies of mobile news narrowed in the 2017–2018 surveys. As shown in Table 3.12, there is no significant difference between male and female respondents in expectancy of interactiveness ($t = 1.62$, $p > .05$). But concerning the expectancy of personal value, female respondents were more likely than male counterparts to regard it as important ($t = -2.94$, $p < .001$). Considering female respondents had higher social needs to meet through consuming news on the mobile phone, this result makes sense. They tended to regard the personal value of mobile news to be important so as to forward or share the news with others. In other words, the opportunity to share news via the phone meant social interaction in and of itself.

The perspectives from male and female focus group participants in Singapore are revealing. A male student in Singapore said this about his reason for reading the news: "I will read about what I am interested in, politics, sports or IT stuff. For me, it is that simple." His male schoolmate added, "Usually I will go out of my way to search for it, but sometimes, they will have notifications, for example, the *Straits Times* will have the notification. I will see these notifications if it interests me, I will see it from top of the screen."

On the other hand, a female student in Singapore said that seeking news on her phone "will not be the first thing I wake up in the morning, and oh let's find out what's the news kind of thing, no. Do I discuss news over breakfast with family or over dinner and over lunch with friends? No. If it is something interesting and will concern us, I will look it up." She included "things like tension between North Korea and South Korea. Things that will concern us."

Table 3.13 EXPECTANCIES OF MOBILE NEWS IN SHANGHAI, HONG KONG, TAIPEI, AND SINGAPORE (2010–2011 SURVEYS)

Expectancies	Shanghai	Hong Kong	Taipei	Singapore	Total	F Value
Interactiveness	2.84 (1.06)	2.24 (.97)	2.10 (.99)	2.39 (1.03)	2.36 (1.05)	82.96***
Personal value	3.33 (.90)	2.73 (.99)	2.49 (1.03)	3.37 (1.03)	2.96 (1.07)	187.05***

Notes: The 5-point scale for expectancy ranged from 1 (not important at all) to 5 (extremely important). Figures in parentheses are standard deviations.
***$p < .001$.

Cross-City Differences in Expectancies of Mobile News

To analyze whether college students in Hong Kong, Taipei, Shanghai, and Singapore differed in their expectancies of mobile news, we conducted a series of one-way ANOVA tests. As Table 3.13 shows, significant differences were found among the four samples in the first wave of surveys. Respondents in Shanghai viewed interactiveness as the highest expectancy associated with mobile news ($M = 2.84$, $SD = 1.06$), followed by those in Singapore ($M = 2.39$, $SD = 1.03$) and Hong Kong ($M = 2.24$, $SD = .97$). Taipei respondents ($M = 2.10$, $SD = .99$) considered it as the least important.

Regarding the expected personal value of mobile news, respondents in Singapore ($M = 2.37$, $SD = 1.03$) and Shanghai ($M = 3.33$, $SD = .90$) considered it as more important than those surveyed in Hong Kong ($M = 2.73$, $SD = .99$) and Taipei ($M = 2.49$, $SD = 1.03$). The prevailing PC culture as well as the relatively low rate of smartphone ownership in Taipei at 28.4% (as compared to 54.3% in Hong Kong, 61.8% in Shanghai, and 70.4% in Singapore in the 2010–2011 surveys) among the four surveyed Asian cities may have contributed to the relatively low expectancies of mobile news held by Taiwan respondents.

The cross-city differences are put into perspective by two focus group participants in Taipei and Hong Kong. A female student in her early 20s in Taipei who had her first mobile phone in third grade said, "I resisted the urge to upgrade to smartphones for a while; I have no particular desire for a smartphone." Like her schoolmates, she carried a laptop on the road. When needing to check the news, she said, "I power on my laptop to catch up what's in the news." Her schoolmate, another female aged 21, added, "If I have my laptop with me, I don't need bother to read news on my phone."

Table 3.14 EXPECTANCIES OF MOBILE NEWS IN SHANGHAI, HONG KONG, TAIPEI, AND SINGAPORE (2017–2018 SURVEYS)

Expectancies	Shanghai	Hong Kong	Taipei	Singapore	Total	F Value
Interactiveness	3.37 (.99)	3.17 (.93)	3.36 (.77)	2.66 (1.00)	3.15 (.96)	58.91***
Personal value	3.74 (.83)	3.67 (.78)	3.83 (.69)	3.96 (.65)	3.80 (.75)	30.97***

Notes: The 5-point scale for expectancy ranged from 1 (not important at all) to 5 (extremely important). Figures in parentheses are standard deviations.
***$p < .001$.

A male student in Hong Kong, however, said, "mobile news is immediate. This is because the apps of some news media will send notifications to me when there are some important news or information in society, such as new cases of Coronavirus confirmed in Hong Kong." His schoolmate, another second-year student, added, "I used Facebook to consume news daily by subscribing or liking their Facebook page of different news media, such as Stand News, Initium Media, Cable News, *Apple Daily*, etc. The Facebook news page uploads posts and they will pop up in my newsfeed."

The expectancies of mobile news increased across the four samples in the second wave of surveys, indicating that the usability attributes of mobile news as interactive and personally usable became more salient eight years after the first wave. However, cross-city differences in expectancies remained significant. Based on results of the one-way ANOVA tests presented in Table 3.14, Shanghai respondents again regarded interactiveness as the highest in importance ($M = 3.37$, $SD = .99$), whereas the expectancy of mobile news as highly interactive by Singaporean respondents was the lowest ($M = 2.66$, $SD = 1.00$). On the other hand, the Singaporeans' expectancy of mobile news as relevant, personal, and valuable was the highest ($M = 3.96$, $SD = .65$), followed by those in Taipei ($M = 3.83$, $SD = .69$), Shanghai ($M = 3.74$, $SD = .83$), and Hong Kong ($M = 3.67$, $SD = .78$). These results reveal that college students in Shanghai and Singapore had high expectancies of mobile news as technologically sophisticated or high in beneficial utility.

Predicting Expectancies of Mobile News

Finally, do demographics, city of residence, and motivations of mobile phone use hold predictive power over expectancies of mobile news? Which of the three mobile phone use motivational factors has the strongest influences on these expectancies or usability attributes of mobile news?

Table 3.15 HIERARCHICAL REGRESSION ANALYSIS PREDICTING EXPECTANCIES OF MOBILE NEWS

Independent Variables	2010–2011		2007–2008	
	Interactiveness	Personal Value	Interactiveness	Personal Value
Block 1: Demographics				
Gender (male)	.02	.08***	−.01	.06***
Age	.04*	.00	.04*	−.10***
City (Shanghai)	.08***	.16***	−.08***	.13***
Adjusted R^2	3.5%	5.9%	1.1%	1.8%
Block 2: Smartphone Ownership				
Smartphone owned	.12***	.03	−.05**	.05**
Incremental Adjusted R^2	10.9%	2.7%	2.1%	1.8%
Block 3: Motives of Mobile Phone Use				
Sociability	.08***	.03	.18***	.04
Entertainment	.07***	.07***	.08***	.04
Surveillance	.38***	.35***	.28***	.25***
Incremental adjusted R^2	16.2%	12.7%	17.3%	7.8%
Total adjusted R^2	27.1%	21.3%	20.5%	9.6%
N	3,429	3,433	2,793	2,799

Note: Beta weights are from final regression equation with all blocks of variables in the model.
***$p < .001$, **$p < .01$, *$p < .05$.

Four separate hierarchical regression analyses were run to address these questions. The regression analyses treated interactiveness and personal value as dependent variables, with gender, age, city, smartphone owner-ship, sociability, entertainment, and surveillance as predictors.

As shown in Table 3.15 (column 1), the 2010–2011 surveys showed socia-bility ($B = .08$, $p < .001$), entertainment ($B = .07$, $p < .001$), and surveillance ($B = .38$, $p < .001$) as significant predictors of the expectancy of interactiveness. Furthermore, the results (column 2) show that entertainment ($B = .07$, $p < .001$) and surveillance ($B = .35$, $p < .001$) were also significant predictors of personal value. However, sociability was not significantly associated with personal value ($B = .03$, $p > .05$). As we expected, surveillance motivation of using the mobile phone to stay informed emerged as the strongest predictor of interactiveness and personal value associated with mobile news.

Regression analyses of the 2017–2018 survey data show (column 3) that sociability (B = .18, p < .001), entertainment (B = .08, p < .001), and surveillance (B = .28, p < .001) were significantly related to interactiveness of mobile news. Moreover, surveillance was a significant predictor of personal value (B = .25, p < .001), while sociability (B = .04, p > .05) and entertainment (B = .04, p > .05) were not after influences of other significant predictors were taken into account.

Consistently, the results indicated that surveillance motivation emerged as the strongest predictor of expectancies of mobile news in terms of being interactive and personally valuable. They provided the empirical evidence in support of the link between surveillance of mobile phone uses and Asian college students' expectancy values of news accessed from the phone.

First-hand accounts of consuming mobile news from participants in our focus groups support these findings. To a 22-year-old male student in Taipei, watching news on TV and reading it on the mobile phone are two different experiences. He elaborated, "TV pushes news to your face once it is on. But for getting news on the phone, you need to make an effort to search for it." His female schoolmate agreed: "Yeah, you need to be in the driver's seat for it. Without the drive, why bother with the news?" The third-year female student in Taipei explained her attachment to her phone for speedily accessing news this way:

> I need my phone for getting news because I want to discuss politics with others. You know, my friends and I are all political junkies of some sort. We skim the news of the day and then come up with something to chat and to debate about. On Facebook, you can see postings and comments on the news. It's a how I get exposed to different perspectives.

Summary of Chapter Key Findings

The key findings of the chapter are summarized as follows:

- Three motivational factors for using the mobile phone are uncovered: surveillance, sociability, and entertainment. Data from two waves of surveys of college students in the four Asian cities show that sociability was the most-sought gratification, followed by entertainment and surveillance. Additionally, the importance of the three motivational factors increased as the wireless telecommunications network updated from 3G to 4G, suggesting the students became more dependent on their phone for meeting diverse needs and goals.

- Two expectancies of mobile news have come to the fore: interactiveness and personal value. The surveys revealed the students' perception of mobile news as something they could interact with and use in a practical sense. The expectancies increased across time in the second survey period, indicating usability attributes of mobile news as critical in deciding whether to consume such news.
- Gender differences in motivations for mobile phone use exist. Male respondents considered surveillance as a more important motivational factor than their female peers, but female respondents tended to view sociability and entertainment as more important to gratify themselves than male respondents. The gender gap in surveillance narrowed in the second survey period due to increases in the three motivational factors among female respondents.
- Gender differences in expectancies of mobile news also exist. Male respondents' expectancies of interactiveness and personal value were higher than those of their female peers. However, the differences decreased in the 2017–2018 surveys. In fact, female respondents tended to regard the personal value expectancy as more important than male respondents to meet their social needs. They expected mobile news to be highly useful personally so as to facilitate their social interaction with others.
- Respondents from the surveyed four cities differ in their civic motivation. In the first wave of surveys, Shanghai respondents rated the helpfulness of the mobile phone for surveillance the highest, while Taipei respondents rated it the lowest. The cross-city differences persisted in the second survey period; Singaporean respondents still attached the greatest importance to surveillance, but Hong Kong respondents ascribed it the least.
- Similarly, cross-city differences exist in expectancies of mobile news. Respondents in Shanghai and Singapore tended to view interactiveness as the highest expectancy. Taipei respondents were inclined to regard it as the least important. These results reveal that college students in Shanghai and Singapore who live in societies where press freedom is restricted to varying degrees have the highest expectancies for mobile news.
- As anticipated, surveillance motivation for mobile phone use turns out to be the strongest predictor of interactiveness and personal value associated with mobile news, suggesting that stronger motivation to stay informed leads to higher expectancies of mobile news as technologically and practically capable to meet the informational need.

GENERALIZATIONS AND THEORETICAL INSIGHTS

This chapter establishes the motivation and expectancies of consuming news accessed from the mobile phone. Findings explain why Asian college students want to use their phone to read and follow news in a high-choice and high-risk media environment—these students surveyed in our study can be characterized as active, purpose-driven news consumers who consider possibilities of consuming mobile news to satisfy their civic interest and fulfill their civic role. As a civic motivation, surveillance stands out as a major underlying reason for their use of the versatile mobile phone, which drives consumption of news (i.e., motivational news use). In other words, civic-minded college students in Asia show a strong need for securing news from the mobile phone to stay in the know; surveillance gratification thus becomes their civic motivation to be informed citizens.

Based on key findings of Chapter 3, three generalizations with theoretical insights into the motivational reasoning concerning mobile news can be made:

First, from the perspective of active users, their reappraisals of technological attributes of mobile news mean expectancies in terms of sharable utility. Expectancies of mobile news stand out as its usability attributes. Thus, accessing news from the mobile phone provides users with news that is interactable and practically usable. Consistent with the literature (LaRose & Eastin, 2004), civic motivation and practical considerations of mobile news seem to go hand in hand, complementing each other in revealing the underlying needs-based reasoning about news expectancies resolving around motives and uses of the mobile phone. In addition, Gen Zers surveyed in the 2017–2018 period regard interactiveness and personal value of mobile news as more important than did millennials surveyed in the 2010–2011 surveys. The changes over time suggest that to consume mobile news efficiently and effectively, Gen Zers consider it more important for mobile news to be interactive and personally usable. The higher expectancy illustrates the newer generation of Asian college students' desire to go beyond access for engaged consumption.

Second, even though the mobile phone can be viewed as fulfilling both relation-oriented and task-oriented needs, male college students tend to take an instrumental view of mobile news, whereas female college students are relationally oriented in their views of the mobile phone. The gender differences are consistent with the expressive versus instrumental divide in telephony communication (Claisse & Rowe, 1993; Dimmick et. al, 1994; Moyal, 1992; Rakow, 1992). The good news is that the gender gap was reversed in the second period of surveys, which showed a greater expectancy by women to use the mobile phone for civic interest. The implications are that in analyzing the behavior of consuming mobile news, it is important to pay attention to the different ways in which male and female users view the mobile phone in general and mobile news in particular. Accordingly, we will incorporate gender analyses in the subsequent chapters.

Third, cross-city differences in the level of civic motivation for consuming mobile news add another dimension to explore in examining the behavior of consuming mobile news. Considering that news media enjoy total freedom in Taiwan where traditional and online media are dynamic and widely available, it is not surprising that Taipei respondents are inclined to regard the mobile phone as less critical to access and consume news. On the other hand, it is not coincidental that the Shanghai and Singapore respondents expressed the greatest need for surveillance and hold the highest expectancy of mobile news. These cross-city differences in motives reveal that societal influences in terms of free flow of information and press freedom should be thoroughly investigated. We will examine if and how those differences at the societal level will influence the pattern of consumption and engagement with mobile news in the next two chapters.

In conclusion, past research (Chan, 2015; Chen et al., 2014a; Shim et al., 2015) has shown sufficient evidence that informational motivation associated with uses of the mobile phone is a reliable predictor of seeking, consuming, and interacting with mobile news. Moreover, past research (R. Yu, 2019) also shows that motivational use of digital news is linked to political knowledge. As such, surveillance motivation and expectancies of mobile news as being interactive and personally valuable will prove to yield strong predictive power over the actual consumption behavior (Chapter 4), engagement with mobile news (Chapter 5), perceptions of mobile news (Chapter 6), and knowledge gain from the news (Chapter 7).

CHAPTER 4

Consumption

Diverse and Rising

MOBILE NEWS IN ASIA'S FOUR LEADING CITIES

Asia's leading cities—Hong Kong, Singapore, Shanghai, and Taipei—are early adopters of information and communications technologies, including the Internet and the mobile phone (Leung, 2007; Leung & Wei, 1998, 2000). They are the most wired and mobile cities in the region. Consuming news from mobile devices dated back to the 2G era—consumers in Chinese societies used the pager to read news and public information (e.g., weather, stock market, and traffic updates). Breaking news pushed to pager users turned the wireless personal communication gadget into a pocket-sized device for consuming news in the 1990s.

Shanghai, China

SMS (short message service) took off in China in 2002, the year Nokia marketed a phone that included the *pinyin* input system supporting simplified Chinese characters.[1] The debut of a Nokia phone supported by 2G networks was a milestone event. Soon afterward, the first news service in the forms of SMS and MMS (Multimedia Message Service) packaged and delivered for the mobile phone, which was called *Shouji Bao* (the Mobile Press), debuted in July 2004. It was a partnership between the *Chinese Women's Daily* and China Mobile, a national mobile network operator and

News in Their Pockets. Ran Wei and Ven-hwei Lo, Oxford University Press (2021). © Oxford University Press.
DOI: 10.1093/oso/9780197523728.003.0004

service provider (Hu, 2009). Other newspapers, including those dailies in Shanghai, followed the trend in marketing mobile news to paid subscribers.

Following network upgrades to 3G in China, more diverse forms of mobile news were introduced, such as web-like news sites (e.g., i-News) supported by WAP (wireless application protocols) for Internet-enabled mobile phones. Responding to the shift to mobile screens for news, newspapers implemented a mobile-first strategy by publishing on WeChat's public accounts. Six of the top 10 accounts are operated by legacy media outlets (M. Li, 2018).

Mobile news gained popularity rapidly because of timely updates and accessibility to news without the constraints of time and location. China's mobile users spend a great deal of time reading news on their smartphones. Over half of active users cited news-getting as the main reason they used WeChat in a 2015–2016 e-marketer survey. Subscribers to mobile news totaled 27 million in 2007, and doubled to 52 million in 2009 (iResearch, 2009).

The business model of mobile news in China, including Shanghai, featured a tri-party model: channel operators (mobile network operators), newspapers (content providers), and third-party IT service providers. In the 3G era, China Mobile sought to expand its network operator's role beyond a channel to become a content provider. Because the Chinese government at all levels did not put telecommunications service under ideological control until the 4G era, publishing news and user-generated content in the forms of SMS and MMS led to the creation of what He (2008) called "the private discourse universe" (p. 182), which means uncensored news in SMS found its way into the mobile sphere.

The most significant development in 2010 was the convergence of smartphones with the Internet, which made it easy to access social media sites on the go. The relatively less regulated SMS for news publishing was replaced by Twitter-like microblogs known as Weibo (*microblogs*). According to a survey of CNNIC (2011), one-third of China's mobile Internet users (e.g., smartphone owners) opened a blog account, thus registering a presence in the microblog sphere.

Similar to the critical role of browsers for PCs as the gateway to access websites in the 2000s, apps served as the major gateway for Chinese smartphone users to access news in the 2010s. Almost half (45.6%) of the Chinese population acquired news through their smartphones thanks to mobile news apps and smartphone-accessed social media platforms like Weibo and WeChat (a popular all-in-one micromessaging app). As a result, more noticeable changes in Chinese mobile phone users' reading habits and news consumption preferences took place in the 4G era. The number of mobile news users reached 631 million (CNNIC, 2018). Over 60% respondents in a survey said that their primary source to access news is mobile social apps such as WeChat (M. Li, 2018).

In Shanghai, to cater to the needs of the digital media market dominated by the young generations, leading newspapers consolidated their businesses and enhanced news content to attract mobile subscribers. *Jiefang Daily*, the oldest and largest-circulated paper controlled by the ruling party, runs a mobile edition of its paper (*Mobile Jiefang Daily*). The Oriental portal, a leading local news website, publishes a mobile version of its site known as the Oriental Mobile News (*Dongfang Shouji Bao*) and has developed a mobile-first strategy in reporting breaking news.

The fact that the mobile phone has opened up new spaces for civic discourse in China reflects the contradictions of the Chinese government's desire to develop new media technologies to catch up with the West (Wallis, 2011) while controlling what it deems as harmful content on new media platforms. R. Wei and Lo (2015) characterized China's media environment as "media rich, information poor" (p. 179). As mobile news has gone mainstream beyond a supplementary to official news media, censorship of news publishing on mobile platforms by the Chinese authorities is increasingly common, including news and messages posted on Weibo and WeChat.

Hong Kong

Hong Kong has long been considered a major telecommunications hub in the Asia-Pacific region. The mobile phone penetration rate topped 120% in 2005 (Office of the Telecommunications Authority [OFTA], 2005). According to the Reuters Institute Digital News Report (2017), Hong Kong is the world's "most mobile" market in terms of news consumption; Nielson (2018) reported that 97% of Hong Kong Internet users access the Internet via mobile phones; and Cheung (2017) found that 31% of respondents who consumed mobile news were mobile-only users. Part of the reason for the popularity of mobile news in the former British colony is that residents of Hong Kong spend an average of 73 minutes on public transit systems (GovHK, 2019).

In an earlier survey conducted in 2013, Chan (2015) reported that the majority of Hong Kong people were multiplatform users, who utilized both the Internet and the mobile phone to access news content. Also, he found that millennials tended to rely solely on the mobile phone for news consumption at the expense of newspapers or television. Two major dailies, *Hong Kong Daily News* and *The Sun,* ceased publishing due to falling circulations (Chan, Chen, & Lee, 2017).

In a tech-savvy city like Hong Kong, the decline of consumption of print newspapers over the past five years has been largely offset by the increasing number of audiences who consume digital versions of newspapers. Almost all of the traditional news media have developed their own mobile apps for distributing news content to meet the rising needs of mobile phone users (Du & Tang, 2019; Kam, 2018).

Posting and publishing news on mobile networks in Hong Kong are regulated under the Unsolicited Electronic Messages Ordinance, which includes email and SMS over mobile networks. The purpose of the 2007 regulations of electronic messages is to protect consumer privacy and re-duce spamming, not exercise censorship by the authorities. Creating and disseminating news for mobile phones is as free as the traditional news outlets in Hong Kong.

Singapore

The first mobile news alert service, known as the SPH Breaking News SMS Alert, debuted in January 2008 in Singapore. Similar to China's experi-ence, it was jointly provided by the dominant newspaper group (Singapore Press Holdings) and a national mobile network operator (Singtel). Singtel sent breaking news as SMS alerts in either Chinese or English to paid subscribers. In the same year, M1, a competitor to Singtel, introduced a paid service called "Info on Demand," which provides financial and other public information in SMS to 3G users.

In Singapore, news consumption shifted toward digital and mobile media as the diffusion of smartphones accelerated in the 4G era. P. C. Goh (2017) found that digital news sites and social media serve as Singapore's primary source of news, with 75% of Singaporeans accessing news through the smartphone. According to surveys in the Reuters Institute Digital News Report (2017), 85% of respondents went online for news, and three-quarters of respondents accessed news via the smartphone. In comparison, only 53% of surveyed Singaporeans remained loyal to print newspapers.

To operate and run SMSs in Singapore, a telecom company needs to apply for a Services-Based Operator (SBO) license from the authorities. Also, on-line sites with a high reach of 50,000 unique IP addresses are subject to more stringent regulations and are required to put up a performance bond of 50,000 Singapore dollars. The authorities may direct SBO operations to block access to certain content. Taking a platform-neutral approach, the 2002 Broadcast Act (latest revision came in 2012) has provisions that regulate all content distributed on electronic channels, including news disseminated over mobile networks and pushed to subscribers, regardless of whether it comes from traditional media or digital platforms.

In October 2019, Singapore passed a controversial anti–fake news law, under which the government has the power to decide whether to act against a piece of online information of what it judges to be falsehood on the Internet and social media platforms. The authorities (i.e., IDA [Infocomm Development Authority of Singapore]) can also order technology companies to block suspicious accounts or be fined for up to one million Singapore dollars. Individuals who violate the law may face jail terms of up to 10 years. Critics (Liotta, 2019) have argued the law provides the government with another means to police chat groups on social media platforms, reducing the already limited freedom of speech in the city nation.

Taipei, Taiwan

Although news media of all sorts have thrived in Taipei, Taiwan's capital city and media center (thanks to the freedom that the press has enjoyed in the past 30 years), the rise of the Internet and the mobile news industry has dealt a major blow to traditional media.[2] The newspaper industry on the island suffered a dramatic fall in readership, which shrank to just 30% in 2015 from 76% in 1992 (Newman et al., 2017). The 2017 Taiwan Communication Survey (TCS) found that nearly 70% of respondents did not read newspapers at all. Only 14% of respondents maintained the habit of reading newspapers every day.

When Global System for Mobile Communications (GSM) was the standard technology for mobile communications in the late 1990s, the total subscribers to 2G services in Taiwan peaked at 25.1 million (out of a population of 23 million). Mobile news in the form of SMS pushed to subscribers appeared Taipei in 1997, among the first in the world. 3G and smartphones further popularized mobile news. Two of the dominant dailies on the island, *China Times* and the *United Daily News*, launched a mobile version of their online papers. In the era of 4G, 88% of Taiwanese citizens accessed news through the Internet (including social media), in which 57% of them used social media via the smartphone, such as Facebook, Line, and YouTube (Newman et al., 2017).

The Taiwan authorities cannot target mobile or online news for censorship. Nevertheless, news content creators and publishers are legally liable for what they publish on mobile devices and platforms. But the law is not clear whether mobile news is yet regulated as a bona fide news medium.

SIGNIFICANCE OF MOBILE NEWS IN ASIA

The wireless network technology that is widely deployed in four of Asia's leading cities is standard, evolving from 2G (GMS) to 3G, and from 3G to 4G (aka Long-Term Evolution [LTE]). But as presented in Table 4.1, the socio-political environments for publishing and consuming mobile news are distinctly different. One example is the approach to regulating news publishing for mobile screens. In Shanghai, it was regulated like a common carrier in the 2G to 3G era. However, as the smartphone has saturated the market in the 4G era, mobile news has been subject to prepublication censorship and ideological control. The year 2013 was considered pivotal when the central government resumed its previous role as what Grigg (2015) called "the sole arbiter of what information the public should be told" in cyberspace (the State Internet Information Office, which is charged with censoring digital content regardless of platforms, was established in 2011; its director is known as China's Internet tsar). For instance, Weibo, a Twitter-like microblogging platform known for exposing corruptions and abuse of power in China, lost users due to tightening of censorship

Table 4.1 REGULATIONS OF MOBILE NEWS IN SHANGHAI, HONG KONG, TAIWAN, AND SINGAPORE

	Shanghai	Hong Kong	Taipei	Singapore
Laws and regulations concerning mobile news	Telecommunications Act 《电信条例》	Unsolicited Electronic Messages Ordinance	The Digital Communications Act	The Broadcasting Act; Protection from Online Falsehoods and Manipulation Act[a,b]
Year passed	2000	2007	Not passed	2012 and 2019
Regulatory agency	Ministry of Information Industry	Office of Communications Authority, HK SAR Government	Concerned Government Agencies	Infocomm Media Development Authority (IMDA)

Sources: [a] Singapore Statutes Online (2012). [b] Lim (2019).

on the site. A law passed in 2013 allows the authorities to put a blogger in jail if their blogs are deemed inaccurate. All it takes is no more than 500 complaints from subscribers (Kuo, 2014).

In Singapore, which adopts a platform-neutral approach, the authorities regulate online and mobile news the same way as traditional media. For instance, news sites are expected to comply within 24 hours to remove content that Infocomm's media development authorities find to be in breach of content standards. In comparison, regulations of digital information and news content distributed via wireless telecommunications networks in Hong Kong focus on reducing spamming and unsolicited messages. In Taipei, content providers to mobile subscribers are legally liable for any accusations of any slander and libel, but they face no prior censorship.

Under these circumstances (e.g., the different censorship mechanisms and regulatory environments), news pushed to mobile phone users and mobile media platforms such as blogs and the micromessaging service WeChat was less regulated in China. Microblogging, for instance, became a new outlet for China's investigative journalists (H. Yu, 2011); journalist bloggers sought to publish uncensored stories first through microblog posting, which is accessible via the mobile phone. Almost all of the influential journalists in China had a blog in which they exposed corruption and wrongdoings (J. Liu, 2013). News bloggers used the mobile platform to crack the tight control of information flow and news reporting (H. Yu, 2011).

Past research (Ying, 2010) indicated that the majority of breaking news was reported first in China on Weibo, not the state media. The Twitter-like microblog Weibo offered a rare outlet of uncensored news in China's tightly controlled media environment. For millions of users in China, the mobile phone served as the platform to get breaking and thrilling unsanctioned news (R. Wei, Lo, Xu, Chen, & Zhang, 2014). It is ironic that the more tightly the Chinese government controls the mainstream news media, the more likely mobile users are to turn to mobile phones for consuming and engaging news, including personalizing it, commenting, rating, voting for top stories, providing tips for reporters, sharing news, offering alternative accounts, and doing a follow-up story (Xu, 2011).

Therefore, in the context of the ubiquity of smartphones and the distinctly different socio-political environments for consuming news on the move in Hong Kong, Shanghai, Singapore, and Taipei, this chapter examines patterns in mobile news consumption among surveyed Asian college students. As the mobile network technologies upgraded from 3G to 4G and smartphones were popularized in the past decade, we expect consuming news on the mobile phone will increase across the two periods of survey. Informed by the findings of Chapter 3 concerning the motives of mobile phone use and expectancies of mobile news as interactive and personally valuable, we anticipate that surveillance and expectances will be positively related to consumption of mobile news. Last but not least, based on our framework presented in Chapter 2, the societal differences among the four studied cities will likely affect the pattern of consumption of mobile news.

FINDINGS

Increased Consumption

How do Asian college students in the four studied cities keep up with news using their phone? Consumption of news accessed from the mobile phone has increased noticeably across the two time periods of survey, which corresponded to the 3G and 4G era. As Table 4.2 shows, in the first wave of surveys conducted in 2010–2011, less than half (between 29% and 53%) of the respondents used their mobile phone to engage in news consumption at least occasionally in diversified ways, such as reading news via websites (53.2%), reading news via mobile sites (42.3%), reading news provided by apps (47.1%), listening to news (44.8%), watching mobile television news (31.3%), and listening to podcasts (28.6%).

In the second wave of surveys conducted in 2017–2018, however, the proportion of respondents who used the mobile phone to consume news at least occasionally doubled (between 54% and 96%). Respondents said that they read news via regular websites (95.7%) the most, followed by reading mobile websites (96.1%), reading mobile news apps (89.3%), listening to news (61.7%), watching mobile television news (69.2%), and listening to podcasts (54%).

Results of an independent t-test indicated that respondents in the 2017–2018 surveys were more likely to use their mobile phone to consume news ($M = 2.43$, $SD = .59$) than their counterparts in the 2010–2011 surveys ($M = 1.72$, $SD = .73$) ($t = 30.70$, $p < .001$). The most common consuming behavior was reading news sites (i.e., regular websites or mobile sites), while the least common was listening to podcasts.

Remarks made by our focus group participants in the four cities put these quantitative findings into perspective. A 22-year-old female student in Taipei, who is in her third year of study, described her choice of using the mobile phone for getting news as necessary due to the changing circumstances. She said:

Table 4.2 CHANGES IN MOBILE NEWS CONSUMPTION BETWEEN 2010–2011 AND 2017–2018

Samples/ News- Consuming Activities	2010–2011			2017–2018			
	No	Yes	Mean	No	Yes	Mean	t Value
To read news via regular websites	46.8%	53.2%	1.98	4.3%	95.7%	2.92	38.17***
To read news via mobile websites	47.7%	42.3%	1.96	3.9%	96.1%	3.00	27.93***
To read mobile news apps	52.9%	47.1%	1.85	10.7%	89.3%	2.86	27.60***
To listen to news	55.2%	44.8%	1.68	39.3%	61.7%	1.90	7.35***
To watch mobile TV news	68.7%	31.3%	1.46	30.8%	69.2%	2.11	24.07***
To listen to news in podcasts	71.4%	28.6%	1.40	46.0%	54.0%	1.80	16.01***
Combined index: Mobile news consumption			1.72 (.73)			2.43 (.59)	30.70***

Note: The scale ranged from 1 to 4, where 1 = never and 4 = often.
***p < .001.

> I used to watch the news on TV during my high school years living with my parents outside Taipei, but living in dorm on campus in Taipei, I lost access to home TV. The phone became the choice for news in a no-choice situation.

A 21-year-old male student in Shanghai, who described himself as a news junkie, said, "Mobile news satisfies my curiosity about major events at home and abroad in a way like eating fast food, quick, easy and inexpensive. I got enough to talk with my schoolmates." He said that his reading includes mobile news sites of ThePaper.cn (*Pengpai*, an online-only paper in Shanghai) and *Beijing News* (a Beijing-based mass paper), and breaking news posted by the two papers on their Weibo and WeChat accounts.

A female student aged 20 in Hong Kong said, "I use my phone to read news from the *South China Morning Post*, *The Guardian*, *RTHK News*, etc. In addition, I follow news on Instagram. News accessible on my phone is fast and handy. What's more, I get to see different perspectives on the same news events." A female student in Singapore explained her news-seeking preferences via her phone. "I like the Facebook page of the *Straits Times* and Channel News Asia. It is more beneficial as the more I click, the more it shows up, and it is a good mix of casual and formal." Her male peer in the same school added, "Most importantly, Facebook tells you what your friends are talking about, and what news you can share with your friends."

Gender and Consumption

We then examined whether and how mobile news consumption was related to gender because previous studies (R. Wei & Lo, 2006) reported gender-based differences in mobile phone usage. As shown in Table 4.3a, results of the 2010–2011 surveys showed that Asian male students (M = 1.83, SD = .78) were more likely than female students (M = 1.65, SD = .69) to consume news via the mobile phone. The gender difference was significant (t = 7.02, p < .001). Specifically, about a third to half (33% and 58%) of the Asian male respondents used their mobile phone for accessing news, including reading news via websites (57.7%), reading news via mobile websites (57.5%), reading mobile news apps (51.6%), listening to news (47.4%), watching mobile television news (35.7%), and listening to podcasts (32.6%).

In comparison, the percentage of Asian female respondents who used mobile phones to consume news was much lower, ranging between 26% and 50%. They read news via websites (50.2%) and mobile websites (48.7%) the most. Reading mobile news apps (44%) was the third most common way to consume news. Listening to news (42.9%), watching television news (28.2%), and listening to podcasts (25.8%) on the mobile phone were less common. These gender differences are consistent with the general pattern of telephone use (Claisse & Rowe; 1993; Moyal, 1992) and mobile phone use (Leung & Wei, 2000; R. Wei & Lo, 2006). Men tend to use the phone as an instrument to acquire information, while women use the phone to express affection.

In the 2017–2018 surveys shown in Table 4.3b, Asian male students were still more likely than female students to use their mobile phone to read news via regular websites (t = 2.13, p < .05), listen to news (t = 3.94, p < .001), watch television news (t = −2.61, p < .01), and listen to podcasts

Table 4.3a DIFFERENCES IN MOBILE NEWS CONSUMPTION BETWEEN MALE
AND FEMALE USERS (2010–2011 SURVEYS)

Samples/News-Consuming Activities	Male (N = 1,466)			Female (N = 2,037)			t Value
	No	Yes	Mean	No	Yes	Mean	
To read news via regular websites	42.3%	57.7%	2.13	49.8%	50.2%	1.88	6.78***
To read news via mobile websites	42.5%	57.5%	2.11	51.3%	48.7%	1.86	6.92***
To read mobile news apps	48.4%	51.6%	1.97	56.0%	44.0%	1.77	5.64***
To listen to news	52.6%	47.4%	1.72	57.1%	42.9%	1.64	2.73**
To watch mobile TV news	64.3%	35.7%	1.55	71.8%	28.2%	1.39	5.80***
To listen to news in podcasts	67.4%	32.6%	1.45	74.2%	25.8%	1.31	5.11***
Combined index: Mobile news consumption			1.83 (.78)			1.65 (.69)	7.02***

Note: The scale ranged from 1 to 4, where 1 = never and 4 = often.
***$p < .001$, **$p < .01$.

($t = 5.50$, $p < .001$). However, they did not differ from their female peers in reading news via mobile websites ($t = 1.56$, $p > .05$) and reading mobile news apps ($t = -1.07$, $p > .05$).

Gender differences in consuming mobile news have narrowed over time largely because mobile news consumption by both male and female respondents increased in the four Asian cities from 2010–2011 to 2017–2018. As shown in Table 4.3b, results of the two waves of surveys show that both males and females reported a higher level of mobile news consumption in the 2017–2018 period than in 2010–2011 period.

Our focus groups also corroborated this trend that female students have a different attitude and usage than male students regarding consuming news on their mobile phones. For instance, a 21-year-old female student in Taipei said, "I had never read news on my phone till I went to college. I cannot live without it in college. I bumped into news reports when I'm

Table 4.3b DIFFERENCES IN MOBILE NEWS USE BETWEEN MALE AND FEMALE USERS (2017–2018 SURVEYS)

Samples/News-Consuming Activities	Male (N = 1,229)			Female (N = 1,699)			t Value
	No	Yes	Mean	No	Yes	Mean	
To read news via regular websites	4.2%	95.8%	2.96	4.1%	95.9%	2.89	2.13*
To read news via mobile websites	4.0%	96.0%	3.03	3.8%	96.2%	2.98	1.56
To read mobile news apps	10.9%	89.1%	2.84	10.5%	89.5%	2.88	–1.07
To listen to news	38.0%	62.0%	1.98	40.4%	59.6%	1.84	3.94***
To watch mobile TV news	30.0%	70.0%	2.16	31.3%	68.7%	2.07	2.61**
To listen to news in podcasts	42.3%	57.7%	1.91	48.9%	51.1%	1.72	5.50***
Combined index: Mobile news consumption			2.48 (.60)			2.40 (.57)	3.72***

Note: The scale ranged from 1 to 4, where 1 = never and 4 = often.
***$p < .001$, **$p < .01$.

using my phone to log in Facebook to catch up with friends." Her school-mate added by saying, "I don't browse a news website unless I need it for doing homework."

A female student in Singapore, in talking about starting the day by reading news on her phone, noted, "I check my email first thing in the morning. I only read when I check my email. That's how I get the news." But a male schoolmate of hers said, "I will read on the way to school on the public transit. I will flip on Facebook or CNN or BBC and scroll up and read headlines." He went on to explain his keen interest in reading hard news this way:

Last year I went to Korea for exchange. Now I'm back in Singapore. Every day, I will read the news to check on the status of the country since there is tension going on between North Korea and South Korea. I will read Yahoo News.

None of the seven female students who participated in the focus group in Shanghai described themselves as news junkies. One of them said, "News content on the mobile phone is not important to me at all. My life goes on without knowing what's in the news." However, three of the male students in Hong Kong said they started reading news on their phones at the age of 13 (the first year in high school).

Smartphone Ownership and Consumption

Next, we examined whether ownership of a smartphone affected how much respondents consumed mobile news. In our first wave of our surveys conducted in 2010–2011, smartphone ownership varied a great deal across the four cities, ranging from 28.4% in Taipei to 54.3% in Hong Kong, 61.8% in Shanghai, and 70.4% in Singapore. As Table 4.4a shows, about half to two-thirds (40.3% and 75.1%) of smartphone users engaged in one of the six mobile news consumption activities, including reading news websites (74.8%), reading mobile news websites (75.1%), reading mobile news apps (67.3%), listening to news (54%), watching mobile television news (44.3%), and listening to podcasts (40.3%).

The proportion of nonsmartphone users who consumed mobile news, on the other hand, was much lower, ranging between one-sixth and one-third (16.1% and 30%). They tended to consume news accessed from their phone by listening to news (34.7%), followed by reading news websites (30%), reading mobile news websites (27.8%), and reading mobile news apps (25.4%). Watching mobile television news (17.2%) and listening to podcasts (16.1%) were the least common.

Results of an independent t-test indicated that the difference between smartphone users ($M = 2.03$, $SD = .73$) and nonsmartphone users in mobile news consumption in the pooled sample ($M = 1.38$, $SD = .57$) was statistically significant ($t = 29.53$, $p < .001$), which indicated that ownership of a smartphone mattered in mobile news consumption.

In the 2017–2018 surveys, ownership of smartphones increased dramatically across the four cities (95% in Hong Kong, 99.5% in Shanghai, 99.6% in Singapore, and 100% in Taipei). As Table 4.4b shows, smartphone users, who outnumbered nonusers, were still more likely than nonusers to use their phone to access news. Half to almost all of them (53.6% and 96.5%) consumed mobile news in one form or another. Among nonsmartphone users, use of their mobile phone to access news also increased (between 68.5% and 76.3%), but still fell behind smartphone users.

Table 4.4a DIFFERENCES IN MOBILE NEWS CONSUMPTION
BETWEEN SMARTPHONE AND NONSMARTPHONE USERS (2010–2011 SURVEYS)

Samples/News-Consuming Activities	Smartphone Users (N = 1,807)			Nonsmartphone Users (N = 1,675)			t Value
	No	Yes	Mean	No	Yes	Mean	
To read news via regular websites	25.2%	74.8%	2.44	70.0%	30.0%	1.49	29.07***
To read news via mobile websites	24.9%	75.1%	2.45	72.2%	27.8%	1.44	31.64***
To read mobile news apps	32.7%	67.3%	2.27	74.6%	25.4%	1.40	26.76***
To listen to news	46.0%	54.0.%	1.82	65.3%	34.7%	1.53	10.03***
To watch mobile TV news	55.7%	44.3%	1.66	82.8%	17.2%	1.23	17.40***
To listen to news in podcasts	59.7%	40.3%	1.57	83.9%	16.1%	1.22	15.33***
Combined index: Mobile news consumption			2.03 (.73)			1.38 (.57)	29.53***

Note: The scale ranged from 1 to 4, where 1 = never and 4 = often.
***$p < .001$.

Further, results of an independent t-test indicated a significant difference between smartphone users (M = 2.44, SD = .59) and nonsmartphone users (M = 2.16, SD = .69) in mobile news consumption in the pooled sample (t = 2.92, $p < .01$). Indeed, owning a smartphone made a difference in accessing news for consumption in both periods of our survey. The smartphone aided its owners to consume more news.

The remarks of focus group participants on the difference the smartphone makes in their preferences for news consumption are revealing. After having her first smartphone, a 23-year-old female student in Shanghai said she did not bother to power on her PC or laptop to access news. "News is readily accessible any time when I picked up my phone. There is so much to choose, websites, apps and WeChat." She said that she particularly liked the features of the multimedia format and visualization of news events on

Table 4.4b DIFFERENCES IN MOBILE NEWS CONSUMPTION BETWEEN SMARTPHONE AND NONSMARTPHONE USERS (2017–2018 SURVEYS)

Samples/News-Consuming Activities	Smartphone Users (N = 2,905)			Nonsmartphone Users (N = 38)			t Value
	No	Yes	Mean	No	Yes	Mean	
To read news via regular websites	3.7%	96.3%	2.94	31.6%	68.4%	1.84	8.44***
To read news via mobile websites	3.5%	96.5%	3.01	26.3%	73.7%	2.13	6.74***
To read mobile news apps	10.5%	89.5%	2.87	23.7%	76.3%	2.47	2.19*
To listen to news	39.3%	60.7%	1.90	31.6%	68.4%	2.16	–1.77
To watch mobile TV news	30.8%	69.2%	2.11	28.9%	71.2%	2.21	–.66
To listen to news in podcasts	46.4%	53.6%	1.80	31.6%	68.4%	2.13	–2.32*
Combined index: Mobile news consumption			2.44 (.59)			2.16 (.69)	2.92**

Note: The scale ranged from 1 to 4, where 1 = never and 4 = often.
***p < .001, ***p < .001, *p < .05.

her smartphone. Her schoolmate, another female student, added, "News on the mobile phone is constantly updated, and it's searchable."

A male student in Taipei in his third year of study likes both his laptop and smartphone, but when it comes to reading news, he said, "I definitely flop on my phone to read news. It's fast, portable and convenient." His 22-year-old female schoolmate in Taipei relied on news apps such as ETtoday.net (a top-rated news aggregator and social networking platform), Line Today (a news aggregator site available on the social media app Line), and Google News. She said, "I never used websites for news, just apps."

The experience of the 18-year-old male student in Hong Kong seems common. He said, "I can gain access to news easily using my smartphone. For example, when I am leaving school, I can simply consume news while I am using Facebook." A second-year male student aged 20 in Hong Kong joined him in saying that he mostly downloaded various applications for consuming news on his smartphone. He continued, "I used Facebook to consume news daily, by subscribing or liking the Facebook page of different news media, such as Stand News (an independent news site), Initium Media (a popular news site known for investigative reports), Cable News, *Apple Daily*, etc."

Surveillance and Consumption

To examine whether the behavior of mobile news consumption is tied to surveillance motivation for using the mobile phone to stay in the know, we distinguished high- and low-motivation users of the mobile phone by splitting the surveillance motivation scale at the median. As we argued in Chapter 2, millennials and centennials have not developed the habit of reading and viewing news as a routine activity, thus surveillance motivation of using the mobile phone would drive them to consume mobile news. We anticipated that respondents in the high-motivation group would consume more news via their phones than their peers in the low-motivation group.

As presented in Table 4.5a, in the 2010–2011 surveys, a third to two-thirds (38% to 68%) of high-surveillance users accessed news from their mobile phone to read news, such as reading news websites (67.5%), reading mobile websites (67.2%), reading news apps (61.1%), listening to news (53.1%), watching mobile television news (41.4%), and listening to podcasts (37.5%). But the number of low-surveillance-motivation users who used their mobile phone to consume news was much lower, ranging from only one-tenth to one-third (13% to 28%). When they did access news via their mobile phone, the most common activities were listening to news (30.3%), reading news websites (28.3%), reading mobile news websites (26.2%), and reading mobile news apps (22.5%). Other options for consuming mobile news were taken much less, such as watching mobile television news (13.6%) and podcast listening (13.1%).

Results of an independent t-test indicated that the differences between the two groups of different surveillance motivation were statistically significant. High-surveillance-motivation users ($M = 1.83$, $SD = .74$) were more likely to use their mobile phone to engage in mobile news consumption activities than were low-surveillance-motivation users ($M = 1.65$, $SD = .52$) ($t = 28.39$, $p < .001$). Such a result underscores the importance of surveillance in motivating the behavior of mobile news consumption.

A similar pattern was found in the 2017–2018 surveys—high-surveillance-motivation users were more likely than low-motivation users in the four studied cities to consume mobile news. According to the

Table 4.5a DIFFERENCES IN MOBILE NEWS CONSUMPTION BETWEEN HIGH-
AND LOW-SURVEILLANCE-MOTIVATION USERS (2010–2011 SURVEYS)

Samples/News-Consuming Activities	High (N = 2,241)			Low (N = 1,273)			t Value
	No	Yes	Mean	No	Yes	Mean	
To read news via regular websites	32.5%	67.5%	2.29	71.7%	28.3%	1.44	26.48***
To read news via mobile websites	32.8%	67.2%	2.28	73.8%	26.2%	1.40	27.92***
To read mobile news apps	38.9%	61.1%	2.14	77.5%	22.5%	1.35	24.99***
To listen to news	46.9%	53.1%	1.80	69.7%	30.3%	1.45	12.24***
To watch mobile TV news	58.6%	41.4%	1.61	86.4%	13.6%	1.18	18.80***
To listen to news in podcasts	62.5%	37.5%	1.53	86.9%	13.1%	1.18	16.06***
Combined index: Mobile news consumption			1.83 (.74)			1.65 (.52)	28.39***

Note: The scale ranged from 1 to 4, where 1 = never and 4 = often.
***$p < .001$.

results presented in Table 4.5b, more than half to nearly all of the high-surveillance-motivation respondents (55% to 98%) used the mobile phone to consume some kinds of news content. However, the proportions of low-surveillance-motivation users who used their phone to engage in similar news consumption activities were still lower, hovering between 52% and 92%.

Another independent t-test showed that the differences between the two groups were statistically significant. Overall mobile news consumption among high-surveillance-motivation users (M = 2.54, SD = .57) was higher than that of low-surveillance-motivation users (M = 2.21, SD = .56) (t = 15.00, $p < .001$). This particular result suggests that the more that Asian college students were civically motivated, the more they consumed news via the mobile phone to satisfy their civic interest.

Table 4.5b DIFFERENCES IN MOBILE NEWS CONSUMPTION BETWEEN HIGH- AND LOW-SURVEILLANCE-MOTIVATION USERS (2017–2018 SURVEYS)

Samples/News-Consuming Activities	High (N = 1,887)			Low (N = 973)			t Value
	No	Yes	Mean	No	Yes	Mean	
To read news via regular websites	2.2%	97.8%	3.07	8.5%	91.5%	2.61	14.97***
To read news via mobile websites	2.3%	97.7%	3.16	7.4%	92.6%	2.66	16.08***
To read mobile news apps	8.0%	92.2%	3.01	16.5%	83.5%	2.54	12.75***
To listen to news	37.4%	62.6%	1.96	43.3%	56.7%	1.79	4.70***
To watch mobile TV news	27.7%	72.3%	2.21	37.2%	62.8%	1.91	8.64***
To listen to news in podcasts	44.8%	55.2%	1.84	48.5%	51.5%	1.74	2.80**
Combined index: Mobile news consumption			2.54 (.57)			2.21 (.56)	15.00***

Note: The scale ranged from 1 to 4, where 1 = never and 4 = often.
***$p < .001$, **$p < .01$.

Participants in the focus groups put these findings into perspective. A third-year female student in Taipei said she has the habit of reading news on her phone while walking. "When I walk, I could not help take a few glances at my phone to catch up with news. News on the phone is so quick, and right there in my hand." Her schoolmate in Taiwan said, "Mobile phone beats all media in getting to know the news quick and easy. For breaking news, I do not want to wait till the evening to watch it on prime-time TV."

To a 25-year-old female student in Shanghai, news accessible from her phone in the form of websites, apps, and social media posts enables her to be well informed. She said, "I pay attention to major international and national news that everyone should know about; this keeps me out of the dark." A second-year male student in Hong Kong cited "when there are some important news or information in the society" as the reason he accessed news via his phone every day. He continued, "I like consuming news from various media outlets. Compared to traditional ways of news consumption like watching TV and listening to radio, using smartphone allows me to consume news from different media at the same time" for the benefit of gaining different perspectives.

Cross-City Differences in Consumption

Given the different socio-political environments for creating and disseminating news to mobile screens, did college students in the four Asian cities differ in their mobile news consumption behavior accordingly? To explore this question, we performed a series of one-way ANOVA tests, which compared the four samples against the means of a range of mobile news consumption activities, results of which are summarized in Tables 4.6a and 4.6b.

As presented in Table 4.6a, in the 2010–2011 surveys, respondents from the four cities differed in consumption of mobile news [F (3, 3511) = 246.13, $p <$ .001]. A Scheffe test revealed that Shanghai respondents were the most

Table 4.6a MOBILE NEWS CONSUMPTION IN SHANGHAI, HONG KONG, TAIPEI, AND SINGAPORE (2010–2011)

Motives/City	Total	Shanghai	Hong Kong	Taipei	Singapore	F Value
To read news via regular websites	1.98	2.69	1.83	1.43	2.21	277.78***
To read news via mobile websites	1.96	2.69	1.85	1.40	2.16	283.81***
To read mobile news apps	1.85	2.63	1.66	1.33	2.01	298.97***
To listen to news	1.68	1.89	1.65	1.66	1.56	21.43***
To watch mobile TV news	1.46	1.75	1.49	1.25	1.46	68,12***
To listen to news in podcasts	1.40	1.64	1.43	1.20	1.43	62.87***
Combined index: Mobile news consumption	1.72 (.73)	2.22 (.65)	1.65 (.70)	1.38 (.57)	1.81 (.75)	246.13***

Note: Values in parentheses are standard deviations.
***$p <$ .001.

Table 4.6b MOBILE NEWS CONSUMPTION IN SHANGHAI, HONG KONG,
TAIPEI, AND SINGAPORE (2017–2018)

Motives/City	Total	Shanghai	Hong Kong	Taipei	Singapore	F Value
To read news via regular websites	2.92	2.96	2.76	3.12	2.80	277.78***
To read news via mobile websites	3.00	2.98	2.80	3.14	3.06	283.81***
To read mobile news apps	2.86	3.32	2.49	2.95	2.63	298.97***
To listen to news	1.90	1.99	2.00	1.81	1.82	21.43***
To watch mobile TV news	2.11	2.15	2.21	2.25	1.79	68.12***
To listen to news in podcasts	1.80	1.89	1.98	1.75	1.57	62.87***
Combined index: Mobile news consumption	2.43 (.59)	2.54 (.57)	2.38 (.63)	2.50 (.55)	2.28 (.58)	31.39***

Note: Values in parentheses are standard deviations.
***$p < .001$.

likely to use their mobile phone for news consumption ($M = 2.22$, $SD = .65$), followed by Singapore respondents ($M = 1.81$, $SD = .75$) and Hong Kong respondents ($M = 1.65$, $SD = .70$). Taipei respondents were the least likely to consume news via the mobile phone ($M = 1.38$, $SD = .57$).

More post hoc Scheffe tests showed that all of the differences in the mobile news consumption behavior among the respondents in Shanghai, Singapore, Hong Kong, and Taipei were significant at the $p < .001$ level. These results demonstrated a pattern in which respondents in Shanghai and Singapore, where governments placed strict control on news media, were more likely to access mobile news than were their counterparts in Hong Kong and Taipei, where news media enjoy a great deal of freedom.

In the 2017–2018 surveys, respondents from the four Asian cities continued to differ in using their mobile phone to consume news [$F (3, 2952) = 31.39$, $p < .001$]. However, the patterns found in the 2010–2011 surveys had changed slightly. As Table 4.6b presents, results of Scheffe tests revealed that Shanghai respondents were still most likely to use their mobile phone to consume news ($M = 2.54$, $SD = .57$), followed by Taipei respondents ($M = 2.50$, $SD = .55$) and Hong Kong respondents ($M = 2.38$, $SD = .63$). The respondents in Singapore were the least likely to consume news via the mobile phone ($M = 2.28$, $SD = .58$). It seems that the changed pattern was largely due to the increased consumption of mobile news across the four samples between the first wave and the second wave of surveys. Overall, respondents in all four cities consumed more news accessed from the mobile phone over time.

Even though Shanghai respondents were the most likely to consume mobile news, there was no difference in the mean level of mobile news consumption behavior between Shanghai and Taipei respondents. The post hoc Scheffe tests further showed that respondents in Shanghai and Taipei were more likely to consume mobile news than were their counterparts in Hong Kong and Singapore.

To illustrate this, a female student in Singapore said, "I don't usually go onto the *Straits Times* website to read, if I want to know the headlines like a quick read, I will just go to Facebook page and whatever articles, I will click the link and read the blog." A male third-year student in Taipei said, "A laptop is more useful to me than my phone. If the news is a long read, I prefer to read it on my laptop. I use my phone to log in Facebook, all I do is putting my fingers on the screen. That is how convenient it is." All of the five students in Hong Kong mentioned the pluralistic nature of news accessed via their phone as an appeal of mobile news.

Predictors of Consumption

To what extent do gender, smartphone ownership, surveillance motivation, personal value of mobile news, and city of residence predict consumption of mobile news? That is, which of these predictor variables has the most effect on explaining the variance in mobile news consumption? To shed light on this question, we ran two separate hierarchical regression analyses for the data collected from the two waves of surveys. The regression runs treated mobile news consumption as a dependent variable, while gender, age, smartphone ownership, surveillance motivation, personal value of mobile news, and city of residence served as predictors. Results of the regressions are presented in Table 4.7.[3]

As shown in Table 4.7 (column 1), in the 2010–2011 surveys, gender ($B = .06$, $p < .001$) and city of residence ($B = .22$, $p < .001$) were positively associated with mobile news consumption, indicating that male and Shanghai (both male and female) respondents were more likely to use the mobile phone to access news for consumption. Furthermore, smartphone ownership ($B = .24$, $p < .001$) and personal value of mobile news ($B = .25$, $p < .001$) were also positively correlated with mobile news consumption.

Table 4.7 HIERARCHICAL REGRESSION ANALYSIS PREDICTING MOBILE NEWS CONSUMPTION

Predictor Variables	Mobile News 2010–2011	Consumption 2017–2018
Block 1: Demographics		
Gender (male = 1)	.06***	.10***
Age	.02	–.02
City (Shanghai = 1)	.22***	.13***
Adjusted R^2	13.3%	1.9%
Block 2: Types of Mobile Phone		
Smartphone ownership (yes = 1)	.24***	–.02
Incremental adjusted R^2	16.2%	0.2%
Block 3: Expectancy of Mobile News		
Personal value	.25***	.18***
Incremental adjusted R^2	11.9%	7.0%
Block 4: Motivation		
Surveillance motivation	.29***	.24***
Incremental adjusted R^2	5.9%	4.7%
Total adjusted R^2	47.3%	13.8%
N	3,425	2,784

Note: Beta weights are from final regression equation with all blocks of variables in the model.
***$p < .001$, **$p < .01$, *$p < .05$.

Among all the significant predictors, surveillance motivation emerged as the strongest predictor of the dependent variable ($B = .29$, $p < .001$).

With all the significant predictors being considered, the equation explained 47.3% of the variance in consumption of mobile news (adjusted R^2), suggesting we included the right set of predictors that affect the level of consuming news from the mobile phone.

Regarding the 2017–2018 surveys, results of the regression analysis showed (column 2 in Table 4.7) that gender ($B = .10$, $p < .001$) and city ($B = .13$, $p < .001$) were significant and positive predictors of mobile news consumption. But smartphone ownership ($B = –.02$, $p > .05$) was no longer a significant predictor. This result makes sense: at a time when almost all the respondents in our study owned a smartphone, its effect on mobile news consumption behavior is neutralized into a constant.

In addition, personal value of mobile news ($B = .18$, $p < .001$) was significantly and positively related to mobile news consumption. Consistently, surveillance motivation was the most powerful predictor of mobile news consumption (B = .24, p< .001). These results provide evidence to support the relationship between surveillance motivation and college students' mobile news consumption activities. Compared to the model built from the 2010–2011 data, the total variance accounted for by the same set of predictors was much less at 13.8% (adjusted R^2), about one-third of the 2010–2011 model. Such change suggests the decreased explanatory power of the equation over time.

SUMMARY OF KEY FINDINGS

Emerging Patterns of Mobile News Consumption

News has become more accessible thanks to the ubiquity of mobile phones and range of options to access news on the move. Findings in this chapter show that Asian college students in the four surveyed cities rode on the momentum of mobile news consumption. The changes and trends of their consumption pattern include:

- Consumption of news accessed from the mobile phone increased across the two periods from 2010–2011 to 2017–2018. College students in the four studied Asian cities were more likely to consume mobile news in the 4G era than in the 3G era.
- Similar to mobile phone usage, gender differences in mobile news consumption also exist. Asian male students proved to be more likely than their female peers to consume more news via their phones. However, gender differences in consuming mobile news narrowed over time largely because mobile news consumption by both male and female respondents increased in the eight-year period from 2010–2011 to 2017–2018.
- The smartphone turned out to be a differentiator in affecting consumption of mobile news. Smartphone owners were likely to consume more news than were nonowner users. Although consumption increased among nonsmartphone users, the second wave of surveys showed they still fell behind smartphone users.
- Consuming mobile news required motivation among Asia's young generations. College students in the four studied cities who believed the mobile phone was helpful to stay informed tended to consume more news from the device. Only a small number of students who had a low surveillance motivation consumed mobile news. This pattern persisted in the second survey.

- Where the surveyed college students lived made a big difference in how much they consumed mobile news. Shanghai residents were the most likely to use the mobile phone to consume news in both waves of surveys, whereas Taipei residents were the least likely to do so. That said, respondents in all four Asian cities consumed more news accessed from the mobile phone over time.

What factors might account for the differences between Shanghai respondents and their counterparts in the other three cities? At the individual level, having a smartphone mattered in consuming mobile news. A female student in her third year of study in Taipei summed it up this way: "I read news because the phone is all that I have on the go."

At the societal level, the absence of press freedom in China appears to create a strong need to access and read news that is unavailable in official media. It seems that the mobile phone, and the less regulated news resources that have emerged to feed it, indeed offers an alternative channel for Shanghai and Singapore college students to stay informed about current affairs and world events. In contrast, college students in Taipei were the least likely among the four Asian cities to use mobile phones to consume news because Taiwan enjoys a great deal of press freedom. News of all sorts finds its way in print, over the air, or online. There is little need for them to access news specifically from the mobile phone.

THEORETICAL INSIGHTS FROM FINDINGS

Findings of this chapter show that news accessible from the mobile phone fulfills Asian college students' needs to be informed. The gratification of surveillance sought from the mobile phone motivates those with interest in hard news to use the mobile phone as a gateway to consume the news. Some predictors of mobile news consumption have remained constant, but others have changed over time.

First, key demographics such as gender and city of residence have persisting predictive power over mobile news consumption behavior. The effects of these social differentiators appear to be enduring as mobile technology evolves from 3G to 4G and smartphones have saturated the four studied cities.

Personal value of mobile news remains a significant predictor in both waves of survey. Using the mobile phone for surveillance drives the consumption behavior. As we anticipated, usability attributes of mobile news as being interactive and useful also affect positively the behavior of mobile news consumption.

On the other hand, other predictors have changed across the two survey periods, including that smartphone ownership, which explained more variance than any predictor in the first wave of surveys, totally lost its predictor power over time because almost all the respondents in the second wave of surveys owned a smartphone. A critical differentiator in the 3G era becomes a constant in the 4G era, indicating that the draw or appeal of technological innovations has worn off. Accordingly, the total variance accounted for by the regression model with the same set of predictors in 2017–2018 was only a third of the 2010–2011 model. Such a change suggests the decreased explanatory power of the equation over time.

More importantly, some societal differences exist in consuming mobile news among the four Asian cities—respondents from Shanghai and Singapore were likelier to consume news on the mobile phone than were their peers in Hong Kong and Taipei. Consistent with past research (e.g., R. Wei et al., 2014), consumption of mobile news is particularly popular in those societies where the press is not free or partially free.

Therefore, it seems to us that consuming mobile news is not simply a matter of convenience and easy access from what Dimmick et al. (2011) characterized as "a 'transit' niche" (p. 34)—serving consumer needs for news and information when they are on the move in space and time. Rather, we conclude that accessing news from mobile phones is tied to the fundamental issue of media access by citizens who seek to be civically informed.

CHAPTER 5

Engagement

The New Dimension

MOBILE NEWS CONSUMPTION AS SOCIAL INTERACTION

The globally popular mobile phone has fueled changes in the ways people consume news. Interacting with the news and other users of news, such as news sharing (D. Goh, Ling, Huang, & Liew, 2017), is common. With a click on embedded links, users can get more of the story beyond breaking-news alerts, headlines, and news summaries. In fact, consumers of mobile news were found to not just passively read news but also take action after accessing the news such as clicking "like," "repost," or "retweet" for links to news (e.g., Twitter feeds or Facebook fan page) and talking with others about the news (Knight Foundation, 2016). As D. Goh et al. (2017) noted, shared news has become a widespread means of news consumption on digital and mobile media, enhancing and expanding users' access to news. Others (Olmstead, Mitchell, & Rosenstiel, 2011) have described the behavior of news sharing as the most important development in the 2010s, as compared to the behavior of searching for news, which was viewed as the most important development of the 2000s.

However, the literature is underdeveloped regarding the key issue of user actions to stay informed anywhere, anytime via the mobile phone. Kümpel, Karnowski, and Keyling (2015) called insufficient theory building of news sharing among networked users "a blind spot" (p. 9). By examining how Asian college students keep track of and interact with news on their mobile phone, Chapter 5 aims to understand their news engagement behavior.

News in Their Pockets. Ran Wei and Ven-hwei Lo, Oxford University Press (2021). © Oxford University Press.
DOI: 10.1093/oso/9780197523728.003.0005

Furthermore, as mobile network technology has continuously improved, offering faster Internet connection, so has the popularity of smartphones. Accordingly, Chapter 5 explores over-time changes from two waves of survey data about users' engagement with mobile news. We will investigate the question of if and how the always-on smartphone supported by 4G networks has enhanced user news engagement behavior compared to that during the 3G era, that is, whether users' news-engaging behavior has changed in the transition from the 3G to 4G networks.

ENGAGEMENT WITH MOBILE NEWS

In Chapter 2, we defined engagement with mobile news as user interactivities with news and others by following and sharing the news. Analytically, we test the idea that mobile news consumption is an engaging and participative behavior by examining two types of user interactive behaviors—user-to-content interactivity (i.e., following news) and user-to-user interactivity (i.e., sharing news with others). This approach is consistent with our user-focused perspective to understand mobile news engagement primarily as a property of users supported by the affordances of the mobile phone (e.g., mobility, personalization, connectivity, interactivity, and modality).

Following Mobile News

Consuming news in the digital era is easy thanks to user-friendly interfaces and more personalized devices with a touch screen, but it can be overwhelming. Reading news on smartphones has moved away from pushing buttons; it means clicking embedded links/video clips, sliding across and tapping thumbs on mobile screens, or scanning a QR code. The Internet-empowered mobile phone has enabled its users to be active.

Following mobile news represents a behavior of making strategic choices in deliberately choosing certain types of news outlets and sources, such as keeping an eye on a breaking story or on reporters on Twitter or subscribing to a news app. Therefore, it exemplifies the character of an active audience—an individual with autonomy who actively makes choices of news outlets to meet their informational needs about current affairs. Past research (S. Lee, 2015; Meijer & Kormelink, 2015; R. Wei, 2008; R. Wei & Lo, 2015) has informed us that those who consume news a great deal on a smartphone with a stronger surveillance motive tend to be engaged with the news by following tweets and blogs.

Sharing Mobile News

Another aspect of news engagement is sharing news with others. In the era of faster 4G networks, news sharing on smartphones takes on multiple forms using multiple methods, expanding the scope of news sharing. Mobile news sharing includes not only forwarding news and redistributing news online with a click of links or emailing a link but also posting, reposting, retweeting, or recommending content with a "like" on popular social media platforms.

News sharing on social media platforms and smartphones is a new issue that has drawn a great deal of scholarly attention (D. Goh et al., 2017; Graves & Konieczna, 2015; Hermida, Fletcher, Korell, & Logan, 2012). Kümpel et al. (2015) defined sharing news online as "the practice of giving a defined set of people access to news content via social media platforms, such as by posting or recommending it" (p. 2). Others (D. Goh et al., 2017) characterized sharing news on digital media as the behavior of users "gifting" news to one another as a form of social interaction in informational exchange (p. 1138).

Moreover, similar to the behavior of following news, the behavior of sharing news among users is "neither haphazard nor casual," according to D. Goh et al. (2017, p. 1139). Rather, the act of news sharing indicates deliberative processing of news accessed from the mobile phone and careful choices in what to share and with whom to share. Past research (Oeldorf-Hirsch & Sundar, 2015) indicated that a user's news-sharing behavior increases their involvement and interest in the news. Thus, news consumption via the smartphone stimulates engagement with the news (Meijer & Kormelink, 2015).

To fully understand mobile news-following and -sharing behavior among Asian college students in Shanghai, Hong Kong, Singapore, and Taipei, we will examine how prevalent news following and sharing is, whether engagement with news has changed in the transition from 3G to 4G networks, and whether owning a smartphone affects a user's news-following and -sharing behavior. Given the motivations of mobile phone use and expectancies of mobile news explicated in Chapter 2, which were empirically verified in Chapter 3, we anticipate that the motivational news use will be positively related to news engagement.

FINDINGS

The 2010–2011 and 2017–2018 surveys included news following as a major dimension of user engagement with news, so our analyses include findings from both surveys. However, the 2010–2011 surveys did not include any data on news sharing. Accordingly, our analysis of mobile news sharing is based solely on data from the second wave.

Patterns of Following

In the first wave of surveys conducted in 2010–2011, following news on the mobile phone in terms of following a journalist or news organization seemed to be uncommon, if not rare. As Table 5.1 shows, only one-third of the respondents engaged in news-following activities. Specifically, one-third to nearly half (37% to 48%) of the respondents used their mobile phone to engage in some kind of news following, such as following a news organization (47.7%), a journalist (41.7%), a news blog (41.1%), a news blogger (39.8%), Twitter updates from a news organization (37.8%), and tweets from a journalist (36.7%). The most common news-following activity was tracking news delivered by a news organization (47.7%), while the least common was trailing Twitter updates from a news organization

Table 5.1 CHANGES IN NEWS-FOLLOWING ACTIVITIES BETWEEN 2010–2011 AND 2017–2018

Samples/ News-Following Activities	2010–2011			2017–2018			t Value
	No	Yes	Mean	No	Yes	Mean	
Following a news organization	52.3%	47.7%	1.75	9.3%	90.7%	2.82	62.94***
Following a journalist	58.3%	41.7%	1.61	20.4%	79.6%	2.38	34.34***
Following a news blog	58.9%	41.1%	1.62	24.0%	76.0%	2.30	29.57***
Following a news blogger	60.2%	39.8%	1.59	26.1%	73.9%	2.23	32.83***
Following Twitter updates from a news organization	62.2%	37.8%	1.60	21.2%	78.8%	2.53	38.27***
Following tweets from a journalist	63.3%	36.7%	1.56	26.7%	73.3%	2.30	31.22**
Combined activities			1.62 (.78)			2.34 (.82)	35.47***

Note: The scale ranged from 1 to 4, where 1 = never and 4 = often.
** $p < .001$, **$p < .01$.

(37.8%). This result is understandable because Twitter, which was launched in July 2006, was a novelty at the time of the first wave of surveys.

The frequency of news-following behavior ranged between "never" and "rarely." The combined mean of all news-following activities was low at 1.62 out of a 4-point scale, indicating that keeping an eye on news when using the mobile phone by following news organizations or journalists was yet to be widespread. When surveyed Asian college students did track news, they tended to follow the familiar news media and providers—news delivered to the mobile phone screen by professional news organizations and journalists.

However, in the second wave of surveys conducted in 2017–2018, following news on the mobile phone by virtue of following a news organization or journalist became more common and prevalent—more than two-thirds of the respondents reported that they used the mobile phone to follow news. Users followed news organizations most often (90.7%), then journalists (79.6%), then Twitter updates from news organizations (78.8%), and finally tweets from journalists (73.3%; refer to Table 5.1).

Moreover, the frequency of news-following activities increased to "seldom" and "sometimes," that is, from "never" in the first wave of surveys to "seldom" in the second wave; the combined mean of all news-following activities was higher at 2.34 out of the same 4-point scale. These results suggest that as news has gone mobile and the diffusion of smartphones has deepened, respondents have become increasingly engaged with mobile news distributed by established news organizations and professional journalists.

Changes in Patterns of Following

We further analyzed the data to ascertain whether the change in mobile news following across the two survey periods from 3G to 4G was statistically significant. As further shown in Table 5.1, respondents surveyed in the 2017–2018 period had a higher level of mobile news following than those surveyed in the 2010–2011 period. In the first surveys, only a third to nearly half (37% to 48%) of the respondents used their mobile phone to engage in some news-following activities. However, in the second surveys, two-thirds to almost all of respondents (74% to 91%) used the mobile phone to engage in similar news-following activities.

Results of an independent t-test ($t = 35.47$, $p < .001$) show that respondents in the second wave of surveys were more likely to follow news posted on blogs (M = 2.34, SD = .82) than their counterparts in the first wave of surveys (M = 1.62, SD = .78). Specifically, following a news organization was most popular (90.7%), followed by following a journalist (79.6%), a news blog (76.0%), a news blogger (73.9%), Twitter updates from an organization (78.8%), and tweets from a journalist (73.3%).

In addition, the change in the frequency of news-following activities from the first period to the second period was significant. Results of a t-test between the two combined means of the activities was t = 35.47, p <.001, indicating the overall increase of following news organizations or journalists to stay informed in the 4G era. These results suggest that as mobile technology evolved from one generation to the next in the 2010s, the faster network and Internet connectivity led to greater engagement with news on the mobile phone. Users seemed to take advantage of the technological advances in increasing their news-following activities.

To demonstrate the use of the vast range of news-following avenues in action, two female college students in Taiwan offered their thoughts on why and how they follow news on their smartphones. One of them said, "If the news is about Taiwan, I follow it up on Facebook; if it is about an international event, I will follow it up on Twitter." The other student added, "My first choice in keeping up with news is apps like Plurk (a microblogging service), Twitter, and PTT (the largest terminal-based bulletin board system in Taiwan), you can quickly see different points of view on the same news story."

A second-year female student in Hong Kong said she follows news from "The Guardian, BBC News, and Stand News because they are reputable news outlets." She has the Guardian app on her phone and subscribed to pages of BBC and Stand News on Facebook. But she shies away from nonmainstream news outlets. She explained, "I do that sometimes, but I doubted the credibility of them. I read it only because I am interested in observing some of the biased news media."

Effect of Smartphone Ownership

As we reported in Chapter 4, ownership of smartphones jumped to 98.7% in the second wave of surveys from 53% in the first wave of surveys, nearly saturating the studied college populations. To address whether mobile news following was related to the increasing ownership of smartphones, the survey data were further analyzed.

As Table 5.2a shows, in the 2010–2011 surveys, more than half of smartphone owners (between 50.8% and 65.9%) engaged in one of the six news-following activities, including following a news organization (65.9%), a journalist (57.5%), a news blog (56.8%), a news blogger (54.9%), Twitter updates from a news organization (52.8%), and tweets from a journalist (50.8%). The percentage of nonsmartphone owners who followed news, on the other hand, was much lower, ranging only between 21.4% and 28.2%. Their most common activities were following news organizations (28.2%), a journalist (24.8%), a news blog (24.2%), and a news blogger (23.3%). Following Twitter updates from a news organization (21.8%) and following tweets of a journalist (21.4%) were the least common. The differences between smartphone owners and nonowners in the combined index of following mobile news were statistically significant ($t = 23.64$, $p < .001$).

In the 2017–2018 surveys, a similar pattern was found, even though almost all of the respondents owned a smartphone—smartphone owners were still more likely than nonowners to follow news accessed from a phone. As presented in Table 5.2b, two-thirds to nearly all (73.2% to 91%) of the respondents who owned a smartphone followed news frequently. On

Table 5.2a DIFFERENCES IN MOBILE NEWS-FOLLOWING ACTIVITIES BETWEEN SMARTPHONE AND NONSMARTPHONE OWNERS (2010–2011 SURVEYS)

Samples/ News-Following Activities	Smartphone Users (N = 1,809)			Nonsmartphone Users (N = 1,672)			t Value
	No	Yes	Mean	No	Yes	Mean	
Following a news organization	34.1%	65.9%	2.09	71.8%	28.2%	1.38	25.05***
Following a journalist	42.5%	57.5%	1.87	75.2%	24.8%	1.32	20.93***
Following a news blog	43.2%	56.8%	1.90	75.9%	24.2%	1.32	21.35***
Following a news blogger	45.1%	54.9%	1.84	76.7%	23.3%	1.31	19.96***
Following Twitter updates from a news organization	47.2%	52.8%	1.87	78.2%	21.8%	1.30	20.33***
Following tweets from a journalist	49.2%	50.8%	1.80	78.6%	21.4%	1.30	18.51**
Combined activities			1.90 (.83)			1.32 (.59)	23.64***

Note: The scale ranged from 1 to 4, where 1 = never and 4 = often.
***$p < .001$, **$p < .01$.

the other hand, nonsmartphone owners, who were small in number (e.g., laggards), followed news less frequently. The percentages of their news-following activities ranged between 81.6% and 84.2%.

Results of an independent t-test indicate no difference between smartphone owners (M = 2.34, SD = .82) and nonsmartphone owners (M = 2.34, SD = .64) in the overall index of following mobile news (t = −0.23, p > .05) in the second wave of surveys, suggesting that owning a smartphone no longer mattered in facilitating the news-following behavior when smartphones saturated the population of Asian college students. Upgrades to smartphones have become routine and common among young people. As a result, the influence of owning a smartphone on news-following behavior has decreased.

Taken together, these results show that in the first wave of surveys, smartphone users seemed to have benefited from owning the Internet-enabled

Table 5.2b DIFFERENCES IN MOBILE NEWS-FOLLOWING
ACTIVITIES BETWEEN SMARTPHONE AND NONSMARTPHONE OWNERS
(2017–2018 SURVEYS)

Samples/ News-Following Activities	Smartphone User (N = 2,830)			Nonsmartphone User (N = 38)			t Value
	No	Yes	Mean	No	Yes	Mean	
Following a news organization	9.0%	91.0%	2.83	18.4%	81.6%	2.05	6.85***
Following a journalist	20.3%	79.7%	2.38	18.4%	81.6%	2.11	2.33*
Following a news blog	23.9%	76.1%	2.31	21.1%	78.9%	2.21	0.75
Following a news blogger	26.2%	73.8%	2.23	15.8%	84.2%	2.34	−0.82
Following Twitter updates from a news organization	21.3%	78.7%	2.54	10.5%	89.5%	2.53	0.09
Following tweets from a journalist	26.8%	73.2%	2.30	15.8%	84.2%	2.53	−1.38
Combined activities			2.34 (.82)			2.34 (.64)	−0.23

Note: The scale ranged from 1 to 4, where 1 = never and 4 = often.
***p < .001, **p < .01.

smartphone to consume more news by following it. However, the difference disappeared across the two survey periods. In the second wave of surveys, in which upgrades to the smartphone became more common, smartphone users and nonusers were similar in following the news via the phone.

Gender Differences

We next explored whether following mobile news was related to gender. As we expected, results in Table 5.3a show that in the 2010–2011 surveys, Asian male college students (M = 1.70, SD = .80) were more likely than their female counterparts (M = 1.56, SD = .75) to follow news on the mobile phone (t = 5.30, p < .001). Nearly half (ranging 41% to 54%) of the male respondents used their mobile phone to engage with news, including following a news organization (53.7%), a journalist (46.9%), a news blog (46.3%), a news blogger (44.3%), Twitter updates from a news organization (41.2%), and tweets from a journalist (40.5%).

Table 5.3a DIFFERENCES IN MOBILE NEWS-FOLLOWING ACTIVITIES BETWEEN MALE AND FEMALE USERS (2010–2011 SURVEYS)

Samples/News-Following Activities	Male			Female			t Value
	No	Yes	Mean	No	Yes	Mean	
Following a news organization	46.3%	53.7%	1.87	56.6%	43.4%	1.66	6.68***
Following a journalist	53.1%	46.9%	1.70	62.1%	37.9%	1.54	5.54***
Following a news blog	53.7%	46.3%	1.71	62.6%	37.4%	1.55	5.12***
Following a news blogger	55.7%	44.3%	1.67	63.5%	36.5%	1.53	4.84***
Following Twitter updates from a news organization	58.8%	41.2%	1.65	64.5%	35.5%	1.56	3.17***
Following tweets from a journalist	59.5%	40.5%	1.61	65.8%	34.2%	1.52	3.33**
Combined activities			1.70 (.80)			1.56 (.75)	5.30***

Note: The scale ranged from 1 to 4, where 1 = never and 4 = often.
***p < .001, **p < .01.

On the other hand, only about one-third (34% to 43%) of Asian female college students used mobile phones to engage with news following. Among them, news organizations (43.4%) were followed the most, then journalists (37.9%), then news blogs (37.4%), and then news bloggers (36.5%). Twitter updates from a news organization (35.5%) and tweets from a journalist (34.2%) were followed the least.

However, the results of the 2017–2018 surveys shown in Table 5.3b revealed narrowed gender differences in following mobile news. Male students did not statistically differ from female users in following a journalist ($t = -1.61$, $p > .05$), a news blog ($t = -1.75$, $p > .05$), a news blogger ($t = -1.10$, $p > .05$), and tweets from a journalist ($t = -1.47$, $p > .05$). Furthermore, female students were even more likely than their male peers to follow a news organization ($t = -2.88$, $p < .001$) and tweet updates from the organizations ($t = -5.17$, $p < .001$). This particular result may be due to the fact that female users tend to spend more time using their phone than male users (DeBailon & Rockwell, 2005; Leung & Wei, 2000).

Table 5.3b DIFFERENCES IN MOBILE NEWS-FOLLOWING ACTIVITIES BETWEEN MALE AND FEMALE USERS (2017–2018 SURVEYS)

Samples/ News-Following Activities	Male			Female			t Value
	No	Yes	Mean	No	Yes	Mean	
Following a news organization	10.9%	89.1%	2.76	8.2%	91.8%	2.86	–2.88***
Following a journalist	21.6%	78.4%	2.34	19.6%	80.4%	2.40	–1.61
Following a news blog	25.2%	74.8%	2.26	23.1%	76.9%	2.33	–1.75
Following a news blogger	27.9%	72.1%	2.20	25.0%	75.0%	2.24	–1.10
Following Twitter updates from a news organization	24.4%	75.6%	2.42	18.9%	81.1%	2.62	–5.17***
Following tweets from a journalist	28.5%	71.5%	2.27	25.6%	74.4%	2.37	–1.47
Combined activities			2.29 (.84)			2.37 (.81)	–2.68***

Note: The scale ranged from 1 to 4, where 1 = never and 4 = often.
***$p < .001$.

Perhaps the most interesting finding from the two waves of survey data was that the mobile news-following behavior of both male and female respondents increased from the 2010–2011 period to the 2017–2018 period (refer to details in Table 5.1). These results indicate that the advances in wireless telecommunications technology from 3G to 4G have led to increased news-following behavior for all mobile phone users regardless of gender. The faster 4G networks and bigger screens make it easy for Asian college student users to follow news updates from either news organizations or new media platforms such as Twitter.

Light versus Heavy Users

We further analyzed whether heavy users of mobile news differed from light users in their mobile news-following behavior. To do so, we distinguished light and heavy users of the mobile news by splitting the mobile news use scale at the median.

As Table 5.4a shows, in the 2010–2011 surveys, more than two-thirds (from 67% to 81%) of heavy mobile news users engaged in following a news organization (80.8%), a journalist (72.7%), a news blog (72.8%), a news blogger (70.2%), Twitter updates from a news organization (67.9%), and tweets from a journalist (66.0%). The proportions of light users who followed news, on the other hand, were much lower, hovering below one-third (ranging from 17% to 26%). The most common activities were following news organizations (25.6%), a journalist (20.5%), a news blog (19.6%), and a news blogger (18.8%). Following Twitter updates from a news organization (17.4%) and following tweets of a journalist (16.6%) were the least common. Statistically, the differences were significant.

A similar pattern was found in the 2017–2018 surveys—heavy mobile news users were more likely than light users to follow news. As Table 5.4b shows, 85.1% and more (up to 96.2%) of the respondents used their mobile phone to engage in some kind of news-following activities. In comparison, the percentages of light users who used the mobile phone to engage in similar news following activities were lower, hovering between 61.6% and 85.5%. Results of an independent t-test also indicate that the differences were significant. Heavy users ($M = 2.66$, $SD = .76$) were consistently more likely to follow news on the mobile phone than light users ($M = 2.04$, $SD = .77$) ($t = 21.56$, $p < .001$).

In summary, these results show that heavy users who accessed news from the mobile phone tend to have a higher level of engagement with the

Table 5.4a DIFFERENCES IN MOBILE NEWS-FOLLOWING ACTIVITIES BETWEEN LIGHT AND HEAVY USERS OF MOBILE NEWS (2010–2011 SURVEYS)

Samples/ News-Following Activities	Heavy User			Light User			t Value
	No	Yes	Mean	No	Yes	Mean	
Following a news organization	19.2%	80.8%	2.33	74.4%	25.6%	1.36	38.78***
Following a journalist	27.3%	72.7%	2.13	79.5%	20.5%	1.25	33.47***
Following a news blog	27.2%	72.8%	2.16	80.4%	19.6%	1.23	32.11***
Following a news blogger	29.8%	70.2%	2.11	81.2%	18.8%	1.24	32.49***
Following Twitter updates from a news organization	32.1%	67.9%	2.13	82.6%	17.4%	1.24	30.74***
Following tweets from a journalist	34.0%	66.0%	2.06	83.4%	16.6%	1.22	30.26**
Combined activities			2.16 (.81)			1.25 (.49)	37.88***

Note: The scale ranged from 1 to 4, where 1 = never and 4 = often.
***$p < .001$, **$p < .01$.

news than light users. The pattern suggests that the more Asian college students use the mobile phone as the gateway to consume news, the more they will follow the news.

Effect of Surveillance Motivation

We also examined whether surveillance motivation of mobile phone use was related to news-following behavior. To accomplish the analysis, we distinguished high-surveillance-motivation users from low-surveillance-motivation users by splitting the surveillance motivation scale at the median. Not surprisingly, results of the surveys show that respondents with high surveillance motivation tend to have a higher

Table 5.4b DIFFERENCES IN MOBILE NEWS-FOLLOWING ACTIVITIES
BETWEEN LIGHT AND HEAVY USERS OF MOBILE NEWS (2017–2018 SURVEYS)

Samples/ News-Following Activities	Heavy User			Light User			t Value
	No	Yes	Mean	No	Yes	Mean	
Following a news organization	3.8%	96.2%	3.07	14.5%	85.5%	2.58	15.07***
Following a journalist	10.4%	89.6%	2.68	30.2%	69.8%	2.08	17.99***
Following a news blog	12.1%	87.9%	2.62	35.7%	64.3%	1.99	18.67***
Following a news blogger	14.2%	85.8%	2.55	37.8%	62.2%	1.92	18.62***
Following Twitter updates from a news organization	10.8%	89.2%	2.84	31.2%	68.8%	2.24	16.24***
Following tweets from a journalist	14.9%	85.10%	2.63	38.4%	61.6%	1.98	18.31**
Combined activities			2.66 (.76)			2.04 (.77)	21.56***

Note: The scale ranged from 1 to 4, where 1 = never and 4 = often.
***$p < .001$, **$p < .01$.

level of mobile news engagement than users with low surveillance motivation.

To be specific, in the 2010–2011 surveys presented in Table 5.5a, around half (from 47% to 61%) of high-motivation users engaged in some kind of news-following activities, including following a news organization (60.7%), following a journalist (53.1%), following a news blog (52.4%), following a news blogger (51.0%), following Twitter updates from an organization (49.2%), and following tweets from a journalist (47.2%). On the other hand, the proportions of low-motivation users who used mobile phones to engage with news were lower, ranging from 18% to 25%. These users tend to follow a news organization (25.2%), a journalist (21.9%), a news blog (21.2%), a news blogger (20.1%), and, to a lesser extent, Twitter updates from an organization (18.1%) and a journalist (18.4%).

Results of another independent t-test indicate that the between-group differences are significant—high motivation users were more likely to

Table 5.5a DIFFERENCES IN MOBILE NEWS-FOLLOWING ACTIVITIES FOR HIGH- AND LOW-SURVEILLANCE-MOTIVATION USERS (2010–2011 SURVEYS)

Samples/ News-Following Activities	High Motivation			Low Motivation			t Value
	No	Yes	Mean	No	Yes	Mean	
Following a news organization	39.3%	60.7%	1.98	74.8%	25.2%	1.35	23.06***
Following a journalist	46.9%	53.1%	1.79	78.1%	21.9%	1.28	20.82***
Following a news blog	47.6%	52.4%	1.81	78.8%	21.2%	1.28	20.51***
Following a news blogger	49.0%	51.0%	1.77	79.9%	20.1%	1.27	19.53**
Following Twitter updates from a news organization	50.8%	49.2%	1.80	81.9%	18.1%	1.24	21.62***
Following tweets from a journalist	52.8%	47.2%	1.74	81.6%	18.4%	1.24	20.37***
Combined activities			1.82 (.85)			1.28 (.52)	23.69***

Note: The scale ranged from 1 to 4, where 1 = never and 4 = often.
***p < .001, **p < .01.

follow news posted on mobile microblogs (M = 1.82, SD = .85) than low motivation users (M = 1.28, SD = .52) in the 2010–2011 surveys (t = 23.69, p < .001).

In the 2017–2018 surveys, the pattern of findings further shows that users with high surveillance motivation were more likely than users with low surveillance motivation to engage in more mobile news-following activities. As shown in Table 5.5b, more than two-thirds (ranging from 76% to 93%) of high-motivation users used their mobile phone to engage in one form or another of news-following activities. However, the percentages of low-motivation users who used the mobile phone to engage in news-following activities were lower, at the range between 67% and 86%. Results of more independent t-test indicate the difference was also significant. That is, respondents with high surveillance motivation were more likely to follow news posted on mobile microblogs (M = 2.44, SD = .82) than respondents with low surveillance motivation (M = 2.13, SD = .78) (t = 9.94, p < .001).

Table 5.5b DIFFERENCES IN MOBILE NEWS-FOLLOWING
ACTIVITIES FOR HIGH- AND LOW-SURVEILLANCE-MOTIVATION
USERS (2017–2018 SURVEYS)

Samples/News-Following Activities	High Motivation			Low Motivation			t Value
	No	Yes	Mean	No	Yes	Mean	
Following a news organization	6.9%	93.1%	2.96	14.2%	85.8%	2.54	11.81***
Following a journalist	18.9%	81.1%	2.46	23.5%	76.5%	2.20	7.22***
Following a news blog	20.8%	79.2%	2.41	30.6%	69.4%	2.09	8.63***
Following a news blogger	23.3%	76.7%	2.31	31.9%	68.1%	2.06	6.84***
Following Twitter updates from a news organization	17.2%	82.8%	2.69	29.1%	70.9%	2.22	11.78***
Following tweets from a journalist	23.6%	76.4%	2.40	33.1%	66.9%	2.09	8.01***
Combined activities			2.44 (.82)			2.13 (.78)	9.94***

Note: The scale ranged from 1 to 4, where 1 = never and 4 = often.
***p < .001.

Cross-City Differences

To analyze whether college students in the four Asian cities differed in their mobile news-following activities due to the different socio-political systems of the city or society in which they lived, we conducted a series of one-way ANOVA tests. As Table 5.6a presents, significant differences were found in the six news-following activities on the mobile phone in the first wave of surveys [F (3, 3512) = 171.29, p < .001]. Respondents in Shanghai (M = 2.01, SD = .88) followed mobile news the most often, followed by those in Singapore (M = 1.79, SD = .80) and Hong Kong (M = 1.49, SD = .66). Taipei respondents (M = 1.30, SD = .56) were the least likely to follow news on the mobile phone. The Scheffe test shows that all the differences in mobile news following among the Shanghai, Singapore, Hong Kong, and Taipei respondents were significant at the p < .001 level.

Accordingly, the general pattern suggests that respondents in China and Singapore (both under authoritarian rule) were more likely to engage in news-following behavior than their counterparts in Hong Kong and Taipei (representing limited or full liberal democracies). It appears that the freer and more liberal a society is, the less residents are inclined to follow the

Table 5.6a MOBILE NEWS-FOLLOWING ACTIVITIES IN SHANGHAI, HONG
KONG, TAIPEI, AND SINGAPORE (2010–2011 SURVEYS)

Samples/News-Following Activities	Shanghai	Hong Kong	Taipei	Singapore	Total	*F* Value
Following a news organization	2.10 (.96)	1.59 (.76)	1.35 (.65)	2.06 (1.02)	1.75 (.92)	177.41***
Following a journalist	1.97 (.94)	1.52 (.73)	1.30 (.59)	1.75 (.88)	1.61 (.82)	124.35***
Following a news blog	2.01 (1.00)	1.49 (.74)	1.32 (.64)	1.76 (.89)	1.62 (.86)	123.86***
Following a news blogger	1.98 (.99)	1.47 (.72)	1.30 (.62)	1.71 (.86)	1.59 (.84)	122.55***
Following Twitter updates from an organization	2.01 (1.02)	1.44 (.70)	1.27 (.58)	1.78 (.99)	1.60 (.88)	146.01***
Following tweets from a journalist	1.98 (1.01)	1.43 (.69)	1.27 (.59)	1.67 (.90)	1.56 (.84)	129.28***
Combined activities	2.01 (.88)	1.49 (.66)	1.30 (.56)	1.79 (.80)	1.62 (.78)	171.29***

Note: The scale ranged from 1 to 4, where 1 = never and 4 = often.
***$p < .001$.

news on the mobile phone. On the other hand, the more illiberal the society is, the more residents living in such societies tend to follow the news.

As Table 5.6b presents, the cross-city differences in using their mobile phone to follow news remained significant in the second wave of surveys [F (3, 2854) = 80.96, $p < .001$]. Results of the post hoc Scheffe test revealed that Shanghai respondents were still most likely to follow news accessible from the mobile phone ($M = 2.56$, $SD = .78$). Although Singapore respondents ($M = 1.98$, $SD = .78$) slightly increased their news following via mobile phones, over the period between the two surveys, Taipei ($M = 2.53$, $SD = .82$) and Hong Kong ($M = 2.26$, $SD = .78$) respondents increased theirs substantially more. The results of the post hoc Scheffe tests also show that respondents in Shanghai and Taipei were more likely to follow microblog news posts than their counterparts in Hong Kong and Singapore. However, there was no difference in the mean of mobile news-following behavior between Shanghai and Taipei respondents.

Consistently, these results indicate that the respondents in Shanghai, China, under an illiberal political system with no free or partially free media, were the mostly likely to follow news in both periods of surveys, while those in Taiwan, who were the least likely to do so in the first wave of surveys, had increased their news-following behavior by the time of

Table 5.6b MOBILE NEWS-FOLLOWING ACTIVITIES IN SHANGHAI, HONG KONG, TAIPEI, AND SINGAPORE (2017–2018 SURVEYS)

Samples/ News-Following Activities	Shanghai	Hong Kong	Taipei	Singapore	Total	F Value
Following a news organization	2.83 (.85)	2.71 (.90)	2.99 (.90)	2.73 (.93)	2.82 (.90)	15.69***
Following a journalist	2.58 (.91)	2.36 (.92)	2.52 (.96)	2.01 (.93)	2.38 (.96)	53.27***
Following a news blog	2.43 (.95)	2.26 (.94)	2.46 (.97)	2.03 (.93)	2.30 (.96)	30.84***
Following a news blogger	2.37 (.94)	2.25 (.95)	2.38 (.97)	1.88 (.87)	2.23 (.95)	44.64***
Following Twitter updates from an organization	2.80 (.89)	2.26 (.99)	2.87 (.98)	2.17 (1.01)	2.53 (1.04)	96.26***
Following tweets from a journalist	2.60 (.92)	2.15 (.97)	2.56 (.99)	1.84 (.97)	2.30 (1.01)	99.77***
Combined activities	2.56 (.78)	2.26 (.78)	2.53 (.82)	1.98 (.78)	2.34 (.82)	80.96***

Note: The scale ranged from 1 to 4, where 1 = never and 4 = often
***$p < .001$.

the second wave. A pattern in news following has emerged from these results—the less liberal and free a society, the more its young citizens engage in following news on mobile phones. Because illiberal societies tend to place tight control on news flow and information (Repnikova, 2017), the mobile phone as a personal and less controlled new medium appears to have become a viable resource for millions of users to stay informed about news and currents events.

Shifting Predictors of Following Behavior

To examine which of the studied independent variables—demographics, mobile news consumption, city of residence, motives for mobile phone use, and expectancies of mobile news—would have the most influence on mobile news-following behavior, two separate hierarchical regression analyses were performed. As shown in Table 5.7 (column 1), in the first wave of surveys, city of residence was a significant but weak predictor of mobile

Table 5.7 HIERARCHICAL REGRESSION ANALYSIS PREDICTING FOLLOWING
NEWS ON MOBILE PHONES

Independent Variables	2010–2011	2017–2018
Block 1: Demographics		
Gender	.01	−.07***
Age	.03*	−.04*
City of residence (Shanghai)	.04**	.12***
Adjusted R^2	7.9%	2.9%
Block 2: Smartphone ownership		
Smartphone ownership	.08***	−.05**
Incremental adjusted R^2	11.4%	0.0%
Block 3: Motivations		
Surveillance	.11***	.03
Incremental adjusted R^2	10.1%	3.6%
Block 4: Expectancies of mobile news		
Personal value	.10***	.11***
Incremental adjusted R^2	3.8%	2.6%
Block 5: Mobile news use		
Mobile news consumption	.49***	.41***
Incremental adjusted R^2	12.7%	14.6%
Total adjusted R^2	45.9%	23.7%
N	3,418	2,674

Note: Beta weights are from final regression equation with all blocks of variables in the model.
***$p < .001$, **$p < .01$, *$p < .05$.

news following (B = .04, $p < .01$), indicating that Shanghai respondents
were more likely to follow news posts on mobile microblogs than were their
counterparts from other cities. Smartphone ownership (B = .08, $p < .001$),
surveillance motivation (B = .11, $p < .001$) and personal value of mobile
news (B = .10, $p < .001$) were also significant and positive predictors of news
following behavior, among which mobile news consumption emerged as
the strongest predictor (B = .49, $p < .001$).

Regression analyses of the 2017–2018 surveys show (column 2 in Table
5.7) that both gender (B = −.07, $p < .001$) and city (B = .12, $p < .001$) were
significantly related to mobile news-following behavior, indicating that
Shanghai respondents of both genders and female respondents in the
other three cities were more likely to use their mobile phone to follow
the news. Smartphone ownership (B = −.05, $p < .01$) and personal value

of mobile news ($B = .11$, $p < .001$) were also significantly related to mobile news-following behavior. The results consistently show that the level of mobile news consumption was again the most powerful predictor of news-following behavior ($B = .41$, $p < .001$), suggesting news following was triggered and amplified by news sought from the mobile phone carried in the respondents' pockets.

The results of these multivariate analyses using two waves of survey data show that the equation, which had the same set of predictors, was more successful in explaining the variance of mobile news-following behavior in the data from the first surveys (45.9%) than that of the second surveys (23.7%). Bata changes presented in Table 5.7 indicate that the effects of owning a smartphone, the surveillance motivation of mobile phone use, and mobile news consumption, to a lesser extent, all decreased across the two periods of survey. However, the effects of gender and city on mobile news-following behavior increased from the 2010–2011 surveys to the surveys of 2017–2018.

What these results indicate is that as the mobile phone evolved from 3G to 4G and the share of smartphones users as well as the number of smartphone-only users increased, individual-level factors, such as motivations, and technology factors, such as types of mobile phone, lost the explanatory power over mobile news-following behavior. In the meantime, socio-political factors like social role and political systems increased their importance in accounting for the behavior.

Remarks made by several participants in our focus groups add meaning to these findings. Regarding her motivation to follow news, a female student in Shanghai said, "I like following news posted on *Sina Weibo* [the biggest microblogging site in China]; it's updated quick and allows me to forward and leave comments on stories." Her male counterpart in Shanghai said something similar: "I use my smartphone to follow news posted on Weibo and WeChat by the *Paper* and *Beijing News*; they are good sources of breaking news."

Likewise, a female student in Singapore provided the following reason that she follows news on her phone: "I feel like it could affect us one way or another. I want to stay aware even if it is overseas. I will be interested in presidential election in Singapore and the U.S. Things happening in Europe and how it will affect Singapore and in turn affect me." Talking about how she follows mobile news specifically, she continued:

I think it depends on if the news is recent and time sensitive. Terrorism and those that happened recently, like the LA shooting or the Vegas shooting. If it is happening right now, so when the Malaysian airline disappears, I was keeping track of the update and the different theories; if it is the news about the presidential election, I won't wake up in the morning, think about what the candidates said.

A male peer of hers in Singapore said he followed news on the U.S. election, because "it is very interesting." Similarly, several students in Taipei said they typically follow hard news the most, followed by entertainment news. A 21-year-old female explained, "The news hole for international news in Taiwan is getting smaller and smaller. A mobile app like *Huffington Post* has all the foreign news that I need." A second-year male student in Hong Kong singled out *Apple Daily* as the news outlet that he followed the most. He said, "I follow its news first for its gossip style of reporting. Then, its serious and critical reporting of the 2019–2020 extradition bill and ensuring civic movement against it draws me to read on."

SHARING MOBILE NEWS

Patterns of Sharing

The results from the 2017–2018 surveys indicate that most respondents in the pooled sample used their mobile phones to engage in all six news-sharing activities. As results presented in Table 5.8 show, sharing news on the mobile phone as a way of consuming news was frequent and popular. The most frequent news-sharing activity was sharing news (87.9%), followed by sharing news photos (83.6%), user-generated news (81.5%), and news videos (81.3%). Sharing news from WhatsApp and WeChat (79.9%), which are micromessaging services for personal communication,

Table 5.8 MOBILE NEWS-SHARING ACTIVITIES (2017–2018 SURVEYS)

Sharing Activities	No	Yes	Mean
Sharing news on the mobile phone	12.1%	87.9%	2.58
Sharing news from WhatsApp/WeChat	21.1%	79.9%	2.39
Sharing user-generated news	18.5%	81.5%	2.40
Sharing news pictures	16.4%	83.6%	2.61
Sharing news video	18.7%	81.3%	2.48
Combined activities			2.48 (.77)

Note: The scale ranged from 1 to 4, where 1 = never and 4 = often.

was less frequent. These results suggest that when sharing mobile news, users tend to share those from traditional news sources as well as user-generated content (UGC; e.g., posts, videos, blogs, digital images, and audio files, among others) via social media platforms.

Smartphone Users versus Nonusers

As presented in Table 5.9 and consistent with the results of news following, smartphone owners were slightly more likely to share mobile news than were nonsmartphone owners. Based on the descriptive results of the 2017–2018 surveys, the majority (ranging between 88.1% and 81.3%) of the respondents who owned a smartphone used it to share news (88.1%), to share news from WhatsApp or WeChat (78.7%), to share user-generated news (81.7%), to share news photos (83.7%), and to share news videos (81.3%). On the other hand, the percentage of nonsmartphone owners who used their phone for news sharing was slightly lower, hovering around 84.2%. The nonsmartphone owners shared news from WhatsApp or WeChat (92.1%) the most, then news photos (86.5%), videos (84.2%), news (84.2%), and user-generated news (79.9%).

In sum, it seems that owning a smartphone still made some difference in affecting mobile news-sharing behavior regardless of the near saturation among the surveyed students. Those who had a smartphone or upgraded to a smartphone tended to share more. Also, with the always-on connectivity,

Table 5.9 DIFFERENCES IN MOBILE NEWS-SHARING ACTIVITIES FOR SMARTPHONE AND NONSMARTPHONE USERS (2017–2018 SURVEYS)

News-Sharing Activities	Smartphone User ($N = 2,830$)			Nonsmartphone User ($N = 38$)			t Value
	No	Yes	Mean	No	Yes	Mean	
Sharing news	11.9%	88.1%	2.59	15.8%	84.2%	2.11	6.85***
Sharing news from WhatsApp/WeChat	21.3%	78.7%	2.40	7.9%	92.1%	2.26	2.33*
Sharing user-generated news	18.3%	81.7%	2.41	21.1%	78.9%	2.21	0.75
Sharing news photos	16.3%	83.7%	2.62	13.5%	86.5%	2.49	−0.82
Sharing news videos	18.7%	81.3%	2.48	15.8%	84.2%	2.32	0.09
Combined activities			2.49 (.77)			2.27 (.57)	2.30*

Note: The scale ranged from 1 to 4, where 1 = never and 4 = often.
***$p < .001$, *$p < .05$.

smartphone owners seem to take advantage of the mobile broadband connection to share news in photos and videos in addition to text.

Gender Differences

As reported in Table 5.10, we found some interesting gender differences in sharing mobile news—Asian female college students were more likely ($M = 2.52$, $SD = .75$) to use the mobile phone to share news than were their male counterparts ($M = 2.44$, $SD = .79$). This was particularly true for sharing news ($t = -3.28$, $p < .01$) and news photos ($t = -4.05$, $p < .001$). The gender differences in the combined index of mobile news sharing are significant ($t = -2.70$, $p < .01$). However, they did not differ from male peers in the other news-sharing activities such as sharing news from WhatsApp or WeChat ($t = -.96$, $p > .05$), sharing user-generated news content ($t = -1.53$, $p > .05$), and sharing news videos ($t = -1.46$, $p > .05$).

Consistent with results concerning news-following behavior, female respondents in the second surveys were more engaged with mobile news by following and sharing such news. These results make sense because female mobile phone users were found to use the mobile phone for social purposes (Leung & Wei, 2000), and sharing news is considered a form of social interaction (D. Goh et al., 2017).

Table 5.10 DIFFERENCES IN MOBILE NEWS-SHARING ACTIVITIES BETWEEN MALE AND FEMALE USERS (2017–2018 SURVEYS)

News-Sharing Activities	Male			Female			t Value
	No	Yes	Mean	No	Yes	Mean	
Sharing news	13.8%	86.2%	2.52	10.5%	89.5%	2.63	−3.28**
Sharing news from WhatsApp/WeChat	21.1%	78.9%	2.37	21.0%	79.0%	2.41	−.96
Sharing user-generated news	20.4%	79.6%	2.37	16.9%	83.1%	2.42	−1.53
Sharing news pictures	18.8%	81.2%	2.53	14.5%	85.5%	2.68	−4.05***
Sharing news videos	19.5%	80.5%	2.44	18.0%	82.0%	2.50	−1.46
Combined activities			2.44 (.79)			2.52 (.75)	−2.70**

Note: The scale ranged from 1 to 4, where 1 = never and 4 = often.
***$p < .001$, **$p < .01$.

Light versus Heavy News Users

Results presented in Table 5.11 shed some light on the question of whether heavy users of mobile news differed from light users of mobile news in sharing the news. Indeed, heavy users of mobile news were more likely to engage in news-sharing activities than light users. Based on the second surveys completed in 2017–2018, a much high proportion— between 88% and 94% of the heavy mobile news users—shared news from news organizations (94.3%), news from WhatsApp/WeChat (88.1%), user-generated news (91.1%), news photos (91.3%), and news videos (89.8%).

In summary, the more Asian college students in the studied cities consumed news from the mobile phone, the more they tended to share the news, which suggests that consuming mobile news itself is an interactive and engaging experience. Furthermore, heavy users of mobile news appear to share all sorts of news, indicating that news accessed on the mobile phone provides a strong drive for engagement.

On the other hand, the proportions of light users of mobile news who shared news via the phone were lower, ranging between 62% and 82%. Specifically, they shared straight news (81.8%) more than news from social media or UGC (WhatsApp or WeChat at 69.8%, user-generated news at 72.1%), news photos (76.0%), and news videos (62.3%). It appears that

Table 5.11 DIFFERENCES IN MOBILE NEWS-SHARING ACTIVITIES BETWEEN LIGHT AND HEAVY USERS (2017–2018 SURVEYS)

News-Sharing Activities	Heavy User			Light User			t Value
	No	Yes	Mean	No	Yes	Mean	
Sharing news	5.7%	94.3%	2.84	18.2%	81.8%	2.34	16.25***
Sharing news from WhatsApp/WeChat	11.9%	88.1%	2.67	30.2%	69.8%	2.12	16.04***
Sharing user-generated news	8.9%	91.1%	2.71	27.9%	72.1%	2.11	18.58***
Sharing news pictures	8.7%	91.3%	2.87	24.0%	76.0%	2.36	14.33***
Sharing news videos	10.2%	89.8%	2.75	27.7%	62.3%	2.20	15.88***
Combined activities			2.75 (.71)			2.22 (.76)	18.31***

Note: The scale ranged from 1 to 4, where 1 = never and 4 = often.
***$p < .001$.

lighter users of mobile news shared more news from the established news sources than from other non-traditional sources such as social media platforms or UGC. In addition, unlike heavy users, they shared less news published in photos and videos, indicating a lower level of interaction with the news content on mobile phones with others.

Results of an independent t-test indicate that the difference in mobile news-sharing behavior between heavy users of mobile news and light users was significant. The former in general were more likely to use a mobile phone to share news ($M = 2.75$, $SD = .71$) than were light users ($M = 2.22$, $SD = .76$) ($t = 18.31$, $p < .001$).

High and Low Surveillance Motivation

Next, the effect of surveillance motivation on news-sharing behavior was examined using data from the 2017–2018 surveys. Table 5.12 shows that respondents with high surveillance motivation were more likely to use their mobile phone to share news than were respondents with low surveillance motivation. According to the survey data, out of the pooled sample, nearly all of the high-surveillance respondents (ranging from 85% to 90%) used a mobile phone to engage in news-sharing activities—news (90.4%), news from WhatsApp or WeChat (81.0%), user-generated news (84.9%), news photos (86.6%), and news videos (84.6%).

Table 5.12 DIFFERENCES IN MOBILE NEWS-SHARING ACTIVITIES
FOR HIGH- AND LOW-SURVEILLANCE-MOTIVATION USERS
(2017–2018 SURVEYS)

News-Sharing Activities	High Motivation			Low Motivation			t Value
	No	Yes	Mean	No	Yes	Mean	
Sharing news	9.6%	90.4%	2.71	17.1%	82.9%	2.33	10.95***
Sharing news from WhatsApp/WeChat	19.0%	81.0%	2.48	25.6%	74.4%	2.20	7.50***
Sharing user-generated news	15.1%	84.9%	2.53	25.5%	74.5%	2.15	10.61***
Sharing news pictures	13.4%	86.6%	2.74	22.5%	77.5%	2.36	9.96***
Sharing news videos	15.4%	84.6%	2.59	25.5%	74.5%	2.23	9.61***
Combined activities			2.60 (.76)			2.25 (.74)	11.53***

Note: The scale ranged from 1 to 4, where 1 = never and 4 = often.
***$p < .001$.

However, the proportions of low-surveillance respondents who used a mobile phone to engage in similar news-sharing activities were lower, ranging from 75% to 83%. They shared news the most (82.9%), then, news photos (77.5%), user-generated news (74.5%), and news videos (74.5%), then news from WhatsApp or WeChat (74.4%). These results are consistent with that of mobile news-following behavior—the more that the respondents were motivated to consume news via the smartphone, the more they became engaged with the news in terms of sharing it with others.

An independent t-test confirmed that these between-group differences were significant. Results indicate that respondents with high surveillance motivation were more likely to use the smartphone to share news ($M = 2.60$, $SD = .76$) than those with low surveillance motivation ($M = 2.25$, $SD = .74$) ($t = 11.53$, $p < .001$). Therefore, whether users shared news accessed from the mobile phone depends on their level of motivation to stay informed about what they consider important, domestically and internationally. High-motivation users have the intrinsic push to share news they consume on the mobile phone.

Cross-City Differences

As reported in Table 5.13, results of the 2017–2018 surveys show that the respondents from the four selected cities also differed in their mobile news-sharing behavior [$F(3, 2871) = 44.98$, $p < .001$]. Results of a post hoc Scheffe test further revealed that Shanghai respondents were most likely to share mobile news ($M = 2.73$, $SD = .69$), followed by Taipei respondents ($M = 2.50$, $SD = .80$), Hong Kong respondents ($M = 2.34$, $SD = .77$), and Singaporean respondents ($M = 2.34$, $SD = .74$).

However, more post hoc Scheffe tests showed no differences in the mean level of mobile news-sharing behavior between Hong Kong and Singaporean respondents. The greatest cross-city differences, therefore, existed between Shanghai respondents and their peers in Taipei, Hong Kong, and Singapore. This pattern in mobile news sharing is consistent with that of mobile news following reported earlier in this chapter.

Predictors of Sharing

To what extent would gender, city of residence, motivation of mobile phone use, expectancies of mobile news, and level of mobile news consumption predict mobile news-sharing behavior in the same way as they predicted

Table 5.13 MOBILE NEWS SHARING IN SHANGHAI, HONG KONG, TAIPEI, AND SINGAPORE (2017–2018 SURVEYS)

News-Sharing Activities	Shanghai	Hong Kong	Taipei	Singapore	Total	F Value
Sharing news	2.78	2.42	2.69	2.41	2.58	33.04***
	(.77)	(.85)	(.91)	(.93)	(.88)	
Sharing news from WhatsApp/WeChat	2.83	2.21	2.31	2.19	2.39	78.65***
	(.81)	(.92)	(.98)	(.98)	(.96)	
Sharing user-generated news	2.73	2.27	2.52	2.04	2.40	81.56***
	(.81)	(.91)	(.92)	(.90)	(.92)	
Sharing news pictures	2.82	2.42	2.57	2.64	2.61	21.87***
	(.83)	(.96)	(1.04)	(1.04)	(.98)	
Sharing news videos	2.50	2.36	2.63	2.39	2.48	12.12***
	(.84)	(.94)	(1.01)	(1.05)	(.97)	
Combined activities	2.73	2.34	2.50	2.34	2.48	44.98***
	(.69)	(.77)	(.80)	(.74)	(.77)	

Notes: The scale ranged from 1 to 4, where 1 = never and 4 = often. Figures in parentheses are standard deviations.
***$p < .001$.

news-following behavior? Further, which of these predictor variables has the strongest effect on sharing mobile news? To address these questions, we ran another hierarchical regression analysis. The equation treated frequency of sharing mobile news as the dependent variable.

As the results of the 2017–2018 surveys presented in Table 5.14 show, city of residence ($B = .12$, $p < .001$), surveillance motivation ($B = .08$, $p < .001$), and personal value of mobile news ($B = .12$, $p < .001$) were all significant predictors of sharing news accessed from the smartphone. Moreover, consuming news from mobile phones ($B = .20$, $p < .001$) and following mobile news ($B = .37$, $p < .001$) were significant and much stronger predictors of sharing mobile news. This particular result reveals a tendency that users who followed the news on their phone tend to share the news with others as well, suggesting that engaged users of mobile news tend to be more deeply engaged with the news. It is consistent with a Pew Research Center (2012) report of mobile news consumption habits that college-educated Americans were inclined to engage with mobile news.

In fact, with the influences of other predictors being taken into consideration, following news accessed from mobile phones was the strongest predictor of sharing the news with others among all the predictors. This particular predictor contributed approximately one-third (10.8%) to the

Table 5.14 HIERARCHICAL REGRESSION ANALYSIS
PREDICTING SHARING NEWS ON THE MOBILE PHONE
(2017–2018 SURVEYS)

Independent Variables	Sharing News
Block 1: Demographics	
Gender	–.04
Age	–.01
City of residence (Shanghai)	.12***
Adjusted R^2	4.5%
Block 2: Smartphone Ownership	
Smartphone ownership	–.02
Incremental adjusted R^2	0.0%
Block 3: Motivations	
Surveillance	.08***
Incremental adjusted R^2	6.4%
Block 4: Expectancies of Mobile News	
Personal value	.12***
Incremental adjusted R^2	4.0%
Block 5: Mobile News Use	
Mobile news consumption	.20***
Incremental adjusted R^2	10.8%
Block 6: News-Following Behavior	
Following mobile news	.37***
Incremental adjusted R^2	10.4%
Total adjusted R^2	36.1%
N	2,616

Note: Beta weights are from final regression equation with all blocks of
variables in the model.
***$p < .001$.

total variance accounted for by all significant predictors (adjusted R^2 of
36.1%).

What these results of multivariate analyses mean is that as the smartphone gained wide popularity and the always-on mobile Internet became
available to millions of smartphone users, consuming news via the phone
became habitual or a routine use of the phone. It seems that checking news
from the phone has gradually slouched from a novelty to the ordinary.
Taking advantage of the new interactive features of news distributed to

smartphones, Asian college students routinely read or view news on the go. The routine of consuming and following mobile news shows the most explanatory power for sharing mobile news with others.

In comparison, demographics (with the exception of city of residence), smartphone ownership, and motivations of mobile phone use turned out to be relatively weak predictors of news-sharing behavior. Such results make sense because when habits of mobile news consumption are formed, users will not need to motivate themselves to seek news from the mobile phone—they just do it.

In explaining what makes people motivated to share news via the phone, the female student in Singapore who spoke about her reasons for following news earlier responded, "When people feel that something has been brought up to light, they feel they should have their opinions heard." Helping others be informed was another reason mentioned for sharing news. In the words of a male student in Singapore, "They may try to look for like-minded people, call it a sort of community building, if you like. You can see the comments in Facebook, they are quite homogenous, and it is pretty interesting like there is sort of like a community there."

A third-year female student in Taipei commented on the importance of news sharing. She said, "Sharing news among my peers enriches the news I get. As the sharing builds up, it's easier to know what really happens." On other hand, another female student in Taipei said she does not like sharing news. She explained, "I feel that I have to be held accountable for what I share. If the story is untrue or biased, something that I would never know or guaranteed, I feel I'm a kind in trouble, so the whole idea of sharing stresses me out." A female student in her second year in Hong Kong expressed the same concern. She said, "Since it is not uncommon for people to extract a paragraph from certain news stories and to generate a piece of fake news, then try to spread it on different social media platforms, so I try to avoid reading news on non-official platforms for the sake of credibility."

Addressing the questions of what they shared and with whom, four out of the five students in Hong Kong mentioned sharing political news with family and sharing environment and entertainment stories with friends on WhatsApp. A second-year female student said, "My family members are not super active online, sometimes I am worried that they might miss out some of the important announcements from the government, or some news that is reported on television." A female student in Shanghai said, "I typically share health news. Then, if it is something big, I definitely share." A second female student in Singapore said she shared news "with family or when the particular topic is of interest to someone like my friend. If I saw such a topic, I will share with my friend or if I am up for a discussion."

A third female student in Singapore explained the type of news she shared via her phone by saying:

> The most recent one will be about presidential election in Singapore. Many of my friends have opinions as to how the president was elected, as there are no other candidate in the race. I think it is interesting as there are many opinions. I didn't know if many of my friends are interested, and it broadens out.

Her male schoolmate in Singapore added that he shares "North Korea related news. I have friends in South Korea. So, when I have news from North Korea, I will share with them because some news is censored. I think because they don't want the citizens to get shock." "Yeah," his peer agreed, "North Korea shoots rockets over Japan. To us, it might be a big news but not in South Korea. It is nothing serious [there]. That is what I share."

SUMMARY OF KEY FINDINGS

The greater capability and ubiquity of smartphones have driven the trend of following and news sharing. To shed light on Asian college students' engagement with mobile news, we focused on the behavior of following and sharing mobile news as two aspects of news engagement and attempted to link the behavior of following and sharing mobile news to a number of antecedents and predictors. Thus, engagement with mobile news includes both user interaction with news content (e.g., use with news embedded with links or video) and user interaction with others (e.g., users or journalists). In doing so, we analyzed mobile news engagement as a property of users, as well as an affordance of the smartphone. The data analyzed in this chapter support the notion that engagement with mobile news results from both user motivation and the empowering tools afforded by the always-on smartphone.

Engagement Behavior

- Findings show that following news on mobile phones was less common in the first period of survey. However, it became more prevalent and frequent as wireless network technologies evolved from 3G networks to 4G in the short span of eight years. The smartphone itself was found to be a significant contributor to the over-time increase.

- The data on news-sharing behavior from the second-wave-only surveys indicate that sharing news was widely reported. Respondents who owned a smartphone tended to share more. Because 95% of the respondents owned a smartphone, sharing news with others became a part of their experience of consuming mobile news. In addition, heavy users of mobile news tended to share all sorts of news they consumed on the smartphone, suggesting that active consumption of news on the mobile phone begets active engagement with it as well.
- Multivariate analyses suggest that an individual who is more motivated to keep an eye on news will consume more news to meet their surveillance need and will be more engaged with the news (e.g., following or sharing). This pattern of mobile news engagement is particularly pronounced among Asian college students living in illiberal societies.
- Results of the two waves of surveys indicate that the more respondents accessed news from their smartphone, the more they tended to follow the news. Further, the more they followed news on the phone, the more they shared the news with others. In fact, the strongest link exists between the behavior of following mobile news and the behavior of sharing such news. We conclude that consuming news via the smartphone enhances the engaging experience.

THEORETICAL INSIGHTS FROM FINDINGS

The general patterns lead to a number of theoretical insights concerning engagement with news accessed and consumed on the mobile phone:

- First, technology matters in affecting user engagement with news accessed from the phone. The smartphone itself was found to be a significant factor contributing to the behavior of consuming and following more news, and thus an enabling factor in facilitating engagement with mobile news.
- Given the low threshold for accessing news on 4G-supported smartphones, sharing news seems to be linked to whether users have an interest in or the habit of consuming news (e.g., the so-called news junkies) in the first place. Users who consume news routinely on the mobile phone tend to share what they consume. Also, their level of motivation to be informed provides the intrinsic push to share news they consume on the phone. This finding suggests that consuming news on the mobile phone is characteristically social, interactive, and participative. Thus, consistent with the recent research on consuming news online

(e.g., Larsson, 2019), consuming news from the mobile phone stimulates and amplifies engagement with the news.

• Surveillance motivation represents a significant and strong predictor of following mobile news in the 3G era and sharing the news in the 4G era, suggesting that the more users perceived the mobile phone as helpful in fulfilling their needs to stay informed anywhere, anytime, the more they used it to follow and share the news. However, the effect of surveillance on mobile news following declined in the 4G era. Consuming mobile news turned out to be a stronger predictor. These findings across the two periods of survey suggest that as mobile phones became always on with Internet connectivity, the newly formed habit of consuming news on one's phone began to drive their news-following and -sharing behavior.

• Finally, results indicate that both following and sharing mobile news were subject to the influence of social-political contexts in which consumption of mobile news took place among the surveyed college students in Shanghai and Singapore, who live in less liberal and free societies and are more likely to engage in news on the mobile phone by following and sharing it largely to circumvent the tightly controlled news flow.

IMPLICATIONS OF FINDINGS FOR CIVIC PARTICIPATION

As R. Wei (2020) argued, permanent connectivity lowers the threshold and cost in sharing political information or recruiting supporters of activist movements and political campaigns. Past research (Ksiazek, Malthouse, & Webster, 2010; S. Lee, 2015) reported a positive relationship of news seeking across digital media channels with civic participation. Therefore, findings of the mobile phone as a gateway to consume news as well as engagement with the news have some far-reaching implications for civic participation in the process of political communication. To be specific, three major implications can be drawn out of the findings in this chapter.

First, what sort of news do people share on mobile phones? Past research (D. Goh et al., 2017) shows that news that was shared belongs to a category of *actionable news* on things that were directly relevant to their everyday lives. Other studies (R. Wei, Huang, & Zheng, 2018; Wen & Wei, 2018) further suggest that engaged users of news tend to take action in public discourse and discussion of the news concerning public issues.

Second, sharing means networking. Following and sharing news content on the smartphone is similar to that on the Internet—*sharing* a link of news to someone who can further *share* that link with more people in a snowballing fashion. The findings of Oeldorf-Hirsch and Sundar (2015) about sharing news on social media suggested that such behavior in sharing news content leads to a sense of community. News sharing among networked users thus leads to a mobile networked sphere (R. Wei, 2016), which facilitates collective actions, when needed. As Putnam (2000) argued, "being connected" online is positively related to political participation. According to evidence collected in Asian societies (e.g., R. Wei, 2016), informational use of mobile phones is conducive to participation in the civic affairs and political movements in Asian countries.

Third, communication on Internet-enabled smartphones is characteristic of a mix of interpersonal and mass communication (R. Wei et al., 2014; Westlund, 2015). Previous research (R. Wei, 2016; Boyd, Zaff, Phelps, Weiner, & Lerner, 2011) suggests that interpersonal communication, such as talks and SMS (short message service) chat, played a key role in bridging news use and participation in discussions of politics. Martin (2015) called it the "bridging function" of mobile phones in political communication. To a large extent, consuming mobile news fulfills an important civic obligation in keeping citizens informed about public affairs. The 4G-supported smartphone empowers Asian college students to not only consume news anywhere, anytime but also become engaged in the news, essentially expanding the opportunity for Asia's young generations to become civically engaged.

CHAPTER 6

Perceptions

The Credibility Factor

EVALUATING NEWS IN THEIR POCKETS: FROM FORM TO SUBSTANCE

The popularity of using the mobile phone to consume news is a global phenomenon (Westlund, 2015). Mobile news expands the reach and coverage of digital news beyond traditional news junkies to their news-averse peers. Living with news accessible from the mobile phone 24/7 has become an integral part of the everyday life of college students. The flip side of the high-choice environment in news consumption is the high risk associated with the flow of ambiguous and questionable news whose sources are difficult to identify or verify. Consuming news accessed via the phone can be risky business. Also, how do Asian college students grapple with the challenge of credibility in news consumption? Specifically, how do they evaluate the quality and credibility of news content they consume via the mobile phone?

This chapter puts the spotlight on the perceptions of mobile news among Asian college students. The goals are to explore how Asian college students evaluate the substance (e.g., credibility of news content) as well as forms (e.g., format, appeal, presentation) of mobile news. In the fake news era, it is worth investigating their views of mobile news as being credible as well as factors such as news reliance and societal differences in press freedom that affect their perceptions of mobile news.

Compaine (2000) made a differentiation of mobile content (or substance) and format. Operationally, we surveyed Asian college students'

News in Their Pockets. Ran Wei and Ven-hwei Lo, Oxford University Press (2021). © Oxford University Press.
DOI: 10.1093/oso/9780197523728.003.0006

evaluation of both substance of mobile news in terms of credibility and forms in terms of appeal, format, and presentation styles. The focus, however, was placed on their perceptions of mobile news credibility as a property of the news source as judged by the consumer: to what extent do surveyed Asian college students perceive mobile news accessed from the phone as believable and trustworthy?

MEDIA CREDIBILITY IN ASIA

Research in Western countries on media source credibility is extensive and broad. The believability of the news is crucial for news organizations to fulfill their democratic function (Gans, 2003). From a news consumer's perspective, the extent to which a news source is considered believable affects the quality of news they consume. Scholars have examined at length popular satisfaction or dissatisfaction with the accuracy of news reports produced by professional news organizations (Gaziano & McGrath, 1986; Tsfati & Cappella, 2003). The bottom line is that consumers will only seek and rely on news sources that they can trust (Tsfati, 2010).

According to Gunther (1992), the formation of credibility perceptions is attributed to users' experience of using the given media for consuming news, which includes the amount of media use, dependency on the media to stay informed about current events, and evaluations of usefulness to users and appeal of news content (e.g., design, layout, and complexity). The generalizations are as follows: the more people use a given media (Flanagin & Metzger, 2000; Johnson & Kaye, 1998), the greater reliance they have on a chosen medium as their source of news (Golan & Day, 2010; Johnson & Kaye, 2004); the more perceived usefulness and value of news (Chen, Chen, Chang, & Abedin, 2017), and the more interactive and appealing the news is (Flanagin & Metzger, 2007; K. Thorson, Vraga, & Ekdale, 2010), the higher perceptions of its credibility.

In addition, literature (R. Wei, Lo, Xu, Chen, & Zhang, 2014; R. Wei, Lo, Chen, Tandoc, & Zhang, 2020; H. Zhang, Zhou, & Shen, 2014) suggests that perceptions of media credibility vary a great deal by country. In countries where press freedom is absent and the media are closely affiliated with the government or under its influence, credibility tends to be high. On the other hand, media are considered less credible by audiences in societies where press freedom is protected and independent media outlets across the ideological spectrum coexist.

Credibility of the media has been an increasingly important topic in Asian communication research as well. The existent literature built on a large number of polls and survey data suggests that the differences in press systems, diversity of media markets, and emerging digital media platforms all play a role in shaping audience perceptions of media credibility in Asia in general, and in the four selected Asian cities in particular.

Media Credibility in Shanghai, China

News consumers in China have been found to place a high level of trust in Chinese news media.[1] In fact, compared to the Western countries such as the United States (T. Liu & Bates, 2009), the overall media credibility ratings in China were high. A survey of 5,807 residents in 10 Chinese cities across the country, including Shanghai, reported that official news organizations like the ruling party's publication—*The People's Daily*—were perceived to be highly credible (H. Zhang et al., 2014). The same study also found that television—China Central Television—which is owned and run by the central government, was perceived to be the most credible news source, followed by newspapers, websites, radio, magazines, and mobile outlets. As X. Li and Zhang (2018) explained, traditional media in China represents the official voice. It is the face of the central government. In the context of China's long history of an authoritarian culture, that "who says" may carry more weight than "says what" in the process of media credibility evaluation (p. 84).

It is interesting to note that although social media platforms available on mobile phones are used widely and have become essential to fulfill Chinese informational and social needs, social media were rated less credible in comparison to traditional news media (X. Li & Zhang, 2018). Similar results were reported about mobile media as an emerging outlet for consuming news. According to H. Zhang's (2013) 10-city survey results completed in 2012, credibility of mobile media was rated below that of traditional media. In fact, among the six media outlets, the mobile channel was considered the least credible, whereas television was viewed as the most credible. Credibility ratings of newspapers, magazines, radio, and news websites fell in between. He speculated that the low rating of mobile media might stem from the low rate of adoption of the mobile phone as a news source back in the early 2010s (only 10% to 15% of the respondents had adopted the mobile phone).

However, new media became increasingly influential as they continued to penetrate China's urban population (smartphone rate reached 68% in 2016; see Pew, 2017). A recent follow-up study by H. Zhang (2018) found that perceived credibility ratings of new media channels, namely websites and mobile devices, increased noticeably from 2012 to 2018. He concluded that users who depended on the nontraditional sources for news content started to view them as credible (in 2016, 45.6% of the Chinese population read or viewed news through their smartphone).

Perceived credibility of newspapers and government-run broadcast services in China's largest city, Shanghai, parallels the trust ratings of Chinese media at the national level. According to a 2014 survey (Wang, Pan, & Qiang, 2014), *Jiefang Daily*, the paper run by the ruling party's Shanghai municipal branch, was rated as the most credible media outlet among over 100 newspapers and 627 periodicals (Shanghai Gov., 2016). The municipal television service—Shanghai Television Station—received high credibility ratings as well. The report also found that although most Shanghai residents rely on news websites and mobile sites for acquiring news, the credibility of digital media outlets was rated lower than legacy official media.

Media Credibility in Hong Kong

With a total of 78 daily newspapers and 573 periodicals (GovHK, 2018), the media landscape in Hong Kong is diverse and market driven. The tabloid press, with its sensationalist approach to journalism, competes for market share. Pro-mainland and anti-China papers coexist. Hong Kong's traditional media had long enjoyed solid credibility ratings. In 1997 (the last year under British rule), they scored an average of 6.73 (on a 10-point scale ranging from 1 to 10) for both electronic and print media (CUHK, 2016). On the same scale, that figure had hardly changed. As of 2009, it stood at 6.59 according to So (2016). *South China Morning Post*, the English daily in the territory, was viewed as the most trusted paid newspaper (CUHK, 2016). The same survey found that RTHK—the Hong Kong government-run radio and television service modeled after the BBC—was the most trusted among the six broadcasters, with a score of 6.76. In comparison, online news media scored an average of only 4.81, the lowest ratings among all media outlets polled.

The relatively high rating of public trust in the Hong Kong news media has suffered a noticeable decline in the last decade. For instance, a survey of 1,023 residents in 2017 indicated that media credibility for all news media had fallen to a 10-year low from 6.19 to 5.73 on the same 10-point scale (HKU, 2018).

Another survey of 907 people in 2016 (So, 2016) reported similar declines. The overall rating for all newspapers in 2016 dropped to 5.58, a decrease from 6.40 in the previous survey conducted in 2009. Over the same period, the overall rating for electronic media in 2016 was 6.36, down from 6.86. Nevertheless, the credibility of social media consistently received the lowest rating of 4.59 (CUHK, 2016).

Media Credibility in Singapore

Singapore's news media are often the target of Western criticism; the city's ranking in press freedom indices declines from year to year. Nevertheless, surveys conducted among Singaporeans have shown a consistently high level of trust in the news media. While Singaporeans recognize the strong influence of the government on the media organizations, especially when it comes to reporting about politics (Hao, 1996), they still regard their nation's news organizations as trustworthy (M. Lee, 2017; Tandoc, 2018).

A recent survey (Tandoc, 2018) found that 47% of respondents in Singapore trust the news media overall. They ranked news outlets, such as the cable news network Channel News Asia and the leading English newspaper *Straits Times,* as the most trusted media outlets. The same survey also found that only 20% said they trust the news from social media, even though social media (63%) have outranked print (43%) and television (55%) as the main sources of news for Singaporeans. This seeming contradiction—relying on digital and mobile news outlets to acquire news but having less trust in them as reliable news sources—is something the four Asian cities have in common.

Media Credibility in Taipei, Taiwan

In Taiwan, the news media enjoy a great deal of freedom—some critics may say too much freedom.[2] Unfortunately, the confidence of Taiwan residents in them as trustworthy sources of news is declining due to the rise of a partisan press that has polarized the public.

According to the Taiwan Social Change Surveys (Lo, 2013), the credibility of newspapers and television declined significantly from 1998 to 2003. In 1998, the credibility rating of newspapers was 6.90 out of a 10-point scale. It fell further to 6.36 in 2003. The credibility rating of television news in 2003 was 7.09, a drop from 7.64 in the 1998 survey.

Other studies consistently have found that people in Taiwan have a low level of trust in news media across the board, even though press freedom has increased year by year. Hsu (2015) compared Taiwan's news media credibility ratings between 2008 and 2012. Results showed that television's and newspaper's credibility had deteriorated from 2008 to 2012. In 2008, television was rated 2.63 and newspapers 2.50 on a 5-point scale. In 2012, the ratings dropped to 2.52 for television and 2.42 for newspapers.

Despite the fact that the Internet has gained popularity as a news source, its rating of 2.46 was lower than that for television but higher than newspapers in the 2012 survey (Hsu, 2015). Consistent with ratings in Hong Kong and Shanghai, the Taiwan public's trust in social media as news sources was the lowest (Newman, Fletcher, Kalogeropoulos, & Nielsen, 2019).

Goals of the Chapter

In summary, perceptions of media credibility vary a great deal across the four Asian cities. In cities where the level of press freedom is low and the media enjoy close ties with the government or are under its heavy influence, media credibility tends to be high in general. On the other hand, in cities where the level of press freedom is high and a range of pluralist media outlets across the ideological spectrum coexists, the media are considered less credible by audiences. Then, we are curious if perceptions of mobile news credibility follow this pattern in the four studied cities and why. Specifically, this chapter aims first to explore how Asian college students perceive the credibility of news accessed from the mobile phone and then to examine contributing factors, including demographics, news reliance, forms of mobile news (appeal and presentation), and societal influences, to perceptions of mobile news credibility.

FINDINGS

In general, respondents viewed mobile news as moderately credible on the 5-item scale we used (i.e., being reliable, complete, balanced, accurate, and fair). As responses to the five items measuring the concept summarized in Table 6.1 indicate, on a 1- to 5-point Likert scale, the credibility rating scores ranged from a mean of 2.97 for reliability to 2.72 for being balanced. The 2,988 respondents agreed more on the two items of "mobile news is reliable" (23.3%) and "mobile news is accurate" (17.6%) than any other items. They disagreed the most with the item "mobile news is balanced" (38.0%). About a third of the respondents (32.9%) also disagreed with the statements that "mobile news is complete" (30.5%) and "mobile

Table 6.1 PERCEIVED CREDIBILITY OF MOBILE NEWS (2017–2018 SURVEYS)

	Agree	Neutral	Disagree	Mean (*SD*)
Mobile news is reliable	23.3%	51.9%	24.8%	2.97 (.84)
Mobile news is complete	19.9%	47.3%	32.9%	2.84 (.88)
Mobile news is balanced	15.5%	46.4%	38.0%	2.72 (.89)
Mobile news is accurate	17.6%	51.9%	30.5%	2.84 (.86)
Mobile news is fair	15.2%	51.9%	32.9%	2.79 (.85)
Combined index: Perceived credibility of mobile news				2.83 (.74)

Notes: The scale ranged from 1 (strongly disagree) to 5 (strongly agree). $N = 2,988$.

news is fair" (32.9%). In short, the respondents appeared to view that news delivered to the mobile screen has integrity (i.e., is reliable and accurate) but lacks alternative perspectives or is less than complete (i.e., is balanced, fair, and complete).

These survey results manifest themselves in attitudes found in focus groups with Asian college students who access news via their phones. On willingness to believe news sources accessed via the mobile phone, a male student in Singapore said, "I think the source is most important to me." He continued, "It has to be credible like the *Straits Times* or *The Guardian*."

A second-year female student in Hong Kong explained her choice of media outlets by saying, "I prefer reading news on a news app, as they are usually original and official content provided by the news organizations, so they are usually of higher credibility." Her male schoolmate in the same year of study in Hong Kong said he prefers to view cable news in Hong Kong "because cable news is famous for its high credibility and neutrality."

Perceived Credibility and Usage

Considering that consumption of mobile news has continued to rise in the four studied cities, we next examined whether heavy users of mobile news differed from light users in terms of their perception of mobile news credibility. Technically, we split the pooled sample by the median of the amount of mobile news consumed. According to results presented in Table 6.2, in general, heavy users tended to have a more positive view of the credibility of mobile news ($M = 3.01$, $SD = .74$) than light users ($M = 2.66$, $SD = .70$). The difference was statistically significant ($t = 12.87$, $p < .001$).

Table 6.2 DIFFERENCES IN PERCEIVED MOBILE NEWS CREDIBILITY
BETWEEN HEAVY AND LIGHT USERS (2017–2018 SURVEYS)

	Heavy Users			Light Users			
	Agree	Disagree	Mean	Agree	Disagree	Mean	t Value
Mobile news is reliable	28.9%	18.4%	3.13	18.2%	30.8%	2.82	9.99***
Mobile news is complete	26.0%	23.6%	3.04	14.0%	41.5%	2.65	12.09***
Mobile news is balanced	21.3%	23.6%	2.91	9.9%	45.8%	2.54	11.59***
Mobile news is accurate	22.6%	23.8%	3.00	13.0%	36.6%	2.69	10.03***
Mobile news is fair	21.3%	25.6%	2.96	9.2%	39.8%	2.62	11.13***
Combined index: Perceived credibility of mobile news			3.01 (.74)			2.66 (.70)	12.87***

Notes: The scale ranged from 1 (strongly disagree) to 5 (strongly agree). $N = 2,988$.
***$p < .001$.

Compared to light users, heavy users tended to perceive mobile news to be significantly more reliable ($t = 9.99$, $p < .001$), complete ($t = 12.09$, $p < .001$), balanced ($t = 11.59$, $p < .001$), accurate ($t = 10.03$, $p < .001$), and fair ($t = 11.13$, $p < .001$), which resulted in significant differences in the overall index of credibility ($t = 12.87$, $p < .001$). Consistent with the literature (Tsfati, 2010), these results suggest that respondents who consume more news on the mobile phone put more trust in the news. Conversely, those who consumed less tended to view it as less credible, which may be why they rarely used the mobile phone to consume news in the first place.

Gender Differences in Credibility

We further examined whether mobile news credibility was related to gender, which was split in the 2017–2018 data. Results in Table 6.3 showed that Asian male college students ($M = 2.91$, $SD = .78$) were more likely to give a higher credibility rating to mobile news than were their female counterparts ($M = 2.78$, $SD = .71$).

Table 6.3 GENDER DIFFERENCES IN PERCEIVED CREDIBILITY OF MOBILE NEWS (2017–2018 SURVEYS)

	Male			Female			
	Agree	Disagree	Mean	Agree	Disagree	Mean	t Value
Mobile news is reliable	26.4%	23.9%	3.01	21.2%	25.4%	2.94	2.33*
Mobile news is complete	24.6%	29.0%	2.93	16.5%	35.5%	2.78	4.68***
Mobile news is balanced	19.2%	34.8%	2.79	13.0%	40.3%	2.67	3.50***
Mobile news is accurate	22.6%	27.6%	2.92	14.5%	32.2%	2.78	4.28***
Mobile news is fair	20.1%	30.2%	2.88	11.7%	34.7%	2.73	4.68***
Combined index: Perceived credibility of mobile news			2.91 (.78)			2.78 (.71)	4.48***

Notes: The scale ranged from 1 (strongly disagree) to 5 (strongly agree). N = 2,988.
***p < .001, *p < .05.

Significant gender differences were found across the five items. The difference was also significant when using the combined credibility index. To be specific, compared to female respondents, male respondents tended to perceive mobile news to be more reliable ($t = 2.33$, $p < .05$), complete ($t = 4.68$, $p < .001$), balanced ($t = 3.50$, $p < .001$), accurate ($t = 4.28$, $p < .001$), and fair ($t = 4.68$, $p < .001$). As such, they also differed in the overall credibility index ($t = 4.48$, $p < .001$). The ratings of all five items by female respondents were lower across the board. As we found in the previous section, male respondents consumed more news accessed from the mobile phone than their female peers, and they also tended to put more trust in mobile news. The finding may explain the gender-based differences.

Credibility and Reliance on Traditional Media for News

Another question worth exploring is whether respondents who relied on traditional media for news a great deal would differ from those whose media reliance was less in perceiving the credibility of mobile news. For this purpose, we categorized the 2,988 respondents into high and low reliance

Table 6.4 DIFFERENCES IN PERCEIVED MOBILE NEWS CREDIBILITY BETWEEN HIGH-RELIANCE AND LOW-RELIANCE USERS (2017–2018 SURVEYS)

	High-Reliance Users			Low-Reliance Users			
	Agree	Disagree	Mean	Agree	Disagree	Mean	*t* Value
Mobile news is reliable	25.7%	22.8%	3.03	20.6%	26.4%	2.91	3.96***
Mobile news is complete	23.1%	29.0%	2.93	16.3%	36.8%	2.74	5.83***
Mobile news is balanced	19.9%	32.6%	2.84	10.7%	43.9%	2.58	8.13***
Mobile news is accurate	20.8%	27.2%	2.92	14.7%	33.7%	2.75	5.41***
Mobile news is fair	20.0%	28.5%	2.91	9.9%	37.4%	2.66	7.93***
Combined index: Perceived credibility of mobile news			2.93 (.72)			2.73 (.74)	7.33***

Notes: The scale ranged from 1 (strongly disagree) to 5 (strongly agree). *N* = 2,988.
***$p < .001$.

on the traditional media by splitting the reliance on traditional media scale at the median. High-reliance users covered respondents whose news consumption depended on traditional media such as newspapers and television. Low-reliance users were respondents who were less dependent on traditional media for getting news. As Table 6.4 shows, respondents in the high-reliance group tended to give mobile news a higher credibility rating (M = 2.93, SD = .72) than did those in the low-reliance group (M = 2.73, SD = .74).

Results of a set of independent t-tests indicated that high-reliance respondents were more likely to rate mobile news to be significantly higher in all of the five credibility items, namely, reliability (t = 3.96, $p < .001$), completeness (t = 5.83, $p < .001$), balance (t = 8.13, $p < .001$), accuracy (t = 5.41, $p < .001$), and fairness (t = 7.93, $p < .001$), as well as the combined credibility (t = 7.33, $p < .001$), than were low-reliance respondents. These results mean that surveyed Asian college students who depended on legacy media to acquire news had the tendency to view mobile news as credible. On the other hand, surveyed college students who were less dependent on legacy media to get news tended to view mobile news as less credible. Therefore, the link between media reliance and consumption of mobile news is empirically supported.

The views expressed by focus group participants in the four cities are revealing, adding contexts to these quantitative findings. When asked about checking news to see if it is credible or not, a male student in Singapore who earlier spoke about his trust in traditional news source said he normally read it and did not check "unless I am interested to find out if the news is authentic." Though he cited news regarding domestic and world politics as topics he would verify, he would not bother fact-checking sports or celebrity news. His peer in the same university in Singapore concurred. She said, "If there is a name to the paper, it is a reliable one. For instance, the blue title of the *Straits Times* gives you a sense of assurance of a reliable source." A third-year female student in Taipei said, "I only read news from sources that are reputable, like BBC mobile site, ET Today, etc."

A 19-year-old second-year student in Hong Kong said, "Prior to college, I relied [on] Yahoo News as my news source. Now in college, I use mobile news apps downloaded on my phone as my sources, including *South China Morning Post*, *The Guardian*, RTHK News, and *The Economist*. From time to time, I followed some news accounts on Instagram." Her male schoolmate said, "Whether mobile news is credible depends on which news outlet is the source." He mentioned the tabloid *Apple Daily* as his news sources on his phone. He explained, "The paper is known for its sensational coverage, but its critical reporting of China and local authorities makes me believe it is a credible news organization."

Credibility and Utility of Mobile News

Among other things, mobile news is quick, easy, and conveniently accessible in one's hand or pocket (Westlund, 2015). Also, news delivered to the screens of mobile devices offers a niche opportunity (Dimmick, Feaster, & Hoplamazian, 2011) as well as "a buffer space" (Wei et al., 2014, p. 650) to stay informed on the move according to users' own schedules; it is plausible that the perceived usefulness of mobile news for filling the gap or downtime in between fixed locations to consume news will influence audiences' perceptions of mobile news credibility.

In our study, we used six items (i.e., mobile news as being updated, helpful, informative, connected, useful, and a time filler) to measure whether and how news as a utility of the mobile phone was related to perceived credibility of mobile news. Analytically, to distinguish respondents between high-utility users and low-utility users, we split the perceived utility scale at

Table 6.5 DIFFERENCES IN PERCEIVED MOBILE NEWS CREDIBILITY
BETWEEN HIGH-UTILITY AND LOW-UTILITY USERS (2017–2018 SURVEYS)

	High-Utility Users			Low-Utility Users			
	Agree	Disagree	Mean	Agree	Disagree	Mean	t Value
Mobile news is reliable	36.6%	13.6%	3.13	12.7%	33.5%	2.82	18.04***
Mobile news is complete	30.6%	21.4%	3.04	11.2%	41.9%	2.65	16.05***
Mobile news is balanced	22.3%	29.5%	2.91	10.1%	44.7%	2.54	11.15***
Mobile news is accurate	26.1%	19.6%	3.00	11.0%	39.0%	2.69	14.02***
Mobile news is fair	22.5%	22.8%	2.96	9.5%	40.8%	2.62	12.65***
Combined index: Perceived credibility of mobile news			3.08 (.75)			2.63 (.68)	16.96***

Notes: The scale ranged from 1 (strongly disagree) to 5 (strongly agree). N = 2,988.
***p < .001.

the median. High-utility users represented the respondents who perceived mobile news to be useful and helpful. Low-utility users were respondents who perceived mobile news to be less informative and helpful.

Table 6.5 shows that high-utility users tended to have a more positive view of mobile news as credible (M = 3.08, SD = .75) than low-utility users (M = 2.63, SD = .68). The difference between the two groups in terms of mean was significant (t = 16.96, p < .001). In fact, respondents who considered mobile news as useful rated the news more positively across all of the five credibility items (refer to Table 6.5). They rated mobile news as being more reliable, complete, balanced, accurate, and fair than did low-utility users. Such results make sense: the more Asian college students believed mobile news as high in utility in terms of being updated, informative, and useful, the more they have trust in it.

To a pair of third-year students in Taipei, quality of news accessed from their phone means clean and neat. One said, "If news on my phone is loaded with pop-ups or embedded with ads that interrupt a read, it annoys me. It's the sort of news that's not trustworthy to me." Another student was also critical of mobile news. She said, "It's like feeding on fast food. It's so fast that the nutrition is lost. *Line Today* is an example of it."

A 20-year-old female student in Hong Kong views mobile news as expanding her horizons. She said, "I like consuming news from various media outlets. Compared to traditional ways of news consumption like watching TV and listening to radio, using smartphone allows me to consume news from different media at the same time."

Credibility and Appeal of Mobile News

Another interesting question to explore was whether the perceived appeal of news presented on mobile screens affects the perceived credibility of mobile news. As detailed in Appendix B, the perceived appeal of news presented on various mobile phones was measured by five semantic differential items bounded by these bipolar adjectives: poor in quality/high in quality, unappealing/appealing, not informative/informative, boring/interesting, and tiring to read/refreshing. In general, as results presented in Table 6.6 show, Asian college students gave moderately positive ratings to the appeal of mobile news.

Participants in our focus groups seem to be sophisticated consumers of digital news. They are aware of tricks and gimmicks embedded in mobile news, which affected their evaluations of mobile news credibility. In the words of a third-year student in Taipei: "I like reading news on my phone because it's neat, simple, and ad-free; I don't like it when the news is too brief, hard to read due to small font size, and difficult to tell if it's authentic or not." Another third-year female student in Taipei described her experience as follows: "In following some newsmakers via my phone, I get to know their own versions of the story directly. Then, I can evaluate which story is credible, which is not."

Table 6.6 RATINGS OF THE FORMAT AND APPEAL OF MOBILE NEWS (2017–2018 SURVEYS)

Format and Appeal	Mean (*SD*)
Quality	3.62 (.93)
Appealing	3.68 (.92)
Informative	3.74 (.94)
Interesting	3.64 (.91)
Refreshing	3.61 (.96)
Combined index: Appeal of mobile news	3.66 (.74)

Notes: The scale ranged from 1 (strongly disagree) to 5 (strongly agree). *N* = 2,949.

The second-year male student in Hong Kong holds a similar view. He said, "In the digital era, immediate access to news has become the most decisive factor of value of news. Sometimes, they may neglect the accuracy of news, just because they want to attract more audience. Doing this may reduce news credibility." To his fellow student in Hong Kong, a 20-year-old female student, "The credibility of mobile news is relatively low," she noted. She blamed it on "gimmicky headlines or clickbait [that] are always used to attract readers in addition to biased posts from social media."

We then distinguished high-appeal raters from low-appeal raters by splitting the appeal of the mobile news presentation scale at the median. High-appeal raters refer to respondents who rated mobile news as having a high-quality, appealing presentation and being informative, interesting, and refreshing. Low-appeal raters were those who evaluated mobile news as having a poor-quality, unappealing presentation and being not informative, boring, and tiring to read. As shown in Table 6.7, the high-appeal group tended to give mobile news a higher rating in credibility ($M = 2.95$, $SD = .75$) than did the low-appeal users ($M = 2.67$, $SD = .70$).

Results of a series of independent t-tests indicated that the difference between the two groups was significant ($t = 10.35$, $p < .001$). High-appeal

Table 6.7 DIFFERENCES IN PERCEIVED MOBILE NEWS CREDIBILITY BETWEEN HIGH-APPEAL AND LOW-APPEAL USERS (2017–2018 SURVEYS)

	High-Appeal Users			Low-Appeal Users			
	Agree	Disagree	Mean	Agree	Disagree	Mean	t Value
Mobile news is reliable	29.4%	20.5%	3.10	15.1%	30.1%	2.79	10.00***
Mobile news is complete	25.4%	28.2%	2.97	12.4%	39.1%	2.66	9.82***
Mobile news is balanced	19.9%	34.5%	2.83	9.5%	42.8%	2.57	7.85***
Mobile news is accurate	22.7%	26.7%	2.96	10.9%	35.3%	2.68	8.85***
Mobile news is fair	19.7%	28.7%	2.90	9.4%	38.3%	2.64	8.05***
Combined index: Perceived credibility of mobile news			2.95 (.75)			2.67 (.70)	10.35***

Notes: The scale ranged from 1 (strongly disagree) to 5 (strongly agree). N = 2,988.
***p < .001.

raters were more likely to believe mobile news to be more reliable, complete, balanced, accurate, fair, and credible than were low-appeal users. These results suggest that the forms and format of mobile news presentation mattered in affecting perceptions of its credibility. The more such news was created with visual appeal and professional layout, the more Asian college students viewed it as being credible.

Remarks made by focus group participants in Taipei, Hong Kong, and Singapore add more perspectives to the aforementioned findings in their reflections about forms of mobile news. A female student in Taipei explained how she evaluates a new story on her phone: "I take a quick read of the headlines. If the headline is sensational, misleading, and reads like a clickbait, I will not bother click[ing] the link to read the rest." She continued, "I rely on sources that I know that are credible for news." A female student in Singapore mentioned that something like a questionable banner at the bottom of the mobile news site would make her suspicious.

The female student in Hong Kong said she simply avoided some news originating from social media. She noted, "Sure, smartphones provide an affordable and convenient option in accessing news. However, I see the need for reading news from various other media, like news on TV and cable, to really get an overall picture of the situation."

Cross-City Differences in Credibility

Finally, we used a series of one-way ANOVA tests to examine whether Asian college students in the four studied cities differed in their perceptions of mobile news credibility. Results of the cross-city comparison are summarized in Table 6.8.

As Table 6.8 presents, respondents from the four cities differed in their levels of perceived credibility of mobile news [F (3, 2968) = 49.89, $p < .001$]. Furthermore, results of a post hoc Scheffe test revealed that Shanghai respondents rated mobile news credibility the highest ($M = 2.99$), followed by Singapore respondents ($M = 2.94$) and Hong Kong respondents (M = 2.83). Taipei respondents gave the lowest rating to mobile news credibility ($M = 2.58$). The Scheffe tests show that all the differences in the mobile news credibility rating among the Shanghai, Singapore, Hong Kong, and Taipei respondents were significant at the $p < .001$ level. Thus, respondents in China and Singapore were more likely to view mobile news as more credible than their counterparts in Hong Kong and Taipei.

These results indicate that respondents in Shanghai and Singapore particularly viewed mobile news as being high in reliability and accuracy, but

Table 6.8 MEAN ESTIMATES OF PERCEIVED CREDIBILITY OF MOBILE NEWS IN SHANGHAI, SINGAPORE, HONG KONG, AND TAIPEI

Sample	Total (N = 2,988)	Shanghai (N = 875)	Singapore (N = 671)	Hong Kong (N = 771)	Taipei (N = 825)	F Value
Mobile news is reliable	2.97 (.84)	3.12 (.80)	3.17 (.84)	2.90 (.90)	2.73 (.77)	46.55***
Mobile news is complete	2.84 (.88)	3.06 (.86)	2.83 (.83)	2.89 (.95)	2.60 (.82)	37.56***
Mobile news is balanced	2.72 (.89)	2.88 (.87)	2.86 (.87)	2.69 (.95)	2.47 (.80)	37.01***
Mobile news is accurate	2.84 (.86)	2.96 (.85)	2.99 (.81)	2.87 (.93)	2.57 (.77)	39.87***
Mobile news is fair	2.79 (.85)	2.94 (.83)	2.89 (.84)	2.81 (.93)	2.54 (.75)	35.45***
Combined index: Perceived credibility of mobile news	2.83 (.74)	2.99 (.74)	2.94 (.70)	2.83 (.79)	2.58 (.67)	49.89***

Notes: The scale ranged from 1 (strongly disagree) to 5 (strongly agree).
Figures in the parentheses are standard deviations.
***$p < .001$.

also viewed the news as lacking different perspectives or being less than complete. Such perceptions fit the reality concerning news media in these two cities—officials dominated the media or official media is the only voice at the expense of nonofficial voices (to illustrate, during the SARS crisis in 2003, and during a similar breakout of COVID-19 in 2019, an official statement was authoritative but delayed; dissident voices were silenced in China); hence, they seem to have a heightened sense of ambivalence toward mobile news.

However, results of the post hoc Scheffe tests revealed no significant difference in the perceived credibility of mobile news between Shanghai and Singapore respondents. Thus, results of the Scheffe tests suggested that surveyed college students in Shanghai and Singapore tended to perceive mobile news as more credible than did their counterparts in Hong Kong and Taipei. Among the four studied cities, college students in Taipei assigned the lowest mean score to the credibility of news consumed on the mobile screen. This finding actually parallels the general low credibility ratings of news media in Taiwan.

Students who participated in our focus groups in the four studied cities explained how they evaluated whether news on their phones is credible and trustworthy. Their accounts help illustrate the cross-city differences. A female student in Singapore cited Singapore's leading English newspaper—the *Straits Times*—as her "most important source of digital news" on her phone. Her peer added, "If it is a national paper, it is a reliable one. The bigger titles are usually more credible."

A female student in Shanghai said she paid attention mostly to established organizations such as the mobile sites of China Central Television (CCTV), *The Paper*, the *People's Daily*, and *China Daily* due to their reputation of being highly credible. She explained, "CCTV represents the official voice, while *The Paper* has a reputation in producing credible and timely in-depth reports." Her schoolmate in Shanghai followed up on her remarks, noting, "I do not enjoy reading news from social media apps like Weibo and WeChat; it is because there seems to be a lot of fake stuff going on in these self-publishing news sites." She continued, "If any news stories posted on these social media platforms step on landmines of ideological control, their accounts will be shut down."

A 23-year-old female student in Taipei said, "I read posts by some KOL [key opinion leaders] on social media sites from time to time, but I don't take what they say on face value at all." Her male schoolmate added, "If I smell something out of a content farm,[3] I will avoid it altogether." He said, "Such stories are politically motivated and ideologically biased. They are [a] no-no to me."

A first-year male student aged 18 in Hong Kong said, "I used mobile apps to access news from established sources like i-Cable news. The apps on my phone are broad and diverse, reflecting different points of view, but I pay no attention to news on social media platforms." A second-year female student in Hong Kong said this about news posted by nonprofessional sources: "I read it sometimes, but I doubted its credibility. I read it only because I am interested in observing some of the biased news media."

Predictors of Credibility

Concerning the strength of the relationships among levels of consumption of mobile news, reliance on traditional media for news seeking, perceived utility and appeal of mobile news, freedom of the press, and credibility of mobile news, we employed two analytical procedures: (1) zero-order correlation concerning the bivariate relationships and (2) multivariate analyses to isolate the effects of a particular independent variable while controlling

Table 6.9 CORRELATION BETWEEN MOBILE NEWS CONSUMPTION, TRADITIONAL MEDIA RELIANCE, PERCEIVED UTILITY, PERCEIVED APPEAL, AND PRESS FREEDOM

Variables	1	2	3	4	5
1. Perceived credibility of mobile news	-----				
2. Mobile news consumption	.30***	-----			
3. Traditional media reliance	.22***	.35***	-----		
4. Perceived utility	.38***	.31***	.06**	-----	
5. Perceived appeal	.25***	.19***	.04*	.35***	-----
6. Freedom of the press	−.21***	−.01	.18***	−.08***	−.14***

Note: N = 2,988.
***p < .001, **p < .01, *p < .05.

for the influences of others. Therefore, with all variables (e.g., mobile news consumption, reliance on traditional media for news seeking, utility of mobile news, appeals of mobile news, and press freedom) being considered simultaneously, multiple regression analyses enabled us to explore which predictor variable would emerge as the strongest predictor in accounting for variance in perceptions of mobile news credibility in the pooled sample.

First, Table 6.9 presents the results of Pearson's correlation tests. As we predicted, level of consuming mobile news was significantly and positively related to perceived credibility of mobile news ($r = .30, p < .001$). Also, the relationship between reliance on traditional media for news and perceived credibility of mobile news was both positive and significant ($r = .22, p < .001$ for reliance on traditional media to stay informed). Additionally, the association between perceived utility of mobile news and perceived credibility of such news was positive ($r = .38, p < .001$). So was the relationship between appeal of mobile news presentation and perceived credibility of mobile news ($r = .25, p < .001$).

Based on these results, it seems that the more the surveyed Asian college students depended on traditional media to be informed of what is important nationally and internationally, the more they consumed news on the mobile phone, and the more they believed mobile-accessed news was credible. At the same time, the more they thought mobile news was useful and appealing in presentation and format, the higher the credibility they assigned to news consumed on the mobile phone.

On the other hand, the association between freedom of the press and perceived credibility of mobile news was significant but negative ($r = −.21, p < .001$), which means that the less freedom the press enjoys in a society, the higher the perceived credibility of news distributed to mobile phones.

Table 6.10 HIERARCHICAL REGRESSION ANALYSIS PREDICTING PERCEIVED CREDIBILITY OF MOBILE NEWS

Independent Variables	Model 1	Model 2	Model 3	Model 4	Model 5
Block 1: Demographics					
Gender	.07***	.05**	.05**	.07***	.07***
Age	.08***	.06***	.08***	.05**	-.01
Block 2: Mobile News Use					
Mobile news consumption		.29***	.24***	.12***	.11***
Block 3: Media Reliance					
Reliance on traditional media for news			.15***	.16***	.19***
Block 4: Perceived Utility/Appeals of Mobile News					
Perceived utility				.29***	.29***
Perceived appeal				.11***	.09***
Block 5: Freedom of the Press					
Press freedom ratings					-.20***
Incremental adjusted R²	1.1%	8.3%	1.9%	10.5%	3.2%
Total adjusted R²	1.1%	9.4%	11.3%	21.8%	25.0%

Note: N = 2,988.
***$p < .001$; **$p < .01$.

This pattern is surprisingly consistent with prior research (X. Li & Zhang, 2018; Tandoc, 2019; H. Zhang et al., 2014) about public trust in traditional versus digital media outlets in Shanghai and Singapore.

Next, we performed a hierarchical multiple regression analysis to identify the strongest predictor of perceived creditability of mobile news. In the regression equation, gender and age were entered first as control variables, followed by level of consuming news on the mobile phone. The third block included reliance on traditional media as news outlets. Perceived utility and appeal of mobile news were entered as the fourth block. The final block entered freedom of the press.[4] Accordingly, five models were generated to predict perceived credibility of mobile news using the pooled data.

Based on regression results summarized in Table 6.10, the fifth model shows that gender was a significant predictor of mobile news credibility ($\beta = .07, p < .001$). Asian male college students were more likely than females to give a higher credibility rating to mobile news. The level of mobile news consumption was also significantly related to credibility of mobile news ($\beta = .11, p < .001$). As anticipated, the more the respondents consumed mobile news, the higher their perceptions of mobile news credibility. In addition, reliance on traditional media as news sources was significantly related to credibility of mobile news ($\beta = .19, p < .001$). The more that respondents relied on traditional media for news, the more they believed mobile news was credible.

The regression analysis further examined whether perceived utility of mobile news and the appeal of news presented on mobile media were significant and positive predictors of credibility of mobile news. Results show that perceived utility (β = .29, p < .001) and the appeal of news presented on mobile media (β = .09, p < .001) were both significant predictors of mobile news credibility. The greater the perceived utility and the greater the appeal of mobile news presentation, the higher the perceived credibility of the news.

Finally, the regression analysis examined the relationship between freedom of the press and credibility of mobile news. As Table 6.10 further shows, freedom of the press was a significant predictor. It was the second strongest predictor after perceived utility, but a negative predictor of credibility of mobile news (β = −.20, p < .001). This result suggests that the lower the freedom of press that a society enjoys, the higher the credibility of news distributed to the mobile screen.

All things considered, Asian college students in our focus groups are satisfied with news accessed through their phones. But they do not simply read what they get. Reflections from the tech-savvy students in Hong Kong dive deeper. A 19-year-old female student in Hong Kong put her overall evaluations of news she consumes on her phone this way: "Overall speaking, I am satisfied with the experience, as smartphones provided an affordable and convenient option in the access of news. However, I see the need for reading news from various outlets, like news broadcast on televisions, to really get an overall picture of the situation." Her male schoolmate in the same year of study agreed. He said, "Yes, based on the convenience and immediateness of news, I am satisfied with my experience of using smartphone to consume news." On the other hand, he continued, "I will not accept information easily without getting any credible sources. I believe that I am able to consume news more critically."

SUMMARY OF KEY FINDINGS

Substance, Form, and Credibility Perceptions

News created and delivered to the mobile phone represents a new domain of media credibility research, which is less understood than those for other digital media outlets and platforms. Findings of this large-scale study shed some light on users' evaluations of the mobile news in the four studied cities of Hong Kong, Shanghai, Singapore, and Taipei. The findings of this chapter indicate that both substance in terms of news content being credible and forms in terms of appeal and presentation of mobile news affect the perceptions of trust in news consumed on the mobile phone. Furthermore, the perceptions are found to be related to a number of predictors. Specifically:

- Respondents totaling 2,988 in the second wave of surveys were inclined to view mobile news as moderately credible; among them, male respondents were more likely to give a higher credibility rating to mobile news than were female respondents.
- Effects of mobile news consumption on perceived credibility of the news: respondents who were heavy users of mobile news tended to have a much more positive view of the credibility of the mobile news than did light users. Conversely, those who consumed less mobile news tended to view it as less credible, which may explain why they use the mobile phone less frequently to access and consume news. Familiarity with mobile news seems to have a positive effect on perceived credibility of such news.
- Respondents whose reliance on traditional media as news sources was high would give mobile news a higher credibility rating than would those in the low-reliance group. This pattern suggests that surveyed Asian college students who depended on legacy media to acquire news viewed mobile news as credible. On the other hand, surveyed Asian college students who were less dependent on legacy media for news viewed mobile news as less credible. These patterns indicate that the habit of relying on traditional news media as news sources generates trust in news consumed on the mobile screen.
- Perceived usefulness of mobile news is positively related to credibility perceptions of such news. Respondents who believed mobile news was highly useful were more likely to view the news as credible than were those who considered mobile news to be of low utility.
- Similarly, perceived appeal of mobile news affects credibility perceptions of mobile news as well. The more respondents thought that mobile news was appealing in presentation and format, the more they viewed the news as credible. Conversely, the more that respondents who did not see mobile news as appealing, the less they perceived it as credible.
- Respondents from the four cities differed in their credibility perceptions of mobile news. Respondents in Shanghai and Singapore tended to perceive mobile news as more credible than did their peers in Hong Kong

and Taipei. The respondents surveyed in Taipei gave the lowest rating to mobile news credibility.

Overall, the findings show that Asian college students in the four studied cities viewed news delivered to the mobile screen as having integrity (i.e., being reliable and accurate) but lacking diversity of perspectives (i.e., being balanced, complete, and fair). Respondents in Shanghai and Singapore in particular held such perceptions, reflecting their impressions of mobile news as being heavily influenced by official or pro-government news outlets. To them, news consumed via the mobile phone is reliable, but something is missing. Hence, the substance of mobile news seems to be a motivating factor for them, but the narrow scope of perspectives is an inhibiting factor (i.e., a disincentive for consuming mobile news). Their overall ambivalence toward credibility of mobile news seems to be an accurate characterization of the mixed views.

However, the more they perceived mobile news as useful and the more appeal such news has (i.e., presentation and layout), the more trust they put in the news. They have no ambivalence in viewing mobile news as usable, appealing, and beneficial. All things considered, mobile news appears to have the potential to meet the civic expectation of surveyed Asian college students.

In conclusion, as the mobile phone has become an indispensable gateway to access and consume news, the credibility of mobile news is a critical condition for the mobile phone to evolve into a viable and significant medium of choice for news. These findings shed light on the question of how Asian college students trust and rely on news accessed from the mobile phone— credibility of mobile news is tied to their usage and news reliance. That is, the more they consume mobile news, the more trust they have in the news. Likewise, the more trust they have in mobile news, the more they consume it. As such, reliance and trust reinforce each other positively; a virtuous cycle in mobile news consumption appears to be in the making.

THEORETICAL INSIGHTS FROM FINDINGS

More importantly, patterns discovered in Chapter 6 suggest that Asian college students evaluate the credibility of mobile news by virtue of its substance (i.e., reliability, completeness, accuracy, balance, and fairness) and consider it as acceptable. This is the good news.

The bad news is that the credibility of mobile news is viewed as inferior to traditional news media. Such a perception is similar to that of other forms of digital news such as news sites and blogs (X. Li & Zhang, 2018; H. Zhang, 2013). This sort of seemingly contradictory view of trust in mobile news the ambivalence held by Asian college students toward the mobile phone as an emerging news outlet. The short history of the mobile phone as a gateway to access and consume news may have something to do with this ambivalent view. It takes time to build trust. To become a trusted news outlet, the mobile phone may have a long way to go.

Among other factors, our finding that the more users use their phone to consume news, the more they view it as being credible, is consistent with the literature that credibility perception is positively associated with regular media use or reliance (Shen, Lu, Guo, & Zhou, 2011; Shen & Zhang, 2014; H. Zhang et al., 2014). Such a pattern persists in mobile news consumption. It is interesting to note that the effect of press freedom as a societal factor on perceptions of mobile news credibility is negative. When the influences of all other predictors are taken into consideration, the less freedom the press enjoys in the surveyed Asian cities, the higher the credibility of news distributed to mobile news.

To make sense of this key finding regarding the societal influences on credibility of mobile news, we put it into the socio-political contexts of the four studied Asian cities. In Shanghai, China, and Singapore, freedom of the press is absent or limited, and the primary role of the press is to support the government or the ruling party. As X. Li and Zhang (2018) have explained, traditional media function as an official government voice in China. "Who says" carries much more weight than "says what" in such an authority-directed context (p. 84). Under such a press system, the government voice overshadows nonofficial voices about important home events and world affairs, resulting in audiences assigning high levels of credibility to news media primarily because they are official sources. This tendency regarding traditional media in Shanghai and Singapore persists in credibility perceptions of mobile news. It is thus understandable that in these two cities, news accessed from mobile devices receives higher credibility.

In the other two cities, Taiwan and Hong Kong, the free press functions as a marketplace of ideas, and political parties and social groups compete to win public attention. During election times, the competition becomes acrimonious, distasteful, and polarizing. Under this system, competing views and interpretations of news events that reflect different political stances find their way into the news media. For example, in Taiwan's popular political TV talk shows, critics (Rawnsley & Rawnsley, 2012) pointed out that anything (e.g., rumors, gossip, half-truths, and downright fake news) goes: ideologically slanted comments are made by guests and biased hosts routinely use foul and inflammatory language. News consumers in Taiwan may believe the press has too much freedom and the freedoms may even be abused, resulting in lower ratings of credibility than in cities without a free press.

This particular finding is both disturbing and ironic: far from increasing credibility, freedom of the press may have diminished it in post–martial law Taiwan. It seems to us that alarm bells should be going off in these societies— if freedom of the press is held to be a bulwark of their democracies, growing distrust of the media may undermine the very concept.

CHAPTER 7
Who Learns from Mobile News?

LEARNING FROM MOBILE NEWS

In the smartphone era, as we have presented in Chapters 1 and 4, mobile phone users in Asia and the rest of the world rely on their phones to stay informed about current affairs, at home and abroad. News content is among the most popular mobile content consumed (Shim, You, Lee, & Go, 2015). Our framework of analysis outlined in Chapter 2 illuminates the link between consuming news via the mobile phone and gaining political knowledge. To us, the stake of the linkage is high because consuming news and knowledgeability about public affairs shape citizenship in the 21st century (Delli Carpini & Keeter, 1996; Tewksbury & Rittenberg, 2012). As Schudson (2003) puts it, news as social knowledge is the critical ingredient for citizens to function and participate in the political process. Kwak, Williams, Wang, and Lee (2005) further argued that political knowledge is positively related to political participation.

From a user's perspective, news that is convenient and easy to read, view, and absorb on a smartphone with a touch screen and user-friendly interface may ultimately increase memory of news content and promote learning (Elenbaas, Vreese, Schuck, & Boomgaarden, 2014; Zaller, 2003). New opportunities may emerge for mobile phone users to engage in civic learning from consumption of news content. Therefore, the effects of consuming news in terms of acquiring political knowledge are examined in this chapter. It seems to us that any effect to be observed from consuming news via the mobile phone should be a result of cognitive engagement, not mindless scrolling on the screen or random browsing of fleeting headlines.

News in Their Pockets. Ran Wei and Ven-hwei Lo, Oxford University Press (2021). © Oxford University Press.
DOI: 10.1093/oso/9780197523728.003.0007

Nevertheless, no study, to date, has examined the effect of mobile news on acquiring political knowledge. Chapter 7 fills this void by investigating how consumption of mobile news as a civic interest of Asian college students is related to and contributes to their civic learning. Considering that mobile phones afford users with convenience and efficiency to track news "on the go" and "in between" around the o'clock, the relationship between following news on the mobile phone among engaged users and political knowledge is also examined.

Specifically, following news via the mobile phone is indicative of a purposive search and motivated approach to obtain news and public information, which drives elaborative processing of the information from the news (Schrøder, 2019). Users who use their mobile phone to follow news will likely learn more from the news. Accordingly, we expect that following news via the mobile phone will be positively related to respondents' political knowledge. The existing scholarship indicates that the use of traditional media (Lo & Chang 2006; Robinson & Levy, 1996) and digital media (Dimitrova, Shehata, Strömbäck, & Nord, 2014) contributes to political knowledge. Similarly, news following through mobile devices, which entails \strong motivation to obtain information, also promotes learning (Weeks & Holbert, 2013).

Given the high threshold of obtaining political knowledge from news, learning as an effect produced by consuming news is subjected to audience's psychological conditions and need for orientation. Weaver (1980) defined the concept as one's interest in news topics and a sense of uncertainty about the interested topics. Generally speaking, the higher the level of uncertainty, the higher the need, which results in a higher level of media use and more cognitive effects. As Matthes (2005) argued, need for orientation accounts for a fundamental reason people would engage in information seeking from the media, and for why some people are more susceptible to the influence of media than others.

Considering that members of the young generations in Asia and elsewhere are just beginning to develop their understanding of international politics, their need for orientation is considered high. Under such circumstances, the need for orientation as a mediator, which promotes learning from the news about current affairs and international events, will likely affect the outcome of consuming news on the mobile phone. We propose that the need for orientation will provide a psychological account of the learning effect of mobile news on political information. Young mobile phone users with a higher need for orientation will likely seek news actively on their phone and process the news thoroughly, resulting in a greater news learning effect.

Finally, we were curious about the extent to which the societal differences in terms of the information accessibility among the four studied cities would affect how college students gained knowledge about major news events. Information accessibility refers to the extent to which citizens in society can have free and full access to digital information, including online news content. We used five benchmark indicators to measure the variable: global outlook, Information and Communication Technology (ICT) Development Index, Internet accessibility, civic freedoms, and diversity of official languages (refer to Chapter 2 for details). As we elaborated in Chapter 2, the more accessible the digital information is in a society, the easier it is for citizens to seek and consume news about domestic and international politics, which in turn facilitates learning from the news. Conversely, in a society where digital information is less accessible due to restrictions and censorship, there are fewer opportunities for its citizens to acquire a broad range of diverse news sources about domestic events and international happenings, which then hinders learning from the news.

TESTING THE LEARNING EFFECT IN NEWS ABOUT NORTH KOREA–U.S. RELATIONS

To empirically test the importance of the role of news media in gaining political knowledge, which in turn shapes citizenship (Hao, Wen, & George, 2014; S. Lee, 2015), we incorporated learning from mobile news about international events as a key aspect of our proposed model concerning the process and effect of mobile news consumption, without which our systematic approach to understanding the motives, user experiences, and effects of news accessed from the mobile phone would be incomplete.

Schrøder (2019) argued that consumers of online news rarely click on stories that have obvious civic focus. Instead, they often consume stories that are amusing, trivial, or downright bizarre. To maintain a clear focus on an important international news event, we decided to center on news about the relationship between North Korea and the United States. The reports affect none of the four studied cities directly or the surveyed respondents personally, but they are relevant to all of the respondents in the four cities because peace and stability on the Korean peninsula concern the entire region.

As a by-product of the Cold War, the on-and-off talks between North Korea and the United States in the fall of 2017 on denuclearizing the Korean peninsula stood out as a piece of prominent international news that would affect stability and peace in the Asia-Pacific region. In fact, the

North Korean nuclear issue has been viewed as a time bomb, threatening the relationship between North Korea and the United States. North Korea has accused the United States of posing a massive threat to its national security, while the United States has insisted on North Korea's abandonment of its ambitious nuclear weapons program. The two sides have engaged in heated exchanges of rhetoric for decades, and the relationship between the two has remained strained.

North Korea's self-defense rhetoric reached a new height in 2017, during which it conducted 25 missile tests; on September 3, it conducted its sixth nuclear test. The next day, the United Nations Security Council passed a U.S.-sponsored resolution to impose new sanctions against North Korea, which made the situation even more intense. In a matter of months, the situation on the Korean peninsula became a flash point in world politics, and a news-making event that was widely reported around the world.

The tension between the United States and North Korea has severely affected the peace and stability of the Asia-Pacific region. Right after the sixth nuclear bomb test was conducted by North Korea, news reports on U.S.–North Korea relations had become one of the major topical events in fall 2017. Accordingly, we focused on the news about North Korea–U.S. relations as an empirical case of political knowledge to test the learning effect of mobile news. To be specific, we intend to examine how mobile news consumption contributes to acquisition of political knowledge concerning the news about U.S.–North Korea relations in this chapter. To do so, we analyzed the role of a set of control (i.e., age, gender) and predictor variables such as need for orientation, consumption of mobile news, following mobile news, and information accessibility in a society in affecting respondents' knowledge about the relationship between North Korea and the United States.

Also, we seek to compare the strength of relationships between individual-level predictors versus societal-level ones and political knowledge. The results will shed light on the question of how information accessibility in society as a strong macro-level variable of societal influence affects the learning of Asian college students from mobile news.

FINDINGS

In the 2017–2018 surveys, respondents in the four studied cities were provided a set of five factual questions that intended to measure their knowledge about the dramatic and tense relationship between the United States and North Korea. The questions requested respondents to identify people,

Table 7.1 KNOWLEDGE ABOUT NORTH KOREA–U.S. RELATIONS

Activity	Correct	Incorrect	Mean (SD)
How many nuclear tests has North Korea performed since 2006?	21.3%	78.7%	.21 (.41)
Who is the current secretary of state of the United States?	21.7%	78.3%	.22 (.41)
What is the purpose of the Otto Warmbier North Korea Nuclear Sanction Act?	31.6%	68.4%	.32 (.47)
On Oct. 9, 2017, a U.S. aircraft carrier sailed into the eastern waters of the Korean Peninsula. The aircraft carrier was?	17.2%	82.8%	.17 (.38)
The U.S. president Donald Trump said at the UN General Assembly that he will "totally destroy" North Korea. Correct or incorrect?	30.9%	69.1%	.31 (.46)
Combined index			1.24 (1.20)

Notes: Figures in parentheses are standard deviations. N = 2,988.
***p < .001; **p < .01; *p < .05.

issues, and prominent events in the news concerning the United States and North Korea. One point was awarded for each question that was answered correctly. Based on this, a knowledge index was created (see Appendix A for details).

As Table 7.1 shows, the mean knowledge score was 1.24, which means respondents correctly answered an average of 1.24 questions out of the five questions provided. Results of univariate analyses show that one-third of the respondents (34.7%) did very poorly, unable to score even one correct answer. In fact, less than 1% of the respondents correctly answered all five questions. Between the two extreme scores, one-sixth of the respondents (15.7%) answered three or more questions correctly.

Such results provide evidence in support of our fundamental assumption about consumption of mobile news—news consumption requires motivation, especially among young people who have yet to form a habit of news consumption. Clearly, consumption of domestically and internationally important news while on the move requires a high cognitive threshold as well.

Gender and Political Knowledge

With the expectation that a gender gap would exist in political knowledge, with men tending to be more knowledgeable (Bode, 2016; Delli Carpini &

Keeter, 1996, 2000; Wolak & McDevitt, 2011), we first examined the role of gender as a social differentiator variable in moderating the relationship between mobile news consumption and gaining knowledge about North Korea–U.S. relations.

Table 7.2 presents results of the surveys in 2017–2018, which show that Asian male college respondents (M = 1.42, SD = 1.26) were more likely than their female peers (M = 1.11, SD = 1.14) to score higher on

Table 7.2 GENDER DIFFERENCES IN KNOWLEDGE BETWEEN MALES AND FEMALES ABOUT NORTH KOREA–U.S. RELATIONS

Questions	Male			Female			t Value
	Correct	Incorrect	Mean	Correct	Incorrect	Mean	
How many nuclear tests has North Korea performed since 2006?	23.4%	76.6%	.23	20.3%	79.7%	.20	1.96
Who is the current secretary of state of the United States?	26.9%	73.1%	.27	18.0%	82.0%	.18	5.71***
What is the purpose of the Otto Warmbier North Korea Nuclear Sanction Act?	38.4%	61.6%	.38	27.1%	72.9%	.27	6.51***
On Oct. 9, 2017, a U.S. aircraft carrier sailed into the eastern waters of the Korean Peninsula. The aircraft carrier was?	18.5%	81.5%	.18	16.4%	83.6%	.16	1.47
The U.S. president Donald Trump said at the UN General Assembly that he will "totally destroy" North Korea. Correct or incorrect?	34.1%	65.9%	.34	28.9%	71.1%	.29	3.17***
Combined index			1.42 (1.26)			1.11 (1.14)	6.72***

Notes: Figures in parentheses are standard deviations. N = 2,988.
***p < .001.

factual questions about the relationship between North Korea and the United States. To be specific, one-fifth (20.2%) of the male respondents answered three or more questions correctly. In contrast, less than one-sixth (14.4%) of the female respondents correctly answered three or more of the questions. Results of an independent t-test indicated that the gender difference in the knowledge scores was significant ($t = 6.72$, $p < .001$).

Consistent with the literature (Bode, 2016; Delli Carpini & Keeter; 2000; Leung & Wei, 1999b), these results reveal that the gender gap in political knowledge exists in the 4G era when news is widely accessible to both male and female college students.

Mobile News Consumption and Political Knowledge

Given the public nature of knowledge about current affairs, past research indicates that media use is a major contributor to political knowledge. The young generations of millennials and centennials are found to rely on digital outlets (websites, mobile apps, and SMS via mobile devices) for news seeking anywhere, anytime (Molyneux, 2018; Struckmann & Karnowski, 2016). Accordingly, we next tested our proposition that mobile news consumption would be positively related to knowledge about the relationship between North Korea and the United States.

As shown in Table 7.3, univariate analyses show that in general, the heavy users of mobile news in the pooled sample ($M = 1.34$, $SD = 1.22$) were more likely than the light users ($M = 1.14$, $SD = 1.17$) to score higher on knowledge questions about North Korea–U.S. relations. More than one-sixth (17.2%) of the heavy users of the mobile news correctly answered three or more questions. Among the light users of mobile news, however, less than one-sixth (14.2%) could do so.

Take the question on the purpose of the Otto Warmbier North Korea Nuclear Sanction Act as an example. The essence of the bill is to suffocate the supply of foreign currency to the isolated country by imposing sanctions against any non-American financial organization that does business with North Korea; violators will meet with civic penalties. As much as a third (33.9%) of the heavy users of mobile news correctly identified the purpose of this act as "enforcing economic sanctions on North Korea." Only 29.7% of the light users, however, were able to identify the purpose of the act. An independent t-test indicated that the difference in the overall

Table 7.3 DIFFERENCES IN KNOWLEDGE BETWEEN HEAVY AND LIGHT USERS ABOUT NORTH KOREA–U.S. RELATIONS

Questions	Heavy Users			Light Users			t Value
	Correct	Incorrect	Mean	Correct	Incorrect	Mean	
How many nuclear tests has North Korea performed since 2006?	23.3%	76.7%	.23	19.7%	80.3%	.20	2.40*
Who is the current secretary of state of the United States?	24.5%	75.5%	.25	19.1%	80.9%	.19	3.55***
What is the purpose of the Otto Warmbier North Korea Nuclear Sanction Act?	33.9%	66.1%	.34	29.7%	70.3%	.30	2.49*
On Oct. 9, 2017, a U.S. aircraft carrier sailed into the eastern waters of the Korean Peninsula. The aircraft carrier was?	21.2%	78.8%	.21	13.3%	86.7%	.13	5.66***
The U.S. president Donald Trump said at the UN General Assembly that he will "totally destroy" North Korea. Correct or incorrect?	29.9%	70.1%	.30	31.7%	68.3%	.32	–1.07
Combined index			1.34 (1.22)			1.14 (1.17)	4.50***

Notes: Figures in parentheses are standard deviations. $N = 2,988$.
***$p < .001$, *$p < .05$.

knowledge scores between heavy users and light users was statistically significant ($t = 4.50, p < .001$).

These results support our proposition that mobile news consumption is positively related to knowledge about current affairs. The more the surveyed Asian college students consumed news on their mobile phone, the more they were knowledgeable about the facts concerning North Korea–U.S. relations.

Following Mobile News and Political Knowledge

Similar to newspaper subscribers, people who sign up to receive digital news tend to receive news from more than one source. As we examined in Chapter 5, mobile users can choose to follow news organizations, professional journalists, news blogs or journalist bloggers, and posts on Twitter by those professional news organizations. Following news on the mobile phone results in continuous, stable, and regular access to news from one's chosen news sources, which in turn facilitates active news consumption and the likelihood of efficient learning.

Therefore, we further analyzed the link between following news through mobile phones and acquisition of political knowledge, because following news represents a purposive behavior that manifests a strong motivation to seek more news about domestic politics, international affairs, or both. In addition, past research (Weeks & Hobert, 2013) indicates that following news may drive news consumers to further elaborate on the news content, thus promoting learning from news. Accordingly, we expect that following the news via mobile phones will enhance respondents' knowledge about the relationship between North Korea and the United States.

As shown in Table 7.4, the survey data revealed that by correctly answering more questions about North Korea–U.S. relations, respondents with high levels of news-following activities ($M = 1.29$, $SD = 1.20$) were more likely than those with low levels of news-following activities ($M = 1.19$, $SD = 1.18$) to learn more from the news. To be specific, one-sixth (16.6%) of respondents with high levels of news-following activities correctly answered three or more of the quiz questions. On the other hand, only less than one-sixth (14.8%) of the respondents who followed mobile news less were able to correctly answer three or more of the factual questions.

To illustrate, about a quarter (24.0%) of the users, who engaged in more news-following activities on their mobile phone, correctly identified Rex Tillerson as U.S. secretary of state. However, less than one-fifth (19.7%) of those who engaged in fewer news-following activities on their phone could correctly identify Tillerson's name. An independent t-test showed that the between-group difference in the combined knowledge index was statistically significant ($t = 2.35$, $p < .05$). As we anticipated, these results indicated that following news delivered to the mobile phone as a type of active news consumption facilitates learning.

Table 7.4 DIFFERENCES IN KNOWLEDGE BETWEEN HIGH-FOLLOWING USERS
AND LOW-FOLLOWING USERS ABOUT NORTH KOREA–U.S. RELATIONS

Questions	High-Following Users			Low-Following Users			
	Correct	Incorrect	Mean	Correct	Incorrect	Mean	*t* Value
How many nuclear tests has North Korea performed since 2006?	21.8%	78.2%	.22	20.5%	79.5%	.21	.89
Who is the current secretary of state of the United States?	24.0%	76.0%	.24	19.7%	80.3%	.20	2.73**
What is the purpose of the Otto Warmbier North Korea Nuclear Sanction Act?	32.9%	67.1%	.33	30.7%	69.3%	.31	1.25
On Oct. 9, 2017, a U.S. aircraft carrier sailed into the eastern waters of the Korean Peninsula. The aircraft carrier was?	20.3%	79.7%	.20	13.7%	86.3%	.14	4.76***
The U.S. president Donald Trump said at the UN General Assembly that he will "totally destroy" North Korea. Correct or incorrect?	29.2%	70.8%	.29	32.5%	67.5%	.33	-1.86
Combined index			1.29 (1.20)			1.19 (1.18)	2.35*

Notes: Figures in parentheses are standard deviations. $N = 2,988$.
***$p < .001$, **$p < .01$, *$p < .05$.

Need for Orientation and Political Knowledge

Next, we explored the role of need for orientation as another variable that promotes learning from the news about current affairs and international events. As we proposed in Chapter 2, individuals with a higher need for orientation would likely seek news actively on their phone and process the news thoroughly, resulting in a greater news learning effect. On the other hand, we expect those with a low need for orientation will be less likely to learn from the news.

To compute a respondent's total score on the need for orientation index, their score on each of the five items in the index was taken and summed up. The total score was then divided at midpoint to create two groups. Those with a score of 3.8 or above out of the 5.0 were classified into the high-need group, whereas those who scored below 3.8 were put into the low-need group.

As results of univariate analysis presented in Table 7.5 show, respondents with a high level of need for orientation ($M = 1.37$, $SD = 1.24$) were more

Table 7.5 DIFFERENCES IN KNOWLEDGE BETWEEN HIGH NEED-FOR-ORIENTATION (NFO) USERS AND LOW NFO USERS ABOUT THE NORTH KOREA-U.S. RELATIONS

Questions	High NFO Users			Low NFO Users			t Value
	Correct	Incorrect	Mean	Correct	Incorrect	Mean	
How many nuclear tests has North Korea performed since 2006?	22.6%	77.4%	.23	19.7%	80.3%	.20	1.92*
Who is the current secretary of state of the United States?	24.6%	75.4%	.25	17.6%	82.4%	.18	4.63***
What is the purpose of the Otto Warmbier North Korea Nuclear Sanction Act?	36.2%	63.8%	.36	25.2%	74.8%	.25	6.49*
On Oct. 9, 2017, a U.S. aircraft carrier sailed into the eastern waters of the Korean Peninsula. The aircraft carrier was?	19.0%	81.0%	.20	14.7%	85.3%	.15	3.09***
The U.S. president Donald Trump said at the UN General Assembly that he will "totally destroy" North Korea. Correct or incorrect?	33.6%	66.4%	.34	27.0%	73.0%	.27	3.87***
Combined index			1.37 (1.24)			1.05 (1.12)	7.27***

Notes: Figures in parentheses are standard deviations. $N = 2,988$.
***$p < .001$, *$p < .05$.

likely than those who had a low level of need for orientation (M = 1.05, SD = 1.12) to score more correct answers on the factual questions concerning North Korea–U.S. relations.

Specifically, nearly one-fifth (18.7%) of respondents with a high level of need for orientation correctly answered three or more questions about the relationship between North Korea and United States. But only one-tenth (11.2%) of the respondents with a low level of need for orientation could answer three or more correctly. An independent t-test indicated that the difference in the combined knowledge scores between respondents whose need for orientation was high and those with a low need for orientation was statistically significant (t = 7.27, p < .001). Similar to news learning from traditional news media, a mobile phone user's interest in current affairs and concern about the uncertainty of unfolding international news events also play a key role in enabling their learning from the news.

Information Accessibility and Political Knowledge

Furthermore, to shed light on the question of how societal differences in terms of the degree of information accessibility across the four studied cities would affect how college students learn about North Korea–U.S. relations, a one-way ANOVA was performed. As we argued in Chapter 2, the more accessible the digital information is in a society, the more news about domestic and international politics is available to news consumers, which in turn facilitates learning from news. In Shanghai, websites such as Google, Facebook, and WhatsApp as well as international media outlets such as the *New York Times* and *Financial Times* are blocked. We were interested in exploring if the restrictions would have any consequences for Chinese college students' learning about a major international event in the region.

Consistent with our expectation, significant cross-city differences were found in the levels of political knowledge in the 2017–2018 surveys [F (3, 2933) = 24.53, p < .001]. As Table 7.6 shows, respondents in Singapore (M = 1.43, SD = 1.21) scored highest in the knowledge index, followed by those in Hong Kong (M = 1.42, SD = .47) and Taipei (M = 1.16, SD = 1.12). In comparison, Shanghai respondents (M = .98, SD = 1.14) had the lowest score on the same set of questions.

The Scheffe test showed that respondents in Singapore and Hong Kong were more likely to score higher on the knowledge index than were their counterparts in Taipei and Shanghai. But there was no difference in the mean level of knowledge score between Singapore and Hong

Table 7.6 MEAN ESTIMATES OF KNOWLEDGE IN SHANGHAI, HONG KONG, TAIPEI, AND SINGAPORE ABOUT NORTH KOREA–U.S. RELATIONS

Sample	Total (N = 2,936)	Shanghai (N = 754)	Hong Kong (N = 721)	Taipei (N = 804)	Singapore (N = 657)	F Value
Knowledge about U.S.–North Korea relations	1.24 (1.20)	.98 (1.14)	1.42 (1.27)	1.16 (1.12)	1.43 (1.21)	24.53***

Note: Figures in parentheses are standard deviations.
***p < .001.

Kong respondents. In addition, Taipei respondents performed better on the political knowledge questions used in the survey than did Shanghai respondents.

Such results underscore the importance of a society's "software" such as access, diversity, and openness of its information environment in learning from the news consumed on the mobile phone. The differences in software account for the results that respondents in Singapore and Hong Kong, two of Asian's most international mega cities with bilingual official languages (Singapore is the most global city in Asia, while Hong Kong positions itself as Asia's world city), outperformed their peers in Taipei and Shanghai. Furthermore, respondents in Taipei, who have free access to a diverse range of news media outlets, domestic and foreign, did better than those in Shanghai, where access to foreign press such as the *New York Times* or *The Times* is off limits, and Google, Facebook, and Twitter are blocked by the infamous "Great Firewall of China."

Predicting Political Knowledge

Finally, with all of the five studied variables, individual and societal, being considered together, which of these variables—gender, need for orientation, mobile news consumption, mobile news-following behavior, and information accessibility—would have the strongest effect on political knowledge? To address the question, we conducted a hierarchical regression analysis, which treated knowledge about North Korea–U.S. relations as the dependent variable. The predictor variables were, respectively, gender, age, need for orientation, mobile news consumption, mobile news following, and accessibility of information. Table 7.7 summarizes the regression results.

As shown in the final model presented in Table 7.7 (column 5), gender was significantly associated with knowledge about the relationship between North Korea and the United States ($B = .12$, $p < .001$), indicating that Asian male college students tended to have a high knowledge score about the relationship. Need for orientation as a predictor was also significantly and positively related to the political knowledge index ($B = .14$, $p < .001$). This means that the more respondents were interested in news about the dramatic North Korea–U.S. relations and were uncertain about the unfolding relations for the region, the more they knew about the topic.

Moreover, mobile news consumption ($B = .06$, $p < .01$) and news-following behavior ($B = .07$, $p < .01$) were both significantly associated with the political knowledge index. But the linkage was weak in terms of beta weights. Among all the significant predictors, information accessibility emerged as the strongest predictor of the overall political knowledge score ($B = .18$, $p < .001$) after influences of other predictors were taken into account. It alone contributed 2.8% to the total variance explained, indicating that accessibility to information in society made a big difference in how respondents learned from the news accessed from the mobile phone.

Taken together, the results of the regression analysis demonstrate that both individual-level predictors, such as gender and need for orientation,

Table 7.7 HIERARCHICAL REGRESSION ANALYSIS PREDICTING KNOWLEDGE ABOUT NORTH KOREA–U.S. RELATIONS

Independent Variables	Model 1	Model 2	Model 3	Model 4	Model 5
Block 1: Demographics					
Gender	.13***	.13***	.13***	.13***	.12***
Age	.00	−.02	−.02	−.02	−.01
Block 2: Need for Orientation					
Need for orientation		.17***	.16***	.16***	.14***
Block 3: Mobile News Use					
Mobile news consumption			.06**	.05*	.06**
Block 4: Mobile News Following					
Following news via mobile phones				.02	.07**
Block 5: Information Environment					
Information accessibility					.18***
Incremental adjusted R²	1.5%	2.9%	0.2%	0.0%	2.8%
Total adjusted R²	1.5%	4.4%	4.6%	4.6%	7.4%

Note: N = 2,101.
***$p < .001$, **$p < .01$, *$p < .05$.

and societal factors, such as information accessibility, account for the most variances in knowledge about a major international event prominently reported in the news media. Mobile news consumption and following mobile news, however, were weak predictors, suggesting that learning from news consumed on the mobile phone is largely subject to the level of information accessibility in a society. However, use of data collected from a one-shot survey limits our ability to further explore the change in those predictors over time.

Thoughts and views of participants in our focus groups in the four Asian cities help us put these findings into perspective. A 22-year-old male student in Taipei elaborated on the advantage of news available on his smartphone. He said, "Mobile apps, like Twitter, Facebook News, and Huffington Post, provide more world news than any other news sources in Taiwan." His schoolmate in Taipei, a second-year female student, viewed the easy access to news on her phone this way. She said, "News on the phone is fast and easy, but very fragmented. You will need to make some efforts to piece things together or get lost." Another female student in Taipei followed up by saying, "Yeah, to catch breaking news, the phone is the choice. But if I want to follow the news to know more, especially why things happen, I will need to power up the laptop, and read the papers for in-depth analysis."

Across the Taiwan Strait, several students in Shanghai explained why they would shy away from news sources on social media sites to stay in the know. A 25-year-old female student said, "It's hard to tell the news is true or not." She continued, "I prefer national media such as CCTV and the *People's Daily* as my sources to get news. It's simple, they're trustworthy. Sometimes, I read the sites of major foreign news organizations. That is only when I can, for the same reason."

A male second-year student aged 20 in Hong Kong said, "I believe that consuming news through the smartphone help[s] me understand what is happening in the world. Sometimes I will use the apps of news media to read international news, such as NOW News (a cable TV service in Hong Kong), BBC News, etc." His schoolmate, another 20-year-old male student, shared his view by saying:

> I read news about Hong Kong only at the time when I relied on newspaper or TV news as my news source. I skip other news. But after I used my phone to consume news, I came to know a much broader range of news, like the mountain fires in Australia and the presidential election in Taiwan. I also log in news sites on social media to follow or share news about world events. Sure, with mobile news, I'm staying updated about happenings around the world.

SUMMARY OF KEY FINDINGS

As a by-product of the Cold War, the on-again/off-again talks on the denuclearization of the Korean peninsula between North Korea and the United States in fall 2017 were a piece of prominent international news that would affect stability and peace in the Asia-Pacific region. In this chapter, we examined the learning effect of mobile news, focusing on the association between consumption of mobile news and factual knowledge about North Korea–U.S. relations. A number of patterns emerged from the results in the 2017–2018 surveys with regard to how Asian college students in the four studied cities acquired knowledge about the eventful North Korea–U.S. relations:

- A gender gap exists in political knowledge, reflected in the higher number of correct answers scored by male respondents compared to females in the same age cohort. The gender difference in the knowledge scores was statistically significant. Although equal numbers of male and female college students owned a mobile phone, the device itself did not narrow the gender-based knowledge gap.
- There is a positive link between level of consumption of mobile news and knowledge of current affairs. The heavy users of mobile news tend to be more knowledgeable about North Korea–U.S. relations than were the light users. Thus, consumption of news accessed from the mobile phone is conducive to learning from the news. Similarly, respondents who engaged in news-following activities show a greater likelihood of correctly answering questions about North Korea–U.S. relations than did those who reported fewer news-following activities. Active consumption of mobile news facilitates learning from the news that they track.
- The need to be oriented also plays an important role in facilitating learning from news accessed through mobile phones. This pattern is similar to the findings concerning learning from traditional news media—as an antecedent of knowledge acquisition from news media. Among the surveyed college students in the four Asian cities, those with a higher need for orientation about news events tend to learn more from the news than those with a low need for orientation.
- Information accessibility of the city matters in impacting how much users learn from mobile news, an external influence beyond individual news-seeking efforts. It shows the strongest relationship with knowledge about a major international issue affecting the Asia-Pacific region. Across the four Asian cities in our study, respondents in Singapore scored the highest on the knowledge index, followed by those in Hong

Kong and Taipei. Surprisingly, the Shanghai respondents, who had the strongest motivation for news seeking, consumed more news from the mobile phone, and engaged in more news-following activities (refer to Chapters 4 and 5), had the lowest score on the same set of factual knowledge questions.

THEORETICAL INSIGHTS FROM FINDINGS

These patterns concerning civic learning from mobile news lead to some theoretical insights into the effects of mobile news consumption as well as the set of predictors that influences the news learning process. The takeaways of Chapter 7 include the following.

First, the relatively low score about U.S.–North Korea relations reported in the news media across the four samples lends support to our assumptions about consumption of mobile news—it requires civic motivation (refer to Chapter 3), but effective consumption with learning effect also demands cognitive involvement. Without being cognitively involved in processing news delivered to the mobile screen, consumption of mobile news will likely amount to mindless scrolling and casual screen touching. On the other hand, when users allocate cognitive resources to process news accessed from their phone (e.g., having an interest in current affairs), they learn more from the news, thereby expanding their knowledgeability about current affairs. Thus, they demonstrate the anticipated civic learning from mobile news.

At the individual level, a strong need for orientation about important news events plays a facilitating role in learning from the news and political information. Gender, on the other hand, works in favor of male news consumers in news learning. Both predictors, which affected political knowledge gained from using traditional media, remain significant in the context of learning from mobile news.

More importantly, cross-city differences in political knowledge scores exist, suggesting some societal-level factors are at work. Respondents in two of Asia's most global and open cities—Singapore and Hong Kong—scored higher on the knowledge index than did their counterparts in Taipei and Shanghai. Further, the Taipei respondents performed better on the political knowledge questions than did their counterparts in Shanghai.

As we found in Chapters 4 and 5, Shanghai respondents consumed more news on their phone and engaged in more news-following activities than did those in the other three surveyed cities. The gap in individual efforts and learning effect appears to be accounted for by the markedly different information environments between Shanghai and the other three cities. All of the three other cities have bilingual official languages, the flow of information is largely free, and access to digital content on the Internet is unrestricted. It seems that, similar to the level of press freedom, these societal differences in information access and openness make a difference in learning from mobile news. Such societal influence appears to cancel out the effects of individual variables, suggesting the limit of individual efforts in learning from news.

The implications of these generalizations are that the hardware of an upgraded network infrastructure and deep diffusion of smartphones alone will not necessarily make young Asian citizens informed. The "software" of their information environment in society is equally important, if not more important, in enabling them to be informed citizens.

To conclude, although mobile technology has significantly reduced barriers to access news anywhere, anytime, the cognitive threshold of effective consumption of such news has become higher. To learn what is important domestically and internationally from news on the mobile phone requires cognitive involvement. In other words, civic learning from mobile news requires something more than unprecedented access. As scholars Tewksbury and Rittenberg (2012) have argued, digital news is critical to citizenship in the 21st century. We would further argue that mere availability of abundant news via the mobile phone in one's pocket does not equate to knowledgeability about current affairs, and hence informed citizenship.

CHAPTER 8

Modeling with Mediation Analysis

MEDIATORS AND MEDIATION EFFECTS

In Chapters 3 to 7, we used multiple regressions to estimate the linear relationships among predictors at the individual level and the societal level and the five dependent variables—motivations, consumption, engaged consumption, perceptions, and knowledge. Results presented in these chapters suggest the presence of a structural relationship among the studied variables. This means that the significant relationships are likely intervened by mediators. The result is that some of the predictors (aka *exogenous variables*, which are unaffected by other variables in the model) have both direct and indirect effects on the studied dependent variables (aka *endogenous variables*, those that are influenced by other factors in the model). The indirect effects of exogenous variables are carried out by mediators (e.g., *mediating variables*). By differentiating predictors in multiple regression into *exogenous, endogenous, and mediating variables*, we are able to clarify the nature of the relationships between the studied independent and dependent variables.

Analytically, we treated societal-level variables in our models as exogenous or independent variables, whose values or changes in value are determined outside the model, while motivation and expectations of mobile news, mobile news consumption, engaged consumption, perceived utility, and appeal were treated as mediators, which intervene in the relationship between independent and dependent variables. Accordingly, to explore *whether* surveillance motivation and expectancies of mobile news enhance or mitigate the impact of exogenous variables (e.g., city of residence,

News in Their Pockets. Ran Wei and Ven-hwei Lo, Oxford University Press (2021). © Oxford University Press.
DOI: 10.1093/oso/9780197523728.003.0008

smartphone ownership, press freedom, and information accessibility) on the endogenous variables, we pursued a series of modeling to empirically test the hypothesized linkages among city of residence, smartphone ownership, surveillance motivation, expectancies of mobile news, and the five studied dependent variables.

Specifically, we employed another multivariate statistical analysis—structural equation modeling (SEM)—to accomplish the goal. SEM is superior to multiple regression analysis and is used to analyze the structural relationships among multiple predictor variables (Kline, 2005), some of which can be differentiated as mediators. All of the models were tested using Amos 25.0.

Consumption

Based on the results of the regression analyses of the 2010–2011 data that were collected during the 3G era (refer to Table 4.7), we propose that city of residence and smartphone ownership will affect Asian college students' motivations for using the mobile phone to consume news and their expectancies of mobile news as having personal value, which will in turn affect the consumption of mobile news. That is, motivational factors are mediators between the two independent variables (e.g., city of residence and smartphone ownership) and the dependent variables (e.g., news consumption). Results of the SEM modeling will demonstrate that the effects of city of residence and smartphone ownership on mobile news consumption are direct and indirect through surveillance motivation and personal value of mobile news.

As Figure 8.1 shows, our model on consuming mobile news specifies that city of residence (Shanghai) will affect smartphone ownership, which provides affordances for surveillance motivation, which then leads to expectancies of mobile news (e.g., mobile news as personal value), which will prompt respondents to consume news via the mobile phone.

Results of SEM testing show that although the chi-square for the model was significant, $X^2 = 1031.65$, $df = 69$, $p < .001$ (X^2/df ratio = 14.95), the comparative fit index (CFI = .97), the normal fit index (NFI = .97), the Tucker Lewis index (TLI = .96), and the root mean square error of approximation (RMSEA = .063) indicated that the model fit was acceptable. The model explained 1.0% of the variance in smartphone ownership, 20.2% of the variance in surveillance motivation, 31.3% in personal value of mobile news, and 62.3% in mobile news consumption.

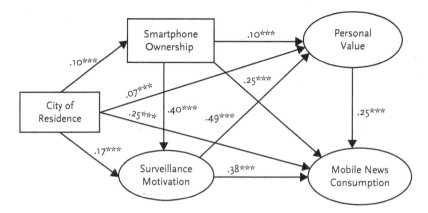

Figure 8.1 Structural Equation Model of Predictors of Mobile News Consumption (2010–2011 Surveys)
Note: Measured variables are represented by squares or rectangles, while latent variables are shown in ovals.
Credit: Ran Wei and Ven-hwei Lo

In terms of strengths of the linkages between the exogenous variables and the endogenous variables, as further shown in Figure 8.1, SEM shows that city of residence had a significant impact on smartphone ownership ($B = .10, p < .001$), surveillance motivation ($B = .17, p < .001$), personal value of mobile news ($B = .07, p < .001$), and mobile news consumption ($B = .25, p < .001$). Smartphone ownership had a significant effect on surveillance motivation ($B = .40, p < .001$), personal value of mobile news ($B = .10, p < .001$), and mobile news consumption ($B = .25, p < .001$). Further, surveillance motivation was significantly associated with expectancies of mobile news as personally valuable ($B = .49, p < .001$), which was also significantly associated with mobile news consumption ($B = .25, p < .001$).

Overall, SEM results validate that city of residence (in this case, Shanghai), smartphone ownership, surveillance motivation, and personal value of mobile news were all significant predictors of mobile news consumption. Furthermore, city of residence and smartphone ownership also had a positive and direct impact on surveillance motivation and perceived personal value of mobile news. They also had a positive and indirect effect on consumption of mobile news through surveillance motivation and personal value of mobile news. What these results mean is that individual-level motivational variables are significant predictors of mobile new consumption, but they are under the influences of exogenous factors such as city of residence and smartphone ownership.

To assess the mediating effects of surveillance motivation and personal value of mobile news in mitigating the effects of city of residence and smartphone ownership on mobile news consumption, we adopted a procedure developed by Sobel (1982) that provides a direct test of an indirect effect. The Sobel test was employed because it performs well for moderate to large effect sizes with a large sample (Preacher & Hayes, 2004). The two mediators in our theoretical model are surveillance motivation and personal value of mobile news. Thus, there are two potential mediating effects between city of residence and mobile news consumption in the model.[1] Results of the Sobel test show that the z score for the mediation path through surveillance motivation was 10.49 ($p < .001$); the path through personal value of mobile news had a z score of 9.90 ($p < .001$). The larger the z score, the stronger the mediation effect. Thus, Sobel tests confirmed that city of residence was indirectly associated with mobile news consumption via surveillance motivation and personal value of mobile news.

Similarly, surveillance motivation and personal value of mobile news are also two potential mediators in the relationship between smartphone ownership and mobile news consumption. Results of the Sobel test indicate that the mediation path through surveillance motivation had a z score of 18.38 ($p < .001$), and the z score for the path through personal value of mobile news was 15.18 ($p < .001$). Accordingly, surveillance motivation and personal value of mobile news were significant mediators in the relationships between city of residence, smartphone ownership, and mobile news consumption.

To further ascertain the mediating effects of surveillance motivation and personal value of mobile news in the relationships among city of residence, smartphone ownership, and mobile news consumption, an additional bootstrapping procedure was conducted using the SPSS version of the PROCESS macro developed by Hayes (2013). The bootstrap method demonstrates that the mediation effects we reported with the Sobel test were accurate and appropriate for our data. Specifically, the bootstrapping procedure was used with 5,000 bootstrap samples and a 95% bias-corrected bootstrap confidence interval. Tables 8.1 and 8.2 show the indirect effects and their associated 95% confidence interval.

Table 8.1 INDIRECT EFFECTS OF CITY OF RESIDENCE ON MOBILE NEWS CONSUMPTION THROUGH HYPOTHESIZED MEDIATORS (2010–2011 SURVEYS)

Variable	B	SE (Boot)	Confidence Interval
Surveillance motivation	.121	.012	[.099, .144]
Personal value of mobile news	.089	.009	[.072, .108]

Note: 5,000 bootstrap samples were used to generate 95% bias-corrected confidence interval.

Table 8.2 INDIRECT EFFECTS OF CITY OF RESIDENCE ON MOBILE NEWS
CONSUMPTION THROUGH HYPOTHESIZED MEDIATORS (2017–2018 SURVEYS)

Variable	B	SE (Boot)	Confidence Interval
Surveillance motivation	.177	.012	[.156, .200]
Personal value of mobile news	.117	.009	[.099, .137]

Note: 5,000 bootstrap samples were used to generate 95% bias-corrected confidence interval.

Taken together, these findings suggest that city of residence and smartphone ownership significantly influence mobile news consumption and that their impacts were mediated by surveillance motivation and personal value of mobile news. Thus, college students who lived in Shanghai, owned a smartphone, had a higher motivation, and perceived mobile news as more valuable personally consumed more mobile news.

Will these results hold when smartphone ownership becomes a constant? To address this question, we propose that city of residence (e.g., living in Shanghai) will affect surveillance motivation, both of which will then affect personal value of mobile news, which will in turn affect mobile news consumption. In modeling from the data collected in the 2017–2018 surveys, smartphone ownership as an exogenous variable was excluded.

To test the model depicted in Figure 8.2, we also implemented SEM. Results show that the chi-square for the model was still significant, $\chi^2 = 565.96$, $df = 56$, $p < .001$ (χ^2/df ratio = 10.11), but other model fit statistics such as the comparative fit index (CFI = .97), the normal fit index (NFI = .97), the Tucker Lewis index (TLI = .94), and the root mean square error of approximation (RMSEA = .055) indicate that the model fit was acceptable. The model explained 0.4% of the variance in surveillance motivation, 28.0% in personal value of mobile news, and 43.6% in mobile news consumption.

As shown in Figure 8.2, SEM indicates that city of residence had a significant effect on surveillance motivation (ß = .07, $p < .001$), personal value of mobile news (ß = −.11, $p < .001$), and mobile news consumption (ß = .12, $p < .001$). Surveillance motivation also had a significant effect on personal value of mobile news (ß = .53, $p < .001$) and mobile news consumption (ß = .47, $p < .01$). SEM further affirms that perceived personal value of mobile news is a significant predictor of mobile news consumption (ß = .27, $p < .001$). Therefore, we generated evidence in support of the proposed model that city of residence, surveillance motivation, and personal value of mobile news are significant predictors of mobile news consumption,

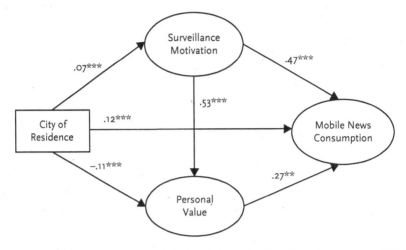

Figure 8.2 Structural Equation Model of Predictors of Mobile News Consumption (2017–2018 Surveys)
Note: Measured variables are represented by squares or rectangles, while latent variables are shown in ovals.
Credit: Ran Wei and Ven-hwei Lo

while surveillance motivation and personal value of mobile news are mediators, whose pathways of influence are subject to the influences of city of residence.

In analyzing the 2017–2018 data collected during the 4G era, we want to explore whether and how surveillance motivation and personal value of mobile news mediate the relationship between city of residence and mobile news consumption. To assess the mediating effect, we also used the Sobel test; results show that the mediation path through surveillance motivation had a z score of 9.90 ($p < .001$), but the z score for the path through personal value of mobile news was –2.41 ($p < .05$). Therefore, surveillance motivation functioned as a significant mediator in the relationship between city of residence and mobile news consumption. However, the presence of personal value of mobile news enhanced rather than reduced the linkage between city of residence and mobile news consumption.[2]

Results of another bootstrap test provided additional evidence in support of the proposed model that surveillance motivation ($B = .010$; CI = .001, .021) is a significant mediator in the relationship between city of residence and mobile news consumption.

These findings provided strong support for the proposed model in the 4G era. Specifically, city of residence had a positive impact on mobile news consumption, but its impact was indirectly influenced by the two motivational variables: surveillance motivation and personal value of mobile news. It is interesting to note that the effect of city of residence on personal value of mobile news was negative. In this case, personal value of mobile news played the role of a suppressor that masked the true strength of the relationship between city of residence and mobile news consumption. At any rate, these results are largely consistent with that from the 3G era—respondents living in Shanghai tended to have a higher motivation even though they perceived mobile news as less valuable personally, which resulted in a higher level of consumption of mobile news.

Following and Sharing

Next, to explore how city of residence and smartphone ownership influence mobile news engagement and whether surveillance motivation, personal value of mobile news, and mobile news consumption mediate the relationship between city of residence, smartphone ownership, and mobile news-following and -sharing behaviors, we developed two separate models using data from the two surveys. The two models are depicted in Figures 8.3 and 8.4.

Specifically, Figure 8.3 includes city of residence, smartphone ownership, surveillance motivation, personal value of mobile news, mobile news consumption, and mobile news following. The model predicts that city of residence and smartphone ownership will directly predict mobile news

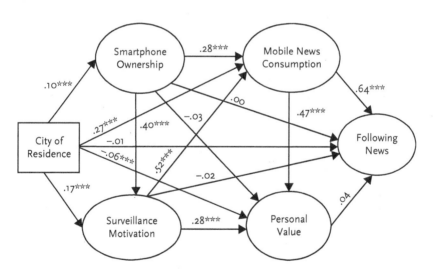

Figure 8.3 Structural Equation Model of Predictors of Mobile News Following (2010–2011 Surveys)
Note: Measured variables are represented by squares or rectangles, while latent variables are shown in ovals.
Credit: Ran Wei and Ven-hwei Lo

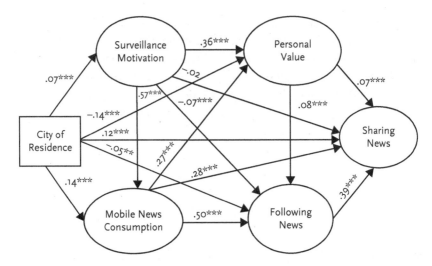

Figure 8.4 Structural Equation Model of Predictors of Mobile News Following and Sharing (2017–2018 Surveys)
Note: Measured variables are represented by squares or rectangles, while latent variables are shown in ovals.
Credit: Ran Wei and Ven-hwei Lo

following. In addition to these direct pathways, it predicts that surveillance motivation will predict mobile news consumption, which next will impact personal value of mobile news, which then will predict mobile news following.

To test the direct and indirect pathways in the model depicted in Figure 8.3, we took the SEM approach. Results show that although the chi-square for the model was significant, X^2 = 2524.85, df = 157, $p < .001$ (X^2/df ratio = 16.08), the comparative fit index (CFI = .96), the normal fit index (NFI = .96), the Tucker Lewis index (TLI = .95), and the root mean square error of approximation (RMSEA = .065) indicate that the model fit was acceptable.

As results in Figure 8.3 show, although city of residence had a significant effect on smartphone ownership ($B = .10$, $p < .001$), surveillance motivation ($B = .17$, $p < .001$), mobile news consumption ($B = .27$, $p < .001$), and personal value of mobile news ($B = -.06$, $p < .001$), it was not significantly associated with news following ($B = -.01$, $p > .05$). Smartphone ownership had a significant effect on surveillance motivation ($B = .40$, $p < .001$) and mobile news consumption ($B = .28$, $p < .001$). But smartphone ownership was not significantly related to personal value of mobile news ($B = -.03$, $p > .05$) and news following ($B = .00$, $p > .05$).

Moreover, surveillance motivation had a significant effect on mobile news consumption ($B = .52$, $p < .001$) and personal value ($B = .28$, $p < .001$).

In addition, mobile news consumption was significantly and positively associated with personal value ($B = .47$, $p < .001$) and news following ($B = .64$, $p < .001$). Finally, SEM results further revealed that surveillance motivation ($B = -.02$, $p > .05$) and personal value of mobile news ($B = .04$, $p > .05$) were not significantly related to news following.

As further shown in Figure 8.3, the direct effects of city of residence and smartphone ownership on following mobile news were not significant; most of their effects on news following were carried out through the three mediators (i.e., motivation, consumption, and personal value). In terms of variance accounted for by the model, these SEM results showed that the model explained 1.0% of the variance in smartphone ownership, 20.3% in surveillance motivation, 61.7% in mobile news consumption, 43.0% in personal value, and 41.0% in news following.

To further assess the mediating effects of surveillance motivation, mobile news consumption, and personal value in the relationships between city of residence and smartphone ownership and news following, we conducted the Sobel test. The three mediators in the model are surveillance, mobile news consumption, and personal value of mobile news. Accordingly, there are three potential mediating effects between city of residence and news-following behavior in the model. Results show that the z score for the mediation path through surveillance motivation was 10.30 ($p < .001$), the path through personal value of mobile news had a z score of 9.68 ($p < .001$), and the path through mobile news consumption had a z score of 19.68 ($p < .001$). Therefore, these results confirmed that surveillance motivation, mobile news consumption, and personal value were indeed significant mediators in the relationship between city of residence and news following.

The three mediators between smartphone ownership and news following in the model are surveillance motivation, mobile news consumption, and personal value of mobile news. Results of the Sobel test show that the z score for the mediation path through surveillance motivation was 16.96 ($p < .001$), the path through personal value of mobile news had a z score of 14.25 ($p < .001$), and the path through mobile news consumption has a z score of 24.41 ($p < .001$). Therefore, these results indicated that surveillance motivation, mobile news consumption, and personal value were also significant mediators in the relationship between smartphone ownership and news following.

Similarly, we pursued another SEM analysis of mobile news-sharing behavior using data collected in the 2017–2018 surveys. As Figure 8.4 illustrates, this model shows that city of residence has a direct effect on mobile news following and sharing. The model also specifies that city of residence affects surveillance motivation of mobile phone use, which affects mobile news consumption, which then leads to personal value of mobile news, which in turn predicts mobile news following and sharing. That is, surveillance motivation, mobile news consumption, and personal value of mobile news are treated as mediators between city of residence and mobile news following as well as mobile news sharing.

To test the hypothesized relationships in the model depicted in Figure 8.4, we used Amos 25.0 to execute the SEM analysis. Results show that the chi-square for the model was significant, $X^2 = 2350.62$, $df = 228$, $p < .001$ (X^2/df ratio = 10.31). On the other hand, the comparative fit index (CFI = .95), the normal fit index (NFI = .94), the Tucker Lewis index (TLI = .92), and the root mean square error of approximation (RMSEA = .056) indicate that the model fit was acceptable. The model explained 0.4% of the variance in surveillance motivation, 35.7% in mobile news consumption, 31.1% in personal value, 25.4% in news following, and 39.7% in news sharing.

As results in Figure 8.4 show, SEM indicates that city of residence had a significant effect on surveillance motivation ($B = .07$, $p < .001$), which was significantly related to mobile news consumption ($B = .57$, $p < .001$), which was significantly associated with personal value ($B = .27$, $p < .001$), news following ($B = .50$, $p < .001$), and news sharing ($B = .28$, $p < .001$). Surveillance motivation also had a significant effect on personal value ($B = .36$, $p < .001$) and news following ($B = -.07$, $p < .001$). Personal value of mobile news was significantly and positively associated with news following ($B = .08$, $p < .001$) and news sharing ($B = .07$, $p < .001$). Consistent with the regression results in Chapter 5, SEM further revealed that news following was the strongest predictor of news sharing ($B = .39$, $p < .001$). The direct effects of city of residence on news following and sharing, however, proved relatively weak.

As further presented in Figure 8.4, surveillance motivation, mobile news consumption, and personal value of mobile news are the three potential mediators in the relationships between city of residence and mobile news following and sharing. Again, to assess the mediating effects of these three mediators, we conducted more Sobel tests. Results indicate that mobile news consumption ($z = 6.06$, $p < .001$) was a significant mediator in the relationship between city of residence and mobile news following. Surveillance motivation ($z = 1.81$, $p > .05$), however, was not a significant mediator in the relationship between city of residence and mobile news following. Moreover, personal value of mobile news ($z = -2.39$, $p < .05$) was found to function as a suppressor that enhanced the relationship between city of residence and mobile news following.

Table 8.3 INDIRECT EFFECTS OF CITY OF RESIDENCE ON MOBILE NEWS
FOLLOWING THROUGH HYPOTHESIZED MEDIATORS (2017–2018 SURVEYS)

Variable	B	SE (Boot)	Confidence Interval
Mobile news consumption	.104	.015	[.075, .133]

Note: 5,000 bootstrap samples were used to generate 95% bias-corrected confidence interval.

In addition, the Sobel test also found that mobile news consumption
($z = 6.05$, $p < .001$) was a significant mediator in the relationship between
city of residence and mobile news sharing. Again, surveillance motivation
($z = 1.83$, $p > .05$) was an insignificant mediator, while personal value of
mobile news ($z = -2.41$, $p < .05$) was a suppressor in the relationship between city of residence and mobile news sharing. The bootstrap test also
confirmed that mobile news consumption mediated the effect of city of
residence on both mobile news following and sharing (results are presented
in Tables 8.3 and 8.4).

Results of SEM also suggest that the influence of surveillance motivation on mobile news following and sharing is affected by mobile news
consumption and personal value of mobile news. Therefore, mobile news
consumption and personal value of mobile news are the two potential
mediators in the relationship between surveillance motivation and mobile
news following and sharing. Again, to assess the mediating effects of these
two mediators, we conducted more Sobel tests. Results indicate that mobile news consumption ($z = 13.73$, $p < .001$) and personal value of mobile
news ($z = 7.47$, $p < .001$) were both significant mediators in the relationship
between surveillance motivation and mobile news following.

In addition, the Sobel test also found that mobile news consumption
($z = 13.30$, $p < .001$) and personal value of mobile news ($z = 9.58$, $p < .001$)
were both significant mediators in the relationship between surveillance
motivation and mobile news sharing. The bootstrap test shown in Tables
8.5 and 8.6 also confirms that mobile news consumption and personal

Table 8.4 INDIRECT EFFECTS OF CITY OF RESIDENCE ON MOBILE NEWS
SHARING THROUGH HYPOTHESIZED MEDIATORS (2017–2018 SURVEYS)

Variable	B	SE (Boot)	Confidence Interval
Mobile news consumption	.083	.012	[.059, .108]

Note: 5,000 bootstrap samples were used to generate 95% bias-corrected confidence interval.

Table 8.5 INDIRECT EFFECTS OF SURVEILLANCE MOTIVATION ON MOBILE NEWS FOLLOWING THROUGH HYPOTHESIZED MEDIATORS (2017–2018 SURVEYS)

Variable	B	SE (Boot)	Confidence Interval
Mobile news consumption	.135	.010	[.115, .156]
Personal value of mobile news	.040	.009	[.023, .057]

Note: 5,000 bootstrap samples were used to generate 95% bias-corrected confidence interval.

Table 8.6 INDIRECT EFFECTS OF SURVEILLANCE MOTIVATION ON MOBILE NEWS SHARING THROUGH HYPOTHESIZED MEDIATORS (2017–2018 SURVEYS)

Variable	B	SE (Boot)	Confidence Interval
Mobile news consumption	.111	.009	[.093, .193]
Personal value of mobile news	.058	.008	[.042, .074]

Note: 5,000 bootstrap samples were used to generate 95% bias-corrected confidence interval.

value of mobile news mediated the effect of surveillance motivation on both mobile news following and sharing.

Perceived Credibility

To examine the direct and indirect effects of freedom of the press, a third exogenous variable at the societal level in our study, on mobile news credibility, we built a fifth model that examines the theoretical linkages among freedom of the press, reliance on traditional media, mobile news consumption, perceived utility of mobile news, perceived appeal of mobile news, and mobile news credibility. In the model presented in Figure 8.5, mobile news credibility was treated as the dependent variable, while the other four predictors (i.e., reliance on traditional media, mobile news consumption, perceived utility of mobile news, and perceived appeal of mobile news) served as mediators.

As illustrated in Figure 8.5, the proposed model predicts that levels of press freedom will affect reliance on traditional media, which affects mobile news consumption, which then impacts perceived utility and perceived appeal of mobile news, which will in turn affect mobile news credibility. SEM analyses show that although the chi-square for the model was significant, $\chi^2 = 2573.30$, $df = 241$, $p < .001$ (χ^2/df ratio = 10.68), the comparative

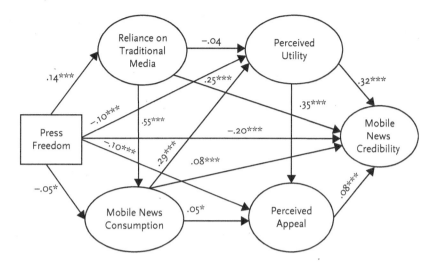

Figure 8.5 Structural Equation Model of Predictors of Mobile News Credibility (2017–2018 Surveys)
Note: Measured variables are represented by squares or rectangles, while latent variables are shown in ovals.
Credit: Ran Wei and Ven-hwei Lo

fit index (CFI = .95), the normal fit index (NFI = .93), the Tucker Lewis index (TLI = .91), and the root mean square error of approximation (RMSEA = .057) indicate that the model stands. The model explained 2.0% of the variance in reliance on traditional media, 29.4% in mobile news consumption, 8.3% in perceived utility of mobile news, 15.0% in perceived appeal of mobile news, and 29.6% in mobile news credibility.

According to results in Figure 8.5, SEM indicated that levels of press freedom had a significantly direct but negative effect on mobile news credibility ($ß = -.20$, $p < .001$). Moreover, press freedom had a direct effect on reliance on traditional media ($ß = .14$, $p < .001$), mobile news consumption ($ß = -.05$, $p < .05$), perceived utility of mobile news ($ß = -.10$, $p < .001$), and perceived appeal of mobile news ($ß = -.10$, $p < .001$). Reliance on traditional news was significantly associated with mobile news consumption ($ß = .55$, $p < .001$) and mobile news credibility ($ß = .25$, $p < .001$). Mobile news consumption had a significant effect on perceived utility of mobile news ($ß = .29$, $p < .001$), perceived appeal of mobile news ($ß = .05$, $p < .05$), and mobile news credibility ($ß = .08$, $p < .01$). Perceived utility of mobile news also had a significant effect on perceived appeal of mobile news ($ß = .35$, $p < .001$) and mobile news credibility ($ß = .32$, $p < .001$). Perceived appeal of mobile news was significantly associated with mobile news credibility ($ß = .08$, $p < .001$).

Although reliance on traditional news significantly enhanced mobile news consumption and mobile news credibility, it did not significantly relate to perceived utility and appeal of mobile news. This makes sense; experience using traditional media for news differs from that of consuming news via the mobile phone.

We conducted mediation analyses next to test the direct and indirect effects of press freedom on mobile news credibility. We were interested in exploring *whether* and *how* perceived utility and perceived appeal of mobile news would mediate the impact of freedom of the press and mobile news consumption on perceptions of mobile news credibility.

Two Sobel tests were conducted. Results show that the z score for the mediation path through perceived utility of mobile news was -4.02 ($p < .001$) and the path through perceived appeal of mobile news had a z score of -6.43 ($p < .001$). These results indicate that perceived utility and perceived appeal of mobile news were statistically significant mediators in the relationship between freedom of the press and mobile news credibility. That is, the two mediators mitigated the effect of press freedom on credibility.

Similarly, perceived utility and perceived appeal of mobile news are also two potential mediators in the relationship between mobile news consumption and mobile news credibility. Results of the Sobel tests indicate that the mediation path through perceived utility of mobile news had a z score of 12.25 ($p < .001$), and the z score for the path through perceived appeal of mobile news was 7.75 ($p < .001$). These results suggest that perceived utility of mobile news and perceived appeal of mobile news mediated the effect of mobile news consumption on credibility.

An additional bootstrap test also demonstrated that perceived utility and perceived appeal of mobile news were significant mediators in the relationship between freedom of the press and mobile news credibility and between mobile news consumption and mobile news credibility.

Results of the bootstrap test are summarized respectively in Tables 8.7 and 8.8.

Table 8.7 INDIRECT EFFECTS OF PRESS FREEDOM ON MOBILE NEWS CREDIBILITY THROUGH HYPOTHESIZED MEDIATORS (2017–2018 SURVEYS)

Variable	B	SE (Boot)	Confidence Interval
Perceived utility of mobile news	−.017	.004	[−.035, −.009]
Perceived appeal of mobile news	−.010	.002	[−.015, −.006]

Note: 5,000 bootstrap samples were used to generate 95% bias-corrected confidence interval.

Table 8.8 INDIRECT EFFECTS OF MOBILE NEWS CONSUMPTION ON MOBILE
NEWS CREDIBILITY THROUGH HYPOTHESIZED MEDIATORS (2017–2018
SURVEYS)

Variable	B	SE (Boot)	Confidence Interval
Perceived utility of mobile news	.112	.011	[.091, .134]
Perceived appeal of mobile news	.027	.006	[.017, .039]

Note: 5,000 bootstrap samples were used to generate 95% bias-corrected confidence interval.

Knowledge

Finally, although there has been plenty of literature regarding the impact
of news media on knowledge about current events, the role of social factors
such as information accessibility in acquiring political knowledge, however,
is rarely explored. To examine the interrelationships among the information accessibility of a society, which represents the exogenous variable at
the societal level; need for orientation; mobile news consumption; news
following; and knowledge about the North Korea–U.S. relationship, we
proposed the sixth model. As Figure 8.6 depicts, the model starts with information accessibility, which affects need for orientation, which leads to
mobile news consumption and following mobile news, which in turn lead
to knowledge acquisition. In doing so, we theorized that learning from
mobile news is a process driven by information accessibility and need for

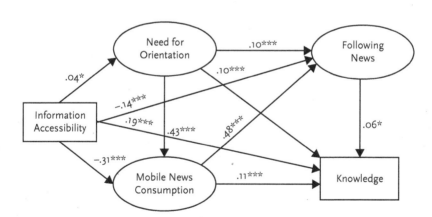

Figure 8.6 Structural Equation Model of Predictors of Knowledge about the North Korea–
U.S. relationship (2017–2018 Surveys)
Note: Measured variables are represented by squares or rectangles, while latent variables are shown in ovals.
Credit: Ran Wei and Ven-hwei Lo

orientation, which are mediated by mobile news consumption and following the news.

Accordingly, in the last model, we anticipated that respondents from societies of lower information accessibility but with a higher need for orientation would be motivated to consume mobile news to be informed about the relationship between North Korea and the United States, engage in following the news, and then learn from the news. Thus, we expected that this learning process by mediators would lead to the most knowledge gain about the North Korea–U.S. relationship.

To test the proposed model, we implemented SEM. Results indicate that although the chi-square for the model was significant, $X^2 = 1318.31$, $df = 114, p < .001$ (X^2/df ratio = 11.56), the comparative fit index (CFI = .96), the Tucker Lewis index (TLI = .93), the normal fit index (NFI = .96), and the root mean square error of approximation (RMSEA = .059) indicate that the model stands. The model explained 0.2% of the variance in need for orientation, 26.7% in mobile news consumption, 33.2% in news-following behavior, and 6.4% in knowledge about the North Korea–U.S. relationship.

As SEM in Figure 8.6 shows, information accessibility had a weak but significant effect on need for orientation ($B = .04, p < .05$), a strong but negative effect on mobile news consumption ($B = -.31, p < .001$), a significant and negative effect on news-following behavior ($B = -.14, p < .001$), and a significant and positive effect on knowledge about the North Korea–U.S. relationship ($B = .19, p < .001$). These results indicate that the more that digital information is accessible in society, the less that respondents living in the society are motivated to consume news via the mobile phone, and the less they follow the mobile news. Conversely, the less that digital information is accessible in society, the more that respondents living in the society feel motivated to consume news on the mobile phone, and the more they followed the mobile news.

In addition, need for orientation had a significant effect on mobile news consumption ($B = .43, p < .001$), news following ($B = .10, p < .001$), and knowledge about the North Korea–U.S. relationship ($B = .10, p < .001$). Mobile news consumption was significantly associated with news following ($B = .48, p < .001$) and knowledge ($B = .11, p < .001$). News following also had a weak but significant effect on the knowledge about the North Korea–U.S. relationship ($B = .06, p < .05$).

Additional tests were performed to examine *whether* and *how* mobile news consumption and mobile news following influenced the impact of information accessibility and need for orientation on knowledge about North Korea–U.S. relations. The two mediators in the relationship between information accessibility and knowledge are mobile news consumption

Table 8.9 INDIRECT EFFECTS OF INFORMATION ACCESSIBILITY ON KNOWLEDGE ABOUT THE NORTH KOREA-U.S. RELATIONSHIP THROUGH HYPOTHESIZED MEDIATORS (2017-2018 SURVEYS)

Variable	B	SE (Boot)	Confidence Interval
Mobile news consumption	−.017	.004	[−.025, −.009]
Following mobile news	−.010	.002	[−.015, −.006]

Note: 5,000 bootstrap samples were used to generate 95% bias-corrected confidence interval.

and mobile news following. Results of the Sobel test showed that the z score for the mediation path through mobile news consumption was −5.81 ($p < .001$); the path through mobile news following had a z score of −5.78 ($p < .001$). Thus, the Sobel tests revealed that mobile news consumption and mobile news following were significant suppressor variables in the relationship between information accessibility and knowledge. The relationship between information accessibility and knowledge was enhanced by mobile news consumption and mobile news following.

Similarly, mobile news consumption and mobile news following are the potential mediators in the relationship between need for orientation and knowledge. Results of more Sobel tests indicate that the mediation path through mobile news consumption had a z score of 3.68 ($p < .001$), and the z score for the path through mobile news following was 2.10 ($p < .05$). Thus, the Sobel tests also confirmed that mobile news consumption and mobile news following were significant mediators in the relationship between need for orientation and knowledge. These indicate that need for orientation can influence knowledge about international events indirectly through mobile news consumption and mobile news following.

An additional bootstrap test also demonstrates that mobile news consumption and mobile news following are significant mediators in the relationship between need for orientation and knowledge. As Tables 8.9 and 8.10 show, these additional analyses suggest that information accessibility

Table 8.10 INDIRECT EFFECTS OF NEED FOR ORIENTATION ON KNOWLEDGE ABOUT THE NORTH KOREA-U.S. RELATIONSHIP THROUGH HYPOTHESIZED MEDIATORS (2017-2018 SURVEYS)

Variable	B	SE (Boot)	Confidence Interval
Mobile news consumption	.112	.011	[.091, .134]
Following mobile news	.027	.006	[.017, .039]

Note: 5,000 bootstrap samples were used to generate 95% bias-corrected confidence interval.

and need for orientation were significantly related to knowledge about North Korea–U.S. relations both directly and indirectly through mobile news consumption and mobile news-following behavior.

SUMMARY OF KEY FINDINGS

Because regression analyses fall short of testing the effects of mediators on dependent variables, we proposed and tested a series of mediation models to examine the direct and indirect effects of exogenous factors (e.g., city of residence, smartphone ownership, press freedom, and information accessibility) on the four dependent variables of our study. The key findings of the mediation analyses are summarized as follows:

- City of residence, smartphone ownership, surveillance motivation, and personal value of mobile news are significant predictors of mobile news consumption with direct and positive effects. Respondents who lived in Shanghai, owned a smartphone, had a higher level of surveillance motivation, and perceived mobile news to be useful were more likely to consume mobile news. Moreover, city of residence at the societal level and smartphone ownership are also indirectly associated with mobile news consumption through the two mediators of surveillance motivation and personal value of mobile news. Taken together, these findings indicate that heightened levels of surveillance motivation and belief that mobile news has more personal value, both of which are conditioned by city of residence and smartphone ownership, are likely to lead to higher levels of mobile news consumption.
- Mobile news consumption and personal value of mobile news are all significantly and positively associated with mobile news following. Further, the relationships between city of residence and mobile news following and between smartphone ownership and mobile news following are mediated by surveillance motivation, mobile news consumption, and personal value of mobile news. The association between surveillance motivation and news following are also mediated by mobile new consumption and personal value of mobile news.
- Freedom of the press, the third exogenous variable; reliance on traditional media; mobile news consumption; perceived utility; and appeal of mobile news all have significant effects on mobile news credibility. The effect of press freedom of a society, however, is negative. Moreover, freedom of the press has an indirect effect on mobile news credibility through reliance on traditional media, mobile news consumption, perceived utility,

and appeal of mobile news. That is, freedom of the press affects reliance on traditional media, which affects mobile news consumption, which then leads to increased perceived utility and appeal of mobile news, which in turn affect perceptions of mobile news credibility. In addition, the relationship between mobile news consumption and mobile news credibility is also mediated by perceived utility and perceived appeal of mobile news. Perceived utility and perceived appeal of mobile news not only influence the relationship between freedom of the press and mobile news credibility but also mediate the relationship between mobile consumption and mobile news credibility.

- All of these variables—information accessibility, need for orientation, mobile news consumption, and news following—were significant predictors of knowledge about the relationship between North Korea and the United States. Additionally, the relationship between information accessibility, a fourth exogenous variable at the societal level, and knowledge about North Korea–U.S. relations was influenced by need for orientation, mobile news consumption, and mobile news following. Need for orientation was also indirectly associated with knowledge about the relationship through mobile news consumption and mobile news following. All these findings indicate that information accessibility can significantly influence knowledge gain from mobile news directly; at the same time, information accessibility has an indirect effect on knowledge through need for orientation, mobile news consumption, and mobile news following.

THEORETICAL INSIGHTS FROM MEDIATION ANALYSES

Previous research on mobile news consumption has overlooked the mediation effects of surveillance motivation and expectancies of mobile news as personally valuable in the relationship between smartphone ownership and mobile news consumption. By proposing a series of mediation models, we intended to clarify the effects of societal-level variables vis-à-vis individual-level variables on the studied dependent variables. The mediation analyses suggest that societal variables tend to have direct effects on mobile news consumption, engaged consumption, perceptions, and knowledge gain. Also, they have indirect effects through individual-level effects on these dependent variables. In other words, the effects of individual-level variables on mobile news consumption, engaged consumption, perceptions, and knowledge gain are derived from societal-level variables.

To illustrate, when the effect of technology on mobile news consumption is neutralized in the data from the second wave of surveys (refer to Figure 8.2), the societal impact (e.g., city of residence) seems to be smaller on the consumption behavior. Perceived personal value of mobile news, which was positively associated with city of residence in the 3G era, turned negative in the 4G era. The change over time makes sense because of China's tightening control of digital news delivered to the mobile screen. News accessed from the mobile phone seems to be recycled straight from official media outlets (i.e., CCTV and the *People's Daily*). College students in Shanghai were still motivated to access news from their phones, but they believed the news to be less usable to them in their personal lives.

Similarly, findings of mediation analyses show that the effect of smartphone ownership on mobile news consumption was also mediated by surveillance and personal value of mobile news. Consistent with the uses and gratifications approach and the expectancy theory, these findings suggest that the more users perceived the smartphone as helpful in fulfilling their informational needs, the more they used the phone for accessing news. More importantly, we clarified the role of motivation and expectancies as key mediators in affecting the behavior of news consumption when societal influences are present in structural relationships.

Findings of this chapter further indicate that mobile news consumption is directly and indirectly associated with mobile news following and sharing. High-level users of mobile news tend to engage more in mobile news-following and -sharing activities than low-level users of mobile news. Those who have a stronger perceived personal value of mobile news are more likely to engage in mobile news following and sharing in the 4G era. These findings reveal that consuming news interactively marks a notable difference between consuming news on traditional media and consuming mobile news on the smartphone.

This chapter also has sought to better understand the factors that influence credibility perceptions of mobile news by examining the societal and individual factors as well as exploring possible mediators of the relationship between press freedom and perceived mobile news credibility. We found that freedom of the press was significantly and negatively related to credibility perceptions, while perceived utility and appeal of mobile news were positively related to credibility perceptions. These findings suggest that freedom of the press was directly related to mobile news credibility; at the same time, its effect on credibility perceptions was mediated by perceived utility and perceived appeal of mobile news. The indirect pathways work as follows: press freedom negatively influences perceived utility and perceived appeal of mobile news, which in turn positively influence mobile news credibility. In addition, our findings suggest that the association between mobile news consumption and mobile news credibility is also mediated by perceived utility and perceived appeal of mobile news. Mobile news consumption positively influences perceived utility and perceived appeal of mobile news, and consequently leads to a higher rating of mobile news credibility.

All things considered, these findings expand our understanding of media credibility by explicating the mechanisms through which freedom of the press and mobile news consumption impact perceived mobile news credibility. Specifically, we found that freedom of the press as a societal variable first influenced perceived utility and perceived appeal and then indirectly influenced mobile news credibility, while the effects of perceived utility and perceived appeal were derived from press freedom. This particular finding provides additional evidence of how societal influences override that of individual-level factors in accounting for credibility perceptions of mobile news.

Similar direct and indirect effects were found regarding the role of information accessibility in influencing acquisition of political knowledge; information accessibility in a society is a significant predictor of political knowledge. But the relationship between information accessibility and knowledge is influenced by mobile news consumption and mobile news following. Although information accessibility was positively related to knowledge in its direct pathway, it had a negative impact on both mobile news consumption and mobile news following in its indirect pathways. These findings validate the incorporation of information accessibility as an exogenous variable in the theoretical model.

Additionally, past research has paid scant attention to the indirect effect of need for orientation to knowledge about international events. We found a direct and indirect pathway between need for orientation and political knowledge. Need for orientation was positively related to political knowledge. Moreover, need for orientation can predict knowledge indirectly through mobile news consumption and following.

In conclusion, information accessibility and need for orientation drive Asian college students to seek, follow, and acquire a great deal of news about international events, hence learning from it. However, college students from societies of higher information accessibility with lower need for orientation are less likely to consume and follow news about international events and learn less about it. Theoretically, these findings indicate that acquisition of political knowledge depends on not only how users are motivated to consume news via the mobile phone and following the news but also how that information accessibility at the societal level facilitates the learning by directly and indirectly influencing motivations, consumption behavior, and engaged consumption.

The implications of these findings for social shaping of new communication technologies are discussed in the next chapter, from which we draw general conclusions of our study.

CHAPTER 9

Conclusions

In Chapters 3 through 8, we analyzed the patterns and consequences of consuming news created and delivered to mobile phones, which is considered the new face of digital news. Also, consuming news anywhere and anytime on the ubiquitous mobile phone with always-on connectivity enables users to access and engage in news content in previously rare contexts such as walking down a street or waiting in line. News consumption has thus become a sort of fluid experience with unpredictable outcomes. To understand the fluid experience of news consumption via the mobile phone and examine the consequence of consuming mobile news, we explored these questions: At a time when news is more accessible than ever, will young adults in Asia actually consume it? If so, why and how? How do they evaluate the news accessed on the mobile phone? And does consuming mobile news make any difference in learning about public affairs and world events?

Taking rapid technological changes from 3G to 4G into consideration, and using two parallel surveys and a cross-societal design to examine societal influences vis-à-vis technological advances on consumption of mobile news, we have shed light on these questions among digitally savvy college students in Asia's four most mobile cities— Shanghai, Hong Kong, Singapore, and Taipei. These mega-cities are among the most technologically, economically, culturally, and politically influential cities in the Chinese-speaking part of Asia. More importantly, by focusing on consuming news via the mobile phone, we aim to situate our comparative analyses within the broad context of linking news consumption to civic interest,

News in Their Pockets. Ran Wei and Ven-hwei Lo, Oxford University Press (2021). © Oxford University Press.
DOI: 10.1093/oso/9780197523728.003.0009

civic motivation, and civic engagement, which are critical to prepare young generations to be active citizens (Tewksbury & Rittenberg, 2012).

CONSUMPTION PATTERNS

Findings from the six chapters (i.e., Chapters 3 through 8) of empirical evidence on the process and effects of mobile news consumption lead to these conclusions concerning the *why, how*, and *effects* of the consumption:

- Surveillance motivation of mobile phone use and expectancies of mobile news as interactive and personally valuable increased from the first period in 2010–2011 to the second period in 2017–2018.
- Driven by the surveillance motivation, consumption of news accessed from the mobile phone has increased noticeably across the two periods.
- Consuming news from the mobile phone stimulates engagement with the news.
- Both motivations (i.e., surveillance) and expectancies (perceived value) of mobile news matter in affecting the news consumption experience.
- Engaged consumption of mobile news is positively related to civic learning from the news.
- Mobile news fills the void left by legacy media in socializing Asia's young generations of millennials (Gen Y) and centennials (Gen Z) into active citizens.

INCREASED CONSUMPTION AND ENGAGEMENT

In Chapter 1, we highlighted two major trends in digital news: the news went mobile in the 3G era, and news that is convenient, quick, brief, and in real time via the mobile phone has gone mainstream in the 4G era. These trends drive the changing patterns of news consumption among the surveyed college students in the four Asian cities.

Taking advantage of the opportunity to access news conveniently via the phones they carry all the time, Asian college students in the four cities rode on the rising momentum of mobile news consumption. In the first wave of surveys conducted in 2010–2011, about half of the students consumed news on their phones. In the short period of eight years, all of the surveyed students became regular consumers of mobile news. The marked increase in consumption of mobile news from 2010–2011 to 2017–2018 was accompanied by the network upgrade from 3G to 4G. In the 4G era, accessing news from the deeply diffused smartphone has become widespread and routine.

Additionally, regardless of 3G or 4G networks, those students who own a smartphone consume more news than do their peers who do not own one. The Internet-empowered iPhone is credited with fueling the increased consumption of mobile news. Thus, as we anticipated, such rising patterns bear evidence of the positive impact of advances in mobile technology in news consumption.

Furthermore, our findings presented in Chapter 3 suggest that mere access to a wide range of digital outlets to read and view news content via the mobile phone does not automatically translate into consumption or increased consumption of news. News accessible via the mobile phone in one's pocket is the necessary condition, but not the only one. Motivated use of the ubiquitous mobile phone for news seeking holds the key. Asian college students who believe the mobile phone is helpful for them to stay informed of current affairs tend to consume more news from the phone. On the other hand, only a small number of students who have a low surveillance motivation consume mobile news.

Findings from our multivariable analyses indicate that surveillance motivation, which refers to the need to search for information about the world at large, is consistently the strongest predictor of mobile news consumption. Such a pattern reveals the important role of civic motivation in consuming news so as to stay informed about domestic events and world politics like presidential elections in the United States and sudden pandemic outbreaks such as COVID-19, among other news events. We have gathered compelling evidence to show that the surveyed Asian college students have become more dependent on their phones for meeting their informational needs thanks to the popular smartphone and deployment of 4G networks.

During this time period, Asian college students increased their expectancies of mobile news to be sharable and personally valuable in deciding whether to consume such news. The more these students believe that mobile news is interactive and helpful to them in schoolwork or civic life, the more they reward themselves with consuming such news.

Taken together, these findings concerning the rising patterns of mobile news consumption validate our premise made in Chapter 1 that consuming mobile news is more than simply a matter of convenience and easy access from the handy mobile phone for a fast-food diet of news content. Rather, driven by the surveillance motivation, news consumption via the mobile phone reveals a process through which Asia's young generations seek to be civically informed.

Moreover, scholars (e.g., Poindexter, 2016; Westlund, 2013) have acknowledged that the deepening diffusion of mobile phones and smart devices has created a new type of news consumer, one who chooses smartphones and tablets over laptops and desktops to access and consume news. These consumers also tend to skip traditional news media as sources of news. Our study shows some support for the observation that the mobile phone entails an emerging media that has become central to the way young people in Asia access and consume news.

Nevertheless, the news outlets they access the most via their phones are mostly legacy media and established news organizations. Students in our focus groups in the four cities mentioned BBC News, *The Guardian*, CNN, the *Straits Times*, *South China Morning Post*, *Apple Daily*, ET Today, CCTV, the *People's Daily*, *The Paper* (Pengbai), and *Beijing News*, among others, as their favorite news sources. They tell us that in a high-choice media environment, they prefer to consume news from trusted outlets over other types of news content online. They appear to regard the legacy media as the gold standard of digital news content. Thus, their reliance on reputable news outlets suggests *a mainstreaming effect* of mobile news on Asia's young generations.

Moreover, we found mobile news consumption exemplifies a type of engaged consumption, which expands users' access to news and enriches their consuming experiences. Findings presented in Chapter 5 show that consumers of mobile news tend to gain a deeper consuming experience by following and sharing news. Taking action after accessing the news such as clicking "like," "repost," or "retweet" for links to news and talking with others about the news have become widespread. Consistent with the literature of consuming news online (e.g., Larsson, 2019; Meijer & Kormelink, 2015), consuming news on the mobile phone stimulates and amplifies engagement with the news. Thus, we conclude that consuming news on the mobile phone is characteristically *social, interactive,* and *participative.*

Similar to the positive effect on increased consumption of mobile news, technology matters in affecting user engagement with news accessed from the phone. The evidence generated from the two surveys supports our prediction that user motivation and the empowering tools afforded by the smartphone on 4G networks will drive engagement with mobile news. Take following news via the mobile phone as an example. Following news on mobile phones was less common in the first period of surveys. However, it became more prevalent and frequent as wireless network technologies evolved from 3G to 4G. The routine of consuming and following mobile news shows the most explanatory power for sharing mobile news with others in the second period of surveys. The smartphone itself was found to be a significant contributor to mobile news consumption, and thus an enabling factor in facilitating engagement with mobile news.

Furthermore, adding new evidence to the literature (S. Lee, 2015; Meijer & Kormelink, 2015; R. Wei & Lo, 2015), we find that those who have a stronger surveillance motivation tend to consume news a great deal on a smartphone and are consequently more likely to be engaged with the news by following tweets and blogs; heavy users of mobile news tend to share all sorts of news they consume on the smartphone. These findings lead to our next conclusion that *it takes both a motivated user and the most updated technology to attain engaged consumption of news.*

Mobile News and Socialization of Young Generations into Citizens

In an era of high risk in news consumption due to the flooding of ambiguous and questionable news sources, our findings indicate that Asian college students are savvy consumers of news accessed from their phones. They do not simply feast on the news that is easy and quick. On the contrary, our findings suggest that they have a healthy dose of skepticism toward news content viewed on the mobile phone. Practically, as we presented in Chapter 6, they critically evaluate the credibility of news sources to decide what to consume and what to avoid. Their heuristic is to rely on familiar and trusted news outlets, online and offline. Given the variety of smartphones, platforms, and news sources targeting the mobile screen, it does not surprise us that the credibility of mobile news in general is thought to be inferior to that of traditional news media. The result is largely consistent with the literature (X. Li & Zhang, 2018; H. Zhang, 2013).

Findings of Chapter 6 further suggest that both form (appeal/format/style) and expectancies (perceived utility) of mobile news matter in affecting the experience of mobile news among the surveyed Asian college students. To be specific, perceived utility and appealing presentation of mobile news positively affect the perceived credibility of such news. Our findings further show that students who rely on traditional media as news sources are likely to rate the credibility of mobile news as high. These patterns indicate that the habit of relying on traditional media as news sources generates trust in news consumed on the mobile screen.

On the other hand, our cross-societal analyses reveal a sense of ambivalence emerging from perceived credibility of mobile news. Asian college students in our study, especially those in Shanghai and Singapore, tend to view mobile news as reliable but are critical about its limited diversity in perspectives and lack of alternatives to the government point of view. To them, news consumed via the mobile phone is reliable, but something is missing. This sort of mixed feeling makes sense. The students in those two cities prefer news outlets that are closely related to the government- or state-run media organizations. Historically, official media are highly rated for being credible because they represent the official voice. And because they are channels of official voices, these media outlets do not offer sufficient alternative perspectives in news reporting.

The most interesting finding about mobile news credibility is a virtuous circle in the making—the more the Asian college students consume mobile news, the more trust they have in the news. The more trust they have in mobile news, the more they consume it. Thus, reliance and trust reinforce each other positively in affecting the consumption of mobile news. These patterns have implications for understanding the most pressing questions of our study: Does mobile news matter? What is the effect of consuming news via the mobile phone?

One of the paradoxes concerning mobile news is that although mobile technology has significantly reduced barriers to accessing news anywhere, anytime, the cognitive threshold of active consumption of such news has become higher. Evidence presented in Chapter 7 shows that consuming news indeed is positively related to civic learning from the news. Using the North Korea and U.S. relationship as a knowledge measure, which requires civic motivation and has a high threshold of cognitive involvement, we examined the learning effects of mobile news.

Findings in Chapter 7 indicate that Asian college students who consumed mobile news heavily tend to be more knowledgeable about North Korea–U.S. relations than were their peers who consumed less news via their phones. Moreover, active consumption of mobile news appears to facilitate learning from the news that they tracked—those who were engaged in news-following activities answered more questions correctly about North Korea–U.S. relations than did those who rarely followed news events from the mobile phone.

These findings lead to the next conclusion, that consuming news via the mobile phone is conducive to acquiring political knowledge. R. Yu (2019) reported that accidental exposure to news, mindless scrolling through the screen, and even random browsing of fleeting headlines were more common than motivated use of news. However, we found that Asian college students who have a higher need for orientation tend to consume more news from the mobile phone and learn more from the news, thereby expanding their overall knowledge about current affairs. The ubiquitous mobile phone not only offers unprecedented access to news but also facilitates civic learning from the news.

We argue throughout the book that the stake in consumption of mobile news is high for shaping young generations into engaged citizens in the 21st century. The systematic empirical evidence we generated from this large-scale study suggests that mobile news plays an important role for civic-minded and motivated Asian college students to seek, engage with, and eventually learn from the news. Accordingly, we conclude that similar to legacy mass media, the mobile phone (i.e., the media in motion) fills the *role to socialize* millennials and centennials in Confucian Asia.

MOBILE TECHNOLOGY AND SOCIAL CHANGE

As we documented in Chapter 1, Asia is at the forefront of the ongoing mobile revolution. The four selected cities in our study are Asia's most mobile cities with world-class IT infrastructure. Our cross-societal comparative approach to understanding consumption of mobile news enables us to explore the broad issues of social change in Asian societies. At the same time, the data from the two parallel surveys provide us with the rare opportunity to examine the impact of technology on social change in the studied cities. Findings from empirical evidence shed light on a number of broad and enduring issues concerning communication technology and society, including the following:

- Mobile news consumption and the tension between technology and social control
- Whether and how the mobile phone as a gateway to access news fulfills a democratic function in keeping citizens informed
- The persisting gender gap in mobile news consumption
- The dynamic interplay between technology and society
- Whether the mobile phone, by bringing personal freedom to millions of users in Asia, will also result in "technologies of freedom" in disseminating news

Communication Technology and Social Change in Asia

First, our large-scale comparative study of trends and patterns in mobile news consumption aims to understand the process of the consumption and effects, with a focus on the role of individual-level variables (e.g., demographics, motivations, perception, and media reliance) versus societal-level factors (e.g., type of press system, level of press freedom, digital information accessibility, and openness of the media environment) in accounting for these trends and patterns. Mobile news as our analytical focus enables us to illuminate the tension between communication technology and social control. The social changes are made amid a tug of war between technological development, which favors grassroots users who can freely choose media outlets to get news that matters to them, and the authorities, who would attempt to place political control over the freedom of media choice and the free flow of digital information.

Specifically, the young generations of millennials and centennials in Asia who grew up with the Internet and the mobile phone expect free flow and exchange of digital information. News is the most popular digital content that they consume via their phones (Shim et al., 2015). From data collected in the two waves of surveys in four of Asia's leading cities, we documented that Asian college students are indeed what Westlund (2013) called "a new type of news consumer" who prefers phones over PCs to seek news, tends to engage with the news, and learns something about currents affairs from the news. Our findings suggest that advances in technology such as the diffusion of smartphones and the network upgrades from 3G to 4G made those possible. The governments in the four studied cities led the rest of Asia in deploying the most updated mobile communications networks. Technologically, they have caught up with the West in building state-of-the-art IT infrastructure. Our data show that consumption of news accessed from the mobile phone among college students in Shanghai, Hong Kong, Singapore, and Taipei doubled in the 4G era as compared to the 3G era.

On the other hand, just as the Internet-powered smartphone has become an essential gateway for young people to consume news in the 4G era, mobile news consumption is increasingly under tightening socio-political control. We documented in Chapter 4 that authorities in Shanghai and Singapore have passed laws (the Broadcasting Act in Singapore and the Telecommunications Act in China) that impose varying degrees of control, such as censorship of news content created and distributed on the mobile phone. The State Internet Information Office was created in China to crack down on user-generated content (UGC). Additionally, the Chinese government at all levels has tightened ideological control over mobile communications by limiting access to digital media and websites, both domestic and foreign. As a result, official media command a dominant presence in mobile news outlets.

These restrictive measures and laws for social control result in marked differences in the software of information technology. Our findings about knowledge gain in Chapter 7 indicate that information accessibility in a city influences how much the surveyed Asian college students learn from mobile news. In fact, the extent to which citizens in a society can have free and full access to digital information is the strongest predictor of knowledge about a major international issue affecting the Asia-Pacific region. The empirical evidence we have gathered suggests that social changes are made amid the tension between tightening socio-political control and rapid technological advances.

Accordingly, with regard to the question of whether the mobile phone as a gateway to access news fulfills a democratic function in keeping young citizens informed, we reach the conclusion that the hardware of mobile communication is important. Moreover, the software also matters. In other words, it takes both hardware (networks and smartphones) and software (global outlook, access, and openness) to produce informed and engaged citizens. The more accessible the information is in a society, the easier for young citizens to seek and consume news about domestic and international politics, which in turn facilitates learning from the news. Conversely, in a society where information is less accessible, there are fewer opportunities for citizens to access a broad range of diverse news outlets about domestic events and international happenings. The restricted access hinders learning from the news.

Gender Gap in News Consumption and Knowledge

Another major and persistent social differentiator in our study turns out to be gender. In all five dependent measures we analyzed in Chapters 3 through 7, a significant gender gap is found, especially in mobile news consumption and political knowledge. Specifically, female college students in the four studied Asian cities love to use the mobile phone to communicate with family and friends, whereas male students prefer to use the phone as a tool for information seeking. Driven primarily by social motives, the female students consumed less news accessed from their phones as compared to their male peers. In addition, they scored lower on knowledge questions than did male students.

All of these gender differences are consistent with the existent literature (Leung & Wei, 2000; Rakow, 1992; R. Wei & Lo, 2006). Our data revalidated the generalization that gender functions as a social differentiator in political communication. In the context of consuming mobile news, our conclusion is mixed. The good news is that the gender gap in terms of owning a smartphone is reduced or eliminated (our second-wave surveys showed that regardless of gender, nearly all students owned a smartphone). Additionally, gender difference in consuming mobile news narrowed over time, largely because mobile news consumption by both male and female respondents increased in the eight-year period from 2010–2011 to 2017–2018.

Nevertheless, the political knowledge gap between male and female college students remains, 20 years after our first study (Leung & Wei, 1999b) in the early years of mobile communication. Although equal numbers of male and female college students own a mobile phone, the device has yet to narrow the gender-based knowledge gap. Thus, social change in terms of equality in gender role seems to be slow; technology offers no quick or magic fix. On the contrary, we consider gender as another headwind that information technology faces in ushering in social change.

Considering that the role of women is still limited in the male-dominated politics of Asia, we speculate that female students in college may have a sense of limited use of news and political knowledge. If this is the case, they are not motivated to seek news actively or use news to empower themselves as much as male students. This is a broader social issue that calls for more thorough research.

The Political Peril Threatening the Promise of Technology of Freedom

The ultimate goal of our study is to examine the interplay between an empowering communication technology and constraining social systems in the context of mobile news consumption. Thus, we have explored the interplay of a decentralizing technology that promises freedom and the socio-political context in which the technology is used, in hopes of shedding light on the great technology-versus-society debate. To achieve this, we have conceptualized consumption of mobile news as a fitting case that exemplifies the conflict between "technology of freedom" (Pool, 1983) and state control of media in hierarchical societies with an authoritarian tradition. We proposed in Chapter 2 that technology would have the potential to positively impact mobile news consumption but that the political structure of a society (democratic vs. authoritarian) that provides the context of consumption might inhibit the technology's potential.

Our empirical findings in general show that the 4G-supported smartphone empowers Asian college students not only to consume news anywhere, anytime, but also to become engaged in the news and gain knowledge from the engaged consumption. However, these patterns did not hold for the Shanghai sample. China's largest city is equally advanced in building

the same worldwide standardized mobile communication technologies—
3G and 4G—as the other three Asian cities. Surveyed college students in
Shanghai were found to have the highest surveillance motivation, to have
the highest expectancies for mobile news, and to consume more news on
their phones, and were more engaged in following and sharing the news
than were their peers in Hong Kong, Singapore, and Taipei.

Nevertheless, their knowledge score was the lowest. Consistent with
past research (e.g., R. Wei et al., 2014), we link the high level of mobile
news consumption to the absence of press freedom in Shanghai. We further attribute the differential result of learning from mobile news in the
Shanghai sample to the lack of accessibility to digital information in the
city. It is clear that the constraints that originate from the socio-political
systems have a negative impact on the outcomes of the consumption. That
is, socio-political factors impede the potential positive outcomes of mobile
news consumption facilitated by the technology.

Further evidence is presented in multivariate analyses, in which the
strengths of relationships between technological factors and the dependent measures are weakened across the two time periods. Smartphone
ownership, which explains more variance than any predictor in the first
surveys, completely lost its predictor power over time because almost all
the respondents in the second surveys owned a smartphone. Accordingly,
the total variance accounted for by the regression model on mobile news
consumption with the same set of predictors in 2017–2018 was only a third
of the 2010–2011 model.

Similarly, in the 4G era, when the share of smartphone users as well as
the number of smartphone-only users increased, individual-level factors,
such as motivations and types of mobile phone, also lost the explanatory
power over mobile news-following behavior. With regard to sharing mobile
news, demographics (with the exception of city of residence), smartphone
ownership, and motivations of mobile phone use have proven to be relatively weak predictors. At the same time, socio-political factors such as
city of residence have emerged as an important predictor of news-sharing
behavior.

Finally, the six structural equation models presented in Chapter 8
generated additional evidence about societal factors as being more important than individual and technological factors in influencing mobile news consumption. Findings of mediation analyses help us clarify
the role of surveillance motivation and expectancies of mobile news
as key mediators in affecting the relationship between societal factors
(e.g., city of residence and smartphone rate) and mobile news consumption. Similarly, level of freedom of the press as a societal variable first

negatively influenced perceived utility and perceived appeal of mobile news, which in turn positively influenced mobile news credibility. Thus, freedom of the press has both direct and indirect effects on mobile news credibility. Additionally, information accessibility at the societal level was found to enhance learning from mobile news directly and indirectly through need for orientation, consumption, and engagement. Taken together, the mediation analyses provide additional evidence of how societal influences override that of individual-level factors in predicting the studied dependent variables.

In sum, our findings support the proposition that technological advances in mobile communication facilitate news consumption. At its early stage, technology enables its users to access news easily and conveniently. But as the technology matures, its potential in bringing about fundamental benefits such as freedom is constrained by socio-political impositions of authorities. In the eyes of an authoritarian government, technology may be nothing but value-free tools to serve the existing political system. Remarks from Ms. Fu Ying, China's former ambassador to the United Kingdom, best illustrate this point of view.

In a Q&A exchange with Nancy Pelosi, the U.S. Speaker of the House, about the West's sanctions of Huawei, the ambassador said:

> We – I think my knowledge of the, how the world works, is that technology is a tool. And, China thinks its reform started forty years ago, have introduced all kinds of Western technologies: Microsoft, IBM, Amazon. They are all active in China. And, since we, since we started with 1st G, 2nd G, 3rd G, 4th G, all the technologies came from Western countries, from the developed world, and China has maintained its political system, the system lead by the Communist Party has become successful, it's not threatened by the technologies. (quote from Fu Ying via Pelosi, 2020)

All things considered, we reach the conclusion that technology is a positive factor in expanding the access of news, in enabling increased consumption, and in stimulating engaged consumption of the news. But the influences of socio-political factors such as political and media systems increased in accounting for effects on mobile news consumption. Therefore, our findings offer insights into the enduring debate of technology determinism in that technological innovations matter in the early stages of its diffusion. However, as the technology matures and its use becomes routinized, the uses are increasingly subject to societal constraints of political power. In short, consumption of mobile news represents an illuminating case of social shaping of technology.

LIMITATIONS OF STUDY AND FUTURE DIRECTIONS OF RESEARCH

The findings of our study should be interpreted in the context of several limitations. First, our study of the process and effects of mobile news consumption focused on audience motivations, behaviors, and perceptions. News content that was actually consumed by the surveyed college students in the four selected cities was not part of our research, which limited our ability to link the content of hard news to consumption patterns. For instance, was political news or sports news consumed the most? What type of news content was followed and shared the most? With whom did users share the most and why? Including news content would shed further light on the questions of news following and sharing, a direction for future research. Future research should include content of mobile news as part of the design to establish an empirical basis to test the relationships between consuming specific types of news via the mobile phone and interest in politics. With news content being part of the study, the effects of mobile news consumption on media credibility ratings and political knowledge would likely be more nuanced.

Related to the first limitation, self-publishing and citizen journalism on mobile social platforms, like WeChat, Line, and WhatsApp, constitute a rising segment of digital journalism. However, news content produced by citizen journalists was not differentiated in the present study. Future research needs to expand the scope of mobile news by analyzing user-generated news content.

Moreover, recent research (R. Yu, 2019) suggests that accidental or random exposure to news via the mobile phone and devices is more common than motivational use of news. Others (Valeriani & Vaccari, 2016) have reported that accidental exposure to political information on social media is positively and significantly correlated with online participation. However, we did not measure or test any irrational use of the mobile phone to access news. To overcome this limitation, future research can expand into the accidental or random use of mobile news.

Analytically, we focused on testing the effects of two macro-level factors—press freedom and information accessibility—on credibility perceptions of mobile news and political knowledge. There is no doubt that the four studied cities also vary across other macro-level measures. Future studies can build on our findings to account for the effects of other macro-level variables. In addition, the samples used in this study included educated, largely affluent people from Confucian Asian societies. Findings may not be generalizable to other East Asian societies such as Japan or Korea, much less the rest of the Southeast Asian countries like Thailand.

Finally, a survey is just a snapshot in time, and conditions may have changed since it was taken. It may be particularly true with the fast-evolving mobile technologies and smartphones. Therefore, we think it helps to remind the reader that our extrapolation and generalizations are based on data that were collected from particular points in the recent past.

THE FUTURE OF MOBILE NEWS

A look into the future of news created and delivered to the mobile phone may be an appropriate way to end this concluding chapter. At the dawn of 5G, ubiquitous mobile communication will speed up trends in delivering news via smaller and smarter mobile devices such as smart watches and wearables, and news accessed from the mobile phone will further evolve. At the same time, newer digital technologies (e.g., virtual reality [VR], algorithm, and big data) will lead to newer tools to package, deliver, and distribute news to mobile phones and devices.

5G and Media Convergence

The hype surrounding the next generation of wireless communications of 5G promises Internet connections that are at least 40 times faster than 4G LTE. The coming together of networks will speed up the trend of media convergence toward the smartphone. 5G smartphones will likely be the information hub and the indispensable interface for interaction with the Internet of Things (IoT), such as driverless cars and smart homes.

4G networks have led to the rise of popular video social network sites such as TikTok. It is expected that ubiquitous mobile communication in the 5G era, which started in 2019, will further increase access to news and public information from home appliances and wearables. In addition, 5G phones will likely be capable of presenting news content in an environment created by fast 3D graphics and forms of 360 videos (augmented reality [AR] and virtual reality [VR]).

AR, VR, and Mobile News

Generated by computers, realistic 3D computer graphics known as VR and related technology AR represent a new type of interface in a digital 3D environment. Storytelling with 360-degree video provides users with a sensory experience of news broader and deeper than just reading or watching it. Experiments in immersion journalism using VR technologies may extend to consumption of news, lending it a sense of being there (Sirkkunen & Uskali, 2019).

Phone-powered Gear VR mobile headsets will be one of the means to experience VR news. Considering the large number of mobile phone users worldwide, mobile VR headsets packaged with different sensing and presentation technologies will take mobile news to the next level—a 3D environment. A report by the Reuters Institute (Watson, 2017) found that leading news organizations such as CNN (CNN VR News), the BBC (BBC VR Hub, Canvas), and the *New York Times* (NYT VR News App) have experimented to integrate VR stories into their news productions in the form of 360-degree videos watched on smartphones.

A FEW FINAL WORDS

In closing, the idea of this book originates from curiosity about the mobile phone's predecessor—the pager—as a mass medium, a kind of marginal idea in the late 1990s; the book is now completed at a time when smartphones serve as a lifeline of critical information and crisis support for millions around the world, during the global COVID-19 pandemic. Thanks to mobile news consumption and high consumer engagement, information about virus testing and quarantines was able to reach millions of residents within hours. The accessibility of such information probably saved lives and served to keep families healthy and communities strong. Without the smartphone, it is possible the pandemic would have been much worse.

The amazing change in only two decades is but one illustration of what the fastest-diffused communication technology in human history means to its users. As 5G dawns, technological advances toward smarter and smaller tools and devices will further shape the future of news created and delivered to the next generation of smartphones supported by 5G networks. The prospect of 5G phones as a converged medium with VR capability will be life changing again and may arrive sooner than we think. There is no doubt that the patterns and issues of mobile news consumption will be more complicated, the relationship between technology and social change will be more complex, and the interplay between technology and society may be more difficult to untangle. In this sense, the best years of mobile news research are yet to come.

APPENDIX A
Survey Methodology

POPULATION OF STUDY

Data were collected from two waves of large-scale parallel surveys of college students in four Asian cities—Hong Kong, Shanghai, Singapore, and Taipei—in 2010–2011 and 2017–2018. Two considerations led to the choice of college students in the four Asian cities as the target population: First, the future of news was believed to be in the hands of young people who grew up with the Internet and the mobile phone. Their news consumption behavior and habits will be critical to the decline and renaissance of news. Second, achieved data show that college students were early adopters of the mobile phone (Leung & Wei, 1999a, 2000). Almost all of them owned a smartphone (e.g., 95.5%, Focus Taiwan, 2018) and relied on the phone to access the Internet. A study of news apps (Weiss, 2013) reported that young adults were heavy consumers of news on their smartphones.

SAMPLING PROCEDURES

A multistage cluster sampling plan was used in drawing the samples across the four cities. In the first step, six universities were selected from the complete lists of existing universities in Hong Kong, Shanghai, and Taipei. The next section lists all the sampled universities. In Singapore, the two largest and most comprehensive universities were selected (the other four universities specializing in particular disciplines such as business were excluded). In the second step, three general education classes were randomly drawn from the selected universities. The research procedures were reviewed and approved by institutional review boards (IRBs).

With prior permission of instructors, self-administered questionnaires in Chinese were distributed in the selected classes in China, Hong Kong, and Taiwan. English questionnaires were used in Singapore. Participation was totally voluntary, and participants were assured of confidentiality and privacy. Respondents in the surveys did not receive any monetary incentive or extra credit. The fieldwork of collecting data started in October–November 2017 and ended in March 2018.

List of Universities Sampled in the Four Asian Cities

1. Shanghai: Shanghai Jiao Tong University, East China Normal University, Shanghai University, Fudan University, University of Shanghai for Science and Technology, Shanghai International Studies University
2. Hong Kong: Chinese University of Hong Kong, City University of Hong Kong, Hang Seng University of Hong Kong, Hong Kong Baptist University, Hong Kong University, Hong Kong Polytechnic University
3. National Taipei University of Technology, National Taipei University of Education, Ming Chuan University, Chinese Culture University, National Taiwan Normal University, and Shih Hsin University (SHU)
4. Singapore: Nanyang Technological University and National University of Singapore

SAMPLE CHARACTERISTICS

	Frist Wave	Second Wave
Time of survey	From December 2010 to January 2011	From October 2017 to March 2018
Mode of survey	Self-administrated questionnaire	Self-administrated questionnaire
Sample size	3,538	2,988
Distribution by Cities		
Shanghai	723 (20.4%)	754 (25.2%)
Hong Kong	587 (16.6%)	734 (24.6%)
Singapore	1028 (29.1%)	671 (22.5%)
Taipei	1200 (33.9%)	829 (27.7%)
Sample Profile		
Have a mobile phone	100%	100%
Types of phones: smartphone	51.9%	98.7%
Non-smartphones	48.1%	1.3%

	Frist Wave	Second Wave
Years of using a mobile phone	$M = 6.41$ years, $SD = 2.8$, ranging from 1 to 15 years	$M = 8.69$ years, $SD = 3.06$, ranging from 1 to 25 years
Calls made per day	4.42 ($SD = 4.71$)	2.16 ($SD = 9.10$)
Calls received per day	4.43 ($SD = 4.72$)	2.49 ($SD = 13.19$)
Text messages sent per day	13.76 ($SD = 19.13$)	32.47 ($SD = 121.60$)
Text messages received per day	14.17 ($SD = 19.28$)	45.78 ($SD = 144.90$)
Gender		
Males	41.9%	58.1%
Females	41.9%	58.1%
Age	$M = 20.73$, $SD = 2.54$, ranging from 17 to 42	$M = 21.05$, $SD = 2.07$, ranging from 17 to 37
Class Standing		
Freshmen	34.5%	17.5%
Sophomores	30.0%	27.3%
Juniors	18.5%	23.6%
Seniors	16.7%	14.9%
Graduate students	0.0%	16.8%

MEASURES OF KEY VARIABLES AND SCALES

To generate comparable measures in the two waves of surveys and across the four cities, uniform items with identical scales were used in the standardized questionnaire. Scales and measures of key variables that were developed for Chapters 3 to 7 are as follows.

Chapter 3: Motivations

Surveillance motivation of mobile phone use. To assess surveillance motivation, respondents were asked to indicate their agreement (5 = strongly agree, 1 = strongly disagree) with three statements adapted from previous research (Leung & Wei, 2000; R. Wei & Lo, 2006) concerning the reasons for using a mobile phone: to get news, to get information about products and services, and to get entertainment information. The three items were averaged to form a measure of "surveillance motivation" ($M = 2.93$, $SD = 1.01$, $\alpha = .91$ for the first wave of surveys; $M = 3.95$, $SD = .76$, $\alpha = .84$ for the second wave of surveys).

Personal value of mobile news. Respondents were further asked to rate the importance of the following attributes of mobile news on a 5-point

Likert scale (1 meant "not important at all" and 5 meant "extremely important"): (1) being important to me personally, (2) giving me useful information, (3) reporting new information, and (4) relating to my job or interests. The four items were combined in building a measure of "personal value of mobile news" (M = 2.92, SD = 1.04, α = .90 for the first wave of surveys; M = 3.80, SD = .75, α = .85 for the second wave of surveys).

Chapter 4: Consumption

Smartphone ownership. Respondents were asked to report the number of years using a mobile phone and indicate whether they owned a smartphone at the time of the survey (1 = yes, 2 = no).

Consumption of mobile news. Consumption of news accessed from the mobile phone distributed by news organizations was operationalized as exposure to such news in terms of reading, listening, and viewing. Six items were employed to measure it. The items reflect the multiple digital formats, forms, and platforms that news organizations use to push news to the mobile phones.

Specifically, on a 4-point scale ranging from 1 (never) to 4 (often), respondents were asked to report how often they used their mobile phone (1) to read news via regular news websites, (2) to read news via mobile websites of news, (3) to read syndicated news feeds like RSS in XML format, (4) to listen to news, (5) to view mobile television news, and (6) to listen to news on podcasts. The average of the six items was used to build an index of "consumption of mobile news" (M = 1.72, SD = .73, α = .87 for the first wave of surveys; M = 2.43, SD = .59, α = .75 for the second wave of surveys).

Chapter 5: Engagement

Smartphone ownership. Respondents were asked to report the number of years using a mobile phone and indicate whether they owned a smartphone at the time of the survey (1 = yes, 2 = no).

Consumption of mobile news. Consumption of news accessed from the mobile phone distributed by news organizations was operationalized as exposure to such news in terms of reading, listening, and viewing. Six items were employed to measure it. The items reflect the multiple digital formats, forms, and platforms that news organizations use to push news to the mobile phones.

Specifically, on a 4-point scale ranging from 1 (never) to 4 (often), respondents were asked to report how often they used their mobile phone

(1) to read news via regular news websites, (2) to read news via mobile websites of news, (3) to read syndicated news feeds like RSS in XML format, (4) to listen to news, (5) to view mobile television news, and (6) to listen to news on podcasts. The average of the six items was used to build an index of "consumption of mobile news" (M = 1.72, SD = .730, α = .87 for the first wave of surveys; M = 2.43, SD = .59, α = .75 for the second wave of surveys).

Following mobile news. Following news accessed on the mobile phone reflects user interactivity with the content created by news organizations and journalists (e.g., bloggers). To measure this dependent variable of the study on the behavior of following a variety of digital news sources, respondents were asked to indicate how often they used their mobile phone (1) to follow a news organization on a social networking site, (2) to follow a journalist on a social network site, (3) to follow a news blog, (4) to follow a news blogger, (5) to follow Twitter updates from a news organization, and (6) to follow Twitter news updates of a journalist. The scale ranged from 1 (never) to 4 (often). The six items were combined to generate an index of "mobile news following" (M = 1.62, SD = .78, α = .92 for the first wave of surveys; M = 2.34, SD = .82, α = .89 for the second wave of surveys).

Sharing mobile news. Sharing news on the mobile phone suggests a higher level of interaction between users and deeper engagement with the news. As the second dependent variable of the chapter, it was measured in another set of five items, which asked respondents to indicate how often they used their mobile phone (1) to share news, (2) to share news from WhatsApp/WeChat, (3) to share user-generated news, (4) to share news photos, and (5) to share news videos. The scale ranged from 1 (never) to 4 (often). These items, which focused on the exchange of information between and among mobile news users, were combined and then averaged to build an index of "mobile news sharing" (M = 2.48, SD = .77, α = .88 for the second wave of surveys only).

Chapter 6: Perceptions

Level of mobile news consumption. To measure the level of using the mobile phone to access news distributed from traditional news organizations, a six-item scale, which was adopted from previous studies (R. Wei et al., 2014), was used. Respondents were asked to report how often they used their mobile phones (1) to read news via regular news websites, (2) to read news via mobile websites of news, (3) to read syndicated news like RSS feeds in XML format, (4) to listen to news, (5) to view mobile television news, and (6) to listen to news on podcasts. The response categories ranged from 1 (never) to 4 (often). The six items were averaged to form an index of "level of mobile news consumption" (M = 2.43, SD = .59, α = .78 for the second wave of surveys only).

Perceived utility of mobile news. Drawing on the domains of information utility identified in previous studies (Li, 2013), respondents were asked to indicate their agreement with the following six statements on a 5-point Likert scale (1 meant "strongly disagree" and 5 meant "strongly agree"): (1) mobile news keeps me well informed when on the road, (2) mobile news helps me become smarter, (3) mobile news helps me understand things that happen in society better, (4) mobile news keeps me connected to the world even when I'm on the move, (5) mobile news helps me better handle daily routines, and (6) mobile news allows me to kill some downtime effortlessly. The averages of six items were combined to form a composite measure of "perceived utility of mobile news" (M = 3.71, SD = .73, α = .88 for the second wave of surveys only).

Appeal of mobile news presentation. To assess how respondents perceived the appeal of news presented on various mobile devices, five semantic differential scale items on a 5-point scale were used; they were bounded by the following bipolar adjectives: poor quality/high quality, unappealing/appealing, informative/not informative, boring/interesting, and tiring to read/refreshing. The items were added and divided by five to create a composite measure of "appeal of mobile news presentation" (M = 3.66, SD = .74, α = .78 for the second wave of surveys only).

Reliance on traditional media for news. Johnson and Kaye (2004) defined media reliance as an attitudinal tendency toward media on which audiences depend for gaining information and acquiring news. Using a 4-point scale that ranges from 1 (never) to 4 (often), respondents were further asked to indicate how often they depended on the following media as sources to stay informed about current affairs: (1) television, (2) newspapers, (3) magazines, and (4) radio. The answers were averaged to build a measure of "reliance on traditional media for news" (M = 2.21, SD = .63, α = .73 for the second wave of surveys only).

Credibility of mobile news. Credibility refers to user subjective assessment of messages in terms of trustworthiness and believability. To assess how respondents perceived the credibility of news accessed from the mobile phone and devices, a five-item credibility scale used in previous studies (Gaziano & McGrath, 1986; Meyer, 1988) was adopted. The five items tapped the conceptual domain of news consumed on the mobile phone.

On a Likert-type scale ranging from 1 (strongly disagree) to 5 (strongly agree), respondents were asked to rate how credible mobile news was. The five statements were (1) "news consumed on mobile media is reliable," (2) "news consumed on mobile media is complete," (3) "news consumed on mobile media is balanced," (4) "news consumed on mobile media is accurate," and (5) "news consumed on mobile media is fair." The five items were averaged to create a composite measure of "credibility of mobile news" ($M = 2.83$, $SD = .74$, $\alpha = .91$ for the second wave of surveys only).

Freedom of the press. Press freedom is defined as the extent to which media are independent and free from legal and political pressures that influence reporting as well as being free from economic factors that affect audience access to news and information in a country (Freedom House, 2014). Based on the Freedom of the Press index from the most recent Freedom House Annual Reports (2019), the level of freedom enjoyed by the press in each city in the study was ranked on a scale of 1 (the least free) to 4 (the freest). Specifically, level of press freedom was coded as an ordinal scale, ranging from 1 = Shanghai, to 2 = Singapore, to 3 = Hong Kong, to 4 = Taipei.

Chapter 7: Who Learns from Mobile News?

Knowledge about North Korea and United States relations. The questions asked respondents to identify people, issues, and events prominent in the news. One point was awarded for each question that was answered correctly. The five items are as follows: (1) How many nuclear tests has North Korea performed since 2006? (2) Who is the current secretary of state of the United States? (3) On October 25, 2017, the U.S. House of Representatives passed the Otto Warmbier North Korea Nuclear Sanction Act; what is the purpose of this act? (4) On October 9, 2017, a U.S. aircraft carrier sailed into the eastern waters of the Korean Peninsula; what is the name of the aircraft carrier? (5) Is it correct that the U.S. president Donald Trump said at the UN General Assembly that he will "totally destroy" North Korea? A knowledge index was created by adding the five questions. The knowledge index ranged from 0 to 5 for each respondent ($M = 1.24$, $SD = 1.20$, ranging from 0 to 5, for the second wave of surveys only).

Need for orientation. On a 5-point Likert scale, respondents were asked about their agreement with the five items, which were adapted from the literature: (1) I need news about current events and world affairs, (2) it is important for me to stay informed about my domestic and foreign affairs, (3) staying informed with current news is important to me, (4) I wish to understand the rapidly changing society we live in, (5) I have a need for in-depth information to understand major social issues. These five items were averaged to construct the scale of need for orientation ($M = 3.78$, $SD = .74$, $\alpha = .78$ for the second wave of surveys only).

APPENDIX B
Protocols of Focus Groups

PARTICIPANTS

Two focus group (FG) sessions were conducted with the same age group prior to the second wave of surveys. Specifically, 12 college students enrolled in a class at National Chiao Tung University of Taiwan were recruited to participate in the FG sessions in April 2016. The discussions focused on experience of accessing and consuming news from smartphones, including their evaluations of the content, style, interface, and format. What they liked and disliked about reading news via the mobile phone was incorporated into the questionnaire.

Following the second wave of surveys, to help us make sense of the quantitative results, four more FG sessions with recruited college students were conducted in the four selected cities between October 2019 and February 2020, respectively, in Taipei (five students, one male and four female), Shanghai (eight students, one male and seven female), Singapore (eight students, four male and four female), and Hong Kong (five students, two male and three female). (The FG session in Hong Kong was conducted online due to the coronavirus outbreaks.)

Each session lasted one hour. A moderator conducted the session. Unstructured questions guided the discussions around the findings in quantitative surveys. Insights from these sessions were reported in Chapters 3 to 7.

UNSTRUCTURED QUESTION GUIDE

1. Questions related to having a mobile phone and upgrades to smartphones:
   - When did you start to have your own mobile phones? Your first smartphones?
   - How important is the smartphone to your daily life? To what extent do you feel you cannot live without it?
   - What do you use your smartphone for? What sorts of things do you like to do on your mobile phone?
     Probe: Listen to music, play games, get news?
   - Describe to me how your life revolves around the smartphone in a typical day?
   - What are the reasons that you spend so much time using your smartphones? What are your expectations from using the phone: to stay connected, to stay informed, or to kill some time?
   - What do you think of using your smartphone to get news?
     Probe: What are the good things/benefits of using mobile news?
2. Questions about consumption of news on smartphones:
   - Can you tell me your experience with news consumption? How do you stay informed?
     Probe: What types of news content do you follow the most? Why? How important is it to read hard news of current affairs? Any particular reasons?
   - Can you tell me your experience with news consumption on smartphones? Please give me an example of how you have used smartphones to access and read news.
     Probe: What are the forms—news alerts, mobile apps, news websites, or social media platforms?
     Probe: When did you start?
   - When do you usually check news on your smartphones?
     Probe: Morning? Anytime? See news alerts?
   - What kind of news do you typically read or view on your smartphones?
     Probe: Breaking news? Sports? Health news?
   - What are the news sources/media you follow the most for news on smartphones?
     Probe: Why? (Credibility? Political ideology? Popularity?)
     Probe: How? (Download the app? Follow them on social media?)
   - How often do you read news from nonprofessional journalists on your smartphones, such as social media influencers or the *Onion*?

- Do you read the whole story or simply browse the headlines? Why? Explain your habits.
- How do you describe your experience of using your smartphones to access and read news? Tell me more about your experiences in terms of what you like the most and what you don't' like.
- Why do you use smartphones for news consumption rather than using desktop or traditional media?
  Probe: Convenience? Accessibility? Multiple sources?
- If you are really interested in certain news events or issues, how do you usually search for relevant information?
  Probe: Search more information from your laptop or desktop? Buy a newspaper? Watch TV news? Why?
3. Questions related to news sharing on smartphones:
   - Following and sharing mobile news is popular. How often do you engage in following and sharing? Why?
     Probe: Knowledge sharing? Getting attention from others? What do you gain from following news?
   - Who would you most like to share news on smartphones?
     Probe: People like you? Friends? Family? Why?
     Probe: What types of news do you enjoy sharing?
     Probe: How? Social media? Text messages? Messaging apps?
4. Broad questions about free press and use of mobile news:
   - How do you feel about the press freedom in Taiwan/Hong Kong/Shanghai/Singapore? Do you feel the news media should be regulated more? If yes, in what way? Do you think self-regulation may be effective?
5. An open-ended question:
   - Any other thoughts and comments on your experience of using mobile news?

NOTES

CHAPTER 1

1. Launched as a trial service on October 1, 2001, Japan's NTT DoCoMo was considered the world's first; it employed the W-CDMA—Wideband Code Division Multiple Access—technology in network design.
2. That is, enhanced freedom in distributing public information enabled by wireless telecommunication technologies that are dispersed, decentralized, easily accessible, and at a low cost.

CHAPTER 2

1. A challenge of new media research is that it is a constantly moving target, which is particularly true with mobile media (Fortunati, 2014). The earliest form of news delivered to 2G phones originated from text messaging sent to pagers. The upgrade to 3G networks led to the global popularity of the smartphone; and G4 ushered in the golden years of the mobile phone.
2. He listed music, gaming, TV, Internet, advertising, and social networking as the other six media.
3. For example, an object's properties that show the possible actions users can do to it, thereby suggesting how they may interact with that object; see Gibson (1975).
4. Shanghai is the largest city of a traditional nation-state, China; Taipei is the capital of a de facto nation-state with limited international recognition; Singapore is a city-state by itself; and Hong Kong is a special administrative region of China. The differences in political systems make it difficult to call these metropolis nation-states in any consistent way. For lack of a better term, we called them cities as the focus/unit of comparative analyses.
5. A comparative study of the three Confucian societies—Hong Kong, Taiwan, and China—by Lin and Ho (2009) indicates that massive sociocultural variations in each society have overshadowed Confucianism, making it marginal, looming in the background.
6. We acknowledge that press freedoms and related laws are not municipal laws. They flow from the national government; in the case of Hong Kong, it is rooted in the Basic Law. Because the rankings are for national governments, not municipal governments, we used national rankings for Shanghai and Taiwan as a key macro-level measure.
7. Due to the lack of rankings of Shanghai and Taipei as separate units, we used the rankings of China and Taiwan as substitutes for Shanghai and Taiwan.

8. They are (1) universal values, (2) freedom of the news media, (3) civil society, (4) civil rights, (5) historical errors of the Chinese Communist Party, (6) crony capitalism, and (7) judicial independence (Vásquez & Porčnik, 2018, p. 4).

CHAPTER 4
1. In cases where statistics for Shanghai are not available, we relied on statistics for China.
2. In cases where statistics for Taipei are not available, we relied on statistics for Taiwan.
3. The standardized regression coefficients reported in the table reflect the strength of relationships between each predictor and the dependent variable while controlling for the influences of other predictors in the equation.

CHAPTER 6
1. Where research of the credibility of Shanghai-based news media is not available, we cited studies about China in general.
2. Where research of the credibility of Taipei-based news media is not available, we cited studies about Taiwan in general.
3. Content farms are websites that publish a large amount of junky content or recycled content with sensational headlines for the benefit of higher ranking by search engines.
4. Multilevel modeling techniques are available to account for the effects of macro-level variables. One such technique is hierarchical linear modeling (HLM); however, HLM and other multilevel modeling tools need more than 10 groups at the higher level to be able to yield meaningful results; unfortunately, our focus on no more than four cities did not meet this threshold. This is the reason we decided to account for press freedom by including it in the regression model, as previous studies have done (see R. Wei et al., 2014).

CHAPTER 8
1. Mediation effect refers to the situation in which the presence of a third variable eliminates or significantly reduces the relationship between the independent variable and dependent variable (Hayes, 2013).
2. The negative z score indicates that the strength of the relationship between city of residence and mobile news consumption increased when personal value of mobile news was included in the model. City of residence was negatively related to personal value of mobile news, which was significantly and positively associated with mobile news consumption. Thus, personal value of mobile news played the role of a suppressor variable that suppressed the relationship between city of residence and mobile news consumption.

REFERENCES

Abonen, T. (2008). *Mobile as 7th of the mass media: Cellphone, cameraphone, iPhone, smartphone*. London: Futuretext.

American Press Institute. (2015). *How millennials get news: Inside the habits of America's first digital generation*. Retrieved from https://www. americanpressinstitute.org/publications/reports/survey-research/ millennials-news/

An, J., & Kwak, H. (2017, May). *Data-driven approach to measuring the level of press freedom using media attention diversity from unfiltered news*. Paper presented at the International AAAI Conference on Web and Social Media, North America.

Babrow, A. S. (1989). An expectancy-value analysis of the student soap opera audience. *Communication Research, 16*(2), 155–178.

Bales, R. F., & Parsons, T. (2014). *Family: Socialization and interaction process*. New York: Routledge.

Banducci, S., & Semetko, H. A. (2002, April 25–27). *Gender and context: Influences on political interest in Europe*. Paper presented at the annual meetings of the Midwest Political Science Association, Chicago, IL.

Bantz, C. (1982). Exploring uses and gratifications: A comparison of reported uses of television and reported uses of favorite program type. *Communication Research, 9*(3), 352–379.

Barthel, M. (2019 July 23). 5 key takeaways about the state of the news media in 2018. Pew Research Center. Retrieved from https://www.pewresearch.org/fact-tank/2019/07/23/key-takeaways-state-of-the-news-media-2018/

Beaudoin, C., & Thorson, E. (2004). Testing the cognitive mediation model. *Communication Research, 31*(4), 446–471.

Blumler, J. G. (1979). The role of theory in uses and gratifications studies. *Communication Research, 6*(1), 9–36.

Bode, L. (2016). Closing the gap: Gender parity in political engagement on social media. *Mass Communication & Society, 20*(4), 587–603.

Boyd, M., Zaff, J., Phelps, E., Weiner, M., & Lerner, R. (2011). The relationship between adolescents' news media use and civic engagement: The indirect effect of interpersonal communication with parents. *Journal of Adolescence, 34*(6), 1167–1179.

Burns, N., Schlozman, K. L., & Verba, S. (2001). *The private roots of public action*. Cambridge, MA: Harvard University Press.

Campbell, S. W., & Ling, R. (2008). Effects of mobile media. In J. Bryant & M. Oliver (Eds.), *Media effects: Advances in theory and research* (3rd ed., pp. 592–606). Mahwah, NJ: Lawrence Erlbaum Associates.

Cellphones Nowadays Blog. (2012). Retrieved March 23, 2013, from http://thecellphonesnowadays.blogspot.com/

Chan, M. (2015). Examining the influences of news use patterns, motivations, and age cohort on mobile news use: The case of Hong Kong. *Mobile Media & Communication*, 3(2), 179–195.

Chan, M., Chen, H., & Lee, F. (2017). Hong Kong. *Reuters Institute Digital News Report 2017*. Oxford, England: Reuters Institute for the Study of Journalism, University of Oxford. Retrieved from https://reutersinstitute.politics.ox.ac.uk/sites/default/files/Digital%20News%20Report%202017%20web_0.pdf

Chan-Olmsted, S., Rim, H., & Zerba, A. (2013). Mobile news adoption among young adults: Examining the roles of perceptions, news consumption, and media usage. *Journalism & Mass Communication Quarterly*, 90(1), 126–147.

Chen, G., Chen, P., Chang, C., & Abedin, Z. (2017). News video quality affects online sites' credibility. *Newspaper Research Journal*, 38(1), 19–31.

Chen, K. Y. N., Lo, V. H., Wei, R., Xu, X. G., & Zhang, G. L. (2014a). Motivations for mobile phone use as predictors of seeking mobile news: A comparative study of college students in Shanghai, Hong Kong, Taipei, and Singapore. *Communication & Society*, 27, 207–237.

Chen, Y. N., Lo, V. H., Wei, R., Xu, X., & Zhang, G. (2014b). A comparative study of the relationship between mobile phone use and social capital among college students in Shanghai and Taipei. *International Journal of Journalism & Mass Communication*, 1, 1–9.

Cheung, K. (2017, August). Hong Kong top "mobile-first" market in news consumption. *Hong Kong Free Press*. Retrieved from https://www.hongkongfp.com/2017/08/07/hong-kong-top-mobile-first-market-news-consumption-print-weighs-last-reuters-study/

China Daily. (2017, May 31). Over 70% Chinese netizens read news on mobile devices. Retrieved from https://www.chinadailyhk.com/articles/181/167/39/1496222013536.html

Chinanews. (2019, November 16). Chinese netizens news consumption report in 5G era report: Mobile news consumption closes to 100%. Retrieved from http://www.chinanews.com/sh/2019/11-16/9009274.shtml

Chung, C., Nam, Y., & Stefanone, M. (2012). Exploring online news credibility: The relative influence of traditional and technological factors. *Journal of Computer-Mediated Communication*, 17(2), 171–186.

Chyi, I., & Chadha, M. (2012). News on new devices: Is multi-platform news consumption a reality? *Journalism Practice*, 6(4), 431–449.

Claisse, G., & Rowe, F. (1993). Domestic telephone habits and daily mobility. *Transportation Research Part A: Policy and Practice*, 27(4), 277–290.

CNNIC. (2011). *The 28th Internet survey report*. Retrieved from http://www.cnnic.cn/research/bgxz/tjbg/201107/t20110719_22120.html

CNNIC. (2018). *The 42nd statistical report on Internet development in China*. Beijing, China: Author.

CNNIC. (2019). *Statistical report on internet development in China*. Retrieved from https://cnnic.com.cn/IDR/ReportDownloads/201911/P020191112539794960687.pdf

Compaine, B. (2000). Who owns the media companies? In B. Compaine & D. Gomery (Eds.), *Who owns the media: Competition and concentration in the media industries* (pp. 499–503). Mahwah, NJ: Lawrence Erlbaum Associates.

CUHK. (2016). *Tracking research: Public evaluation on media credibility survey results.* Retrieved October 16, 2018, from http://www.com.cuhk.edu.hk/ccpos/en/research/Credibility_Survey%20Results_2019_ENG.pdf

Dalton, R. J., & Ong, N. T. (2003). *Authority orientations and democratic attitudes in East Asia: A test of the Asian values hypothesis.* Irvine, CA: Center for the Study of Democracy, University of California, Irvine.

DeBailon, L., & Rockwell, P. (2005). Gender and student-status differences in cellular telephone use. *International Journal of Mobile Communications, 3*(1), 82–98.

Deci, E. L., & Ryan, R. M. (1985). *Intrinsic motivation and self-determination in human behavior.* New York: Plenum.

Delli Carpini, M., & Keeter, S. (1996). *What Americans know about politics and why it matters.* New Haven, CT: Yale University Press.

Delli Carpini, M., & Keeter, S. (2000). Gender and political knowledge. In S. T. Rinehart & J. Josephson (Eds.), *Gender and American politics: Women, men, and the political process* (pp. 21–52). Armonk, NY: M. E. Sharpe.

Digital Marketing Blog. (2018, August 20). *38 Singapore's digital and social media stats and facts.* Retrieved from https://www.soravjain.com/digital-and-social-media-stats-facts-singapore

Dimitrova, D., Shehata, A., Strömbäck, J., & Nord, L. (2014). The effects of digital media on political knowledge and participation in election campaigns: Evidence from panel data. *Communication Research, 41*(1), 95–118.

Dimmick, J., Feaster, J., & Hoplamazian, G. (2011). News in the interstices: The niches of mobile media in space and time. *New Media & Society, 13*(1), 23–39.

Dimmick, J. W., Sikand, J., & Patterson, S. J. (1994). The gratifications of the household telephone: Sociability, instrumentality, and reassurance. *Communication Research, 21*(5), 643–663.

Donald, S., Anderson, T., & Spry, D. (2010). *Youth, society and mobile media in Asia.* London: Routledge.

Dow, J. K. (2009). Gender differences in political knowledge: Distinguishing characteristics-based and returns-based differences. *Political Behavior, 31*(1), 117–136.

Du, R., & Tang, A. (2019). Social media in Hong Kong's changing ecology of news production and consumption. In Y. Huang & Y. Song (Eds.), *The evolving landscape of media and communication in Hong Kong* (pp. 99–113). Hong Kong: City University of Hong Kong Press.

Dunaway, J., Searles, K., Sui, M., & Paul, N. (2018). News attention in a mobile era. *Journal of Computer-Mediated Communication, 23*(2), 107–124.

Dutton, W. (Ed.). (2013). *The Oxford handbook of Internet studies.* Oxford: Oxford University Press.

Dutton, W. H., & Peltu, M. (1996). *Information and communication technologies: Visions and realities.* Oxford: Oxford University Press.

Eastin, M. S., Cicchirillo, V., & Mabry, A. (2015). Extending the digital divide conversation: Examining the knowledge gap through media expectancies. *Journal of Broadcasting & Electronic Media, 59*(3), 416–437.

Elenbaas, M., de Vreese, C., Schuck, A., & Boomgaarden, H. (2014). Reconciling passive and motivated learning: The saturation-conditional impact of media coverage and motivation on political information. *Communication Research, 41*(4), 481–504.

Ellison, N. (2004). *Telework and social change: How technology is reshaping the boundaries between home and work.* Santa Barbara, CA: Greenwood Publishing Group.

Fishbein, M. (1979). A theory of reasoned action: Some applications and implications. *Nebraska Symposium on Motivation, 27,* 65–116.

Fishbein, M., & Ajzen, I. (1976). Misconceptions about the Fishbein model: Reflections on a study by Songer-Nocks. *Journal of Experimental Social Psychology, 12*(6), 579–584.

Flanagin, A., & Metzger, M. (2000). Perceptions of internet information credibility. *Journalism and Mass Communication Quarterly, 77*(3), 515–540.

Flanagin, A., & Metzger, M. (2007). The role of site features, user attributes, and information verification behaviors on the perceived credibility of web-based information. *New Media & Society, 9*(2), 319–342.

Flavián, C., & Gurrea, R. (2006). The role of readers' motivations in the choice of digital versus traditional newspapers. *Journal of Targeting, Measurement and Analysis for Marketing, 14*(4), 325–335.

Focus Taiwan. (2018, October 30). *Over 85% of youth in Taiwan use mobile phones: poll.* Retrieved from https://focustaiwan.tw/society/201810300016

Fortunati, L. (2014). Understanding the role of mobile media in society: Models and theories. In G. Goggin & L. Hjorth (Eds.), *The Routledge companion to mobile media* (pp. 45–55). New York: Routledge.

Frankel, R. (2010). The global cities index 2010. *Foreign Policy.* Retrieved from http://www.foreignpolicy.com/articles/2010/08/11/the_global_cities_index_2010

Freedom House. (2004). *Press freedom survey.* Retrieved April 12, 2019, from https://freedomhouse.org/sites/default/files/inline_images/2004.pdf

Freedom House. (2019). *Freedom and the media: A downward spiral.* Retrieved June 10, 2019, from https://freedomhouse.org/report/freedom-media/freedom-media-2019

Gans, H. J. (2003). *Democracy and the news.* New York: Oxford University Press.

Gayomali, C. (2012, December 3). The text messaging turns 20: A brief history of SMA. *The Week.* Retrieved from https://theweek.com/articles/469869/text-message-turns-20-brief-history-sms

Gaziano, C., & McGrath, K. (1986). Measuring the concept of credibility. *Journalism Quarterly, 63*(3), 451–462.

Gibson, J. (1975). Affordances and behavior. In E. S. Reed & R. Jones (Eds.), *Reasons for realism: Selected essays of James J. Gibson* (pp. 410–411). Hillsdale, NJ: Lawrence Erlbaum Associates.

Go-Global. (2014, August 11). *Smartphone usage in Hong Kong—Statistics and trends.* Retrieved from https://www.go-globe.hk/smartphone-usage-hong-kong/

Goh, D., Ling, R., Huang, L., & Liew, D. (2017). News sharing as reciprocal exchanges in social cohesion maintenance. *Information, Communication & Society, 22*(8), 1128–1144.

Goh, P. C. (2017). *Reuters Institute digital news report 2017.* Reuters Institute for the Study of Journalism, University of Oxford. Retrieved from http://www.digitalnewsreport.org/survey/2017/singapore-2017/

Golan, G., & Day, A. (2010). In God we trust: Religiosity as a predictor of perceptions of media trust, factuality, and privacy invasion. *American Behavioral Scientist, 54*(2), 120–136.

GovHK. (2018). Hong Kong: The facts: Media. Retrieved from http://www.gov.hk

GovHK. (2019). HK Facts: Transportation. Retrieved from https://www.gov.hk/en/about/abouthk/factsheets/docs/transport.pdf

Grant. A. (2018). The communication technology ecosystem. In A. Grant & J. Meadows (Eds.), *Communication technology update and fundamentals* (16th ed., pp. 1–8). New York: Routledge.

Graves, L., & Konieczna, M. (2015). Sharing the news: Journalistic collaboration as field repair. *International Journal of Communication*, 9, 1966–1984.

Greenfield, A. (2018). *Radical technologies: The design of everyday life*. New York: Verso.

Grigg, A. (July 4, 2015). How China stopped its bloggers. *Financial Review*. Retrieved from https://www.afr.com/technology/how-china-stopped-its-bloggers-20150702-gi34za

Gunther, A. (1992). Biased press or biased public? Attitudes toward media coverage of social groups. *Public Opinion Quarterly*, 56(2), 147–167.

Ha, L., Xu, Y., Yang, C., Wang, F., Yang, L., Abuljadail, M., & Gabay, I. (2018). Decline in news content engagement or news medium engagement? A longitudinal analysis of news engagement since the rise of social and mobile media 2009–2012. *Journalism*, 19(5), 718–739.

Hao, X. (1996). The press and public trust: The case of Singapore. *Asian Journal of Communication*, 6(1), 111–123.

Hao, X., Wen, N., & George, C. (2014). News consumption and political and civic engagement among young people. *Journal of Youth Studies*, 17(9), 1221–1238.

Hayes, A. (2013). *Introduction to mediation, and conditional process analysis: A regression-based approach*. New York: Guilford Press.

He, Z. (2008). SMS in China: A major carrier of the nonofficial discourse universe. *Information Society*, 24(3), 182–190.

Hermida, A., Fletcher, F., Korell, D., & Logan, D. (2012). Share, like, and recommend. *Journalism Studies*, 13(5–6), 815–824.

Hill, S., & Bradshaw, P. (2018). *Mobile-first journalism: Producing new for social and interactive media*. New York: Routledge.

HKU. (2018). Credibility rating of Hong Kong news media in general. Hong Kong University Public Opinion Program. Retrieved October 16, 2019, from https://www.hkupop.hku.hk/english/popexpress/press/nm_credibility/index.html

Hofstede, G. (1991). *Cultures and organizations: Software of the mind*. Maidenhead, UK: McGraw-Hill.

Hofstede, G. (n.d.). *National cultural dimensions*. Retrieved November 7, 2019, from https://geerthofstede.com/culture-geert-hofstede-gert-jan-hofstede/6d-model-of-national-culture/

Hoffman, L. (2019). Political knowledge. *Oxford Bibliographies*. Retrieved February 12, 2020, from https://www.oxfordbibliographies.com/view/document/obo-9780199756841/obo-9780199756841-0098.xml

Hong Kong Telecoms. (2010). *Hong Kong—telecoms, mobile and broadband*. Retrieved from http://www.budde.com.au/Research/2009-Hong-Kong-Telecoms-Mobile-and-Broadband.html?r=51

Hsu, M. (2015). Factors affecting news credibility and efficacy of news literacy. *Chinese Journal of Communication Research*, 27, 99–136.

Hu, W. (2009). *A content analysis of mobile news: The case study of i-news* (MA thesis, Shanghai Jiao Tong University).

Incollingo, J. (2018). "I'm a news junkie . . . I like being informed": Mobile news use by a newspaper's digital subscribers. *Newspaper Research Journal*, 39(2), 134–144.

International Telecommunications Union (ITU). (2017). *ICT development index, IDI ranking, 2017.* Retrieved from https://www.itu.int/net4/ITU-D/idi/2017/

iResearch. (2009). *Mobile text service subscribers in China.* Retrieved from http://www.Iresearch.com.cn

Iyengar, S., Curran, J., Lund, A. B., Salovaara-Moring, I., Hahn, K. S., & Coen, S. (2010). Cross-national versus individual-level differences in political information: A media systems perspective. *Journal of Elections, Public Opinion & Parties, 20*(3), 291–309.

Jackson, L., Ervin, K., & Gardner, P. (2001). Gender and the Internet: Women communicating and men searching. *Sex Roles, 44*(5), 363–379.

Johnson, T., & Kaye, B. (1998). Cruising is believing? Comparing internet and traditional sources on media credibility measures. *Journalism and Mass Communication Quarterly, 75*(2), 325–340.

Johnson, T., & Kaye, B. (2004). Wag the blog: How reliance on traditional media and the Internet influence credibility perceptions of weblogs among blog users. *Journalism & Mass Communication Quarterly, 81*(3), 622–642.

Joo, J., & Sang, Y. (2013). Exploring Koreans' smartphone usage: An integrated model of the technology acceptance model and uses and gratifications theory. *Computers in Human Behavior, 29*(6), 2512–2518.

Kam, K. (2018, July). Why Hong Kong's traditional media is alive and kicking in the digital age. *South China Morning Post.* Retrieved from https://www.scmp.com/comment/insight-opinion/article/2071749/why-hong-kongs-traditional-media-alive-and-kicking-digital

Kamba, M. A., & Mansor, Y. (2010). From information-poverty to information-rich: ICT as enabler. In *Proceeding of the 3rd International Conference on Information and Communication Technology for the Moslem World (ICT4M) 2010.*

Katz, E., Blumler, J., & Gurevitch, M. (1973). On the use of the mass media for important things. *American Sociological Review, 38*(2), 164–181.

Katz, J., & Aakhus, M. (Eds.). (2001). *Perpetual contact: Mobile communication, private talk, public performance.* New York: Cambridge University Press.

Kauffman, R. J., & Techatassanasoontorn, A. A. (2010). New theoretical perspectives on technology adoption. *Information Technology and Management, 11*(4), 157–160.

Kearney. (2019). *Global Cities Index (GCI), 2018–2019.* Retrieved from https://www.kearney.com/global-cities/2019

Kleinberg, M., & Lau, R. (2019). The importance of political knowledge for effective citizenship: Differences between the broadcast and Internet generations. *Public Opinion Quarterly, 83*(2), 338–362.

Kline, R. B. (2005). *Principles and practice of structural equation modeling* (2nd ed.). New York: Guilford Press.

Knight Foundation. (2016, May). *Mobile-first news: How people use smartphones to access information.* Retrieved October 2018, from https://knightfoundation.org/reports/mobile-first-news-how-people-use-smartphones-acces/

Kopomaa, T. (2000). *The city in your pocket: Birth of the mobile information society.* Bloomington, IN: Indiana University Press.

Ksiazek, T., Malthouse, E., & Webster, J. (2010). News-seekers and avoiders: Exploring patterns of total news consumption across media and the relationship to civic participation. *Journal of Broadcasting & Electronic Media, 54*(4), 551–568.

Ksiazek, T., Peer, L., & Lessard, K. (2016). User engagement with online news: Conceptualizing interactivity and exploring the relationship between online news videos and user comments. *New Media & Society, 18*(3), 502–520.

Kümpel, A., Karnowski, V., & Keyling, T. (2015). News sharing in social media: A review of current research on news sharing users, content, and networks. *Social Media & Society, 1*(2), 1–14.

Kuo, J. (2014, January 17). Sina Weibo just lost 28 million users to censorship and WeChat. *Quarts.com*. Retrieved from https://qz.com/india/1799646/amul-rival-mother-dairy-bets-on-cafe-delights/

Kwak, N., Williams, A. E., Wang, X., & Lee, H. (2005). Talking politics and engaging politics: An examination of the interactive relationships between structural features of political talk and discussion engagement. *Communication Research, 32*(1), 87–111.

LaRose, R., & Eastin, M. S. (2004). A social cognitive theory of Internet uses and gratifications: Toward a new model of media attendance. *Journal of Broadcasting & Electronic Media, 48*(3), 358–377.

Larsson, A. (2019). News use as amplification: Norwegian national, regional, and hyperpartisan media on Facebook. *Journalism & Mass Communication Quarterly, 96*(3), 721–741.

Lasica, J. D. (1997). When push comes to news. *American Journalism Review, 19*(4), 32–40.

Lee, F. L. (2018). Changing political economy of the Hong Kong media. *China Perspectives, 3*, 9–18.

Lee, M. K. (2017, November). Digital news consumption in Singapore on the rise; The Straits Times remains most-read English paper: Nielsen survey. *Straits Times*. Retrieved from https://www.straitstimes.com/singapore/digital-news-consumption-in-singapore-on-the-rise-the-straits-times-remains-most-read

Lee, S. (2015). News engagement vs. news consumption: Does online news use promote civic engagement? *Electronic News, 9*(2), 75–90.

Leung, L. (2007). Unwillingness-to-communicate and college students' motives in SMS mobile messaging. *Telematics & Informatics, 24*(2), 115–129.

Leung, L., Lee, P., Lo, V., Xiong, C., & Wu, T. (2009). *The ascendancy of Internet communication: A comparative study of four Chinese cities.* Hong Kong: Hong Kong Institute of Asia-Pacific Studies, Chinese University of Hong Kong.

Leung, L., & Wei, R. (1998). Factors influencing the adoption of interactive TV in Hong Kong: Implications for advertising. *Asian Journal of Communication, 8*(2), 124–147.

Leung, L., & Wei, R. (1999a). Seeking news via the pager: A value-expectancy study. *Journal of Broadcasting & Electronic Media, 43*(3), 299–315.

Leung, L., & Wei, R. (1999b). Who are the mobile phone have-nots? Influences and consequences. *New Media & Society, 1*(2), 209–226.

Leung, L., & Wei, R. (2000). More than just talk on the move: A use-and-gratification study of the cellular phone. *Journalism & Mass Communication Quarterly, 77*(2), 308–320.

Levinson, P. (2004). *Cellphone*. New York: Palgrave & St. Martin's.

Li, M. (2018, January 10). *How WeChat became the primary news source in China.* Retrieved from https://www.cjr.org/tow_center/how-wechat-became-primary-news-source-china.php

Li, X. (2013). Innovativeness, personal initiative, news affinity and news utility as predictors of the use of mobile phones as news devices. *Chinese Journal of Communication, 6*(3), 350–373.

Li, X., & Zhang, G. (2018). Perceived credibility of Chinese social media: Toward an integrated approach. *International Journal of Public Opinion Research, 30*(1), 79–101.

Lievrouw, L. A., & Livingstone, S. (2002). *Handbook of new media: Social shaping and consequences of ICTs.* London: Sage.

Lim, C. K. (2019). *Singapore: Telecoms, media & Internet 2020.* Retrieved from https://iclg.com/practice-areas/telecoms-media-and-internet-laws-and-regulations/singapore

Lin, C., & Atkin, D. (2014). *Communication technology and social change: Theory and implications.* Mahwah, NJ: LEA.

Lin, L., & Ho, Y. (2009). Confucian dynamism, culture and ethical change in Chinese societies – A comparative study of China, Taiwan, and Hong Kong. *The International Journal of Human Resource Management, 20*, 2402–2417.

Ling, R. (2008). *New tech, new ties: How mobile communication is reshaping social cohesion.* Cambridge, MA: MIT Press.

Liotta, E. (2019, October 2). Here's all you need to know about Singapore's "fake news" law. *Vice Asia.* Retrieved October 20, 2019, from https://www.vice.com/en_in/article/7x5eee/heres-all-you-need-to-know-about-singapores-fake-news-law

Liu, J. (2013). Mobile communication, popular protests and citizenship in China. *Modern Asian Studies, 47*(3), 995–1018.

Liu, T., & Bates, B. (2009). What's behind public trust in news media: A comparative study of America and China. *Chinese Journal of Communication, 2*(3), 307–329.

Livingstone, S., & Markham, T. (2008). The contribution of media consumption to civic participation. *British Journal of Sociology, 59*(2), 351–371.

Lo, V. (1994). Media use, involvement and knowledge of the Gulf war. *Journalism Quarterly, 71*(1), 45–56.

Lo, V. (2013). A comparative study of newspaper and television news credibility in 1993, 1998, and 2008. In M. Chang, V. H. Lo, & H. Shyu (Eds.), *Social change in Taiwan, 1985–2005: Mass communication and political behavior* (pp. 65–91). Taipei: Institute of Sociology, Academia Sinica.

Lo, V., & Chang, C. (2006). Knowledge about the Gulf Wars: A theoretical model of learning from the news. *Harvard International Journal of Press/Politics, 11*(3), 135–155.

Lubrano, A. (1997). *The telegraph: How technology innovation caused social change.* New York: Routledge.

MacKenzie, D., & Wajcman, J. (1985). *The social shaping of technology.* Milton Keynes: Open University Press.

Martin, J. (2015). Mobile news use and participation in elections: A bridge for the democratic divide? *Mobile Media & Communication, 3*(2), 230–249.

Matthes, J. (2005). The need for orientation towards news media: Revising and validating a classic concept. *International Journal of Public Opinion Research, 18*(4), 422–444.

McQuail, D. (2000). *McQuail's mass communication theory* (4th ed.). London: Sage Publications.

Meijer, I., & Kormelink, T. (2015). Checking, sharing, clicking and linking. *Digital Journalism, 3*(5), 664–679.

Meyer, P. (1988). Defining and measuring credibility of newspapers: Developing an index. *Journalism Quarterly, 65*(3), 567–574.

Miconi, A., & Serra, M. (2019). On the concept of medium: An empirical study. *International Journal of Communication, 13*, 3444–3461.

MIIT. (2020). Monthly telecommunications statistical report by province. Retrieved from http://www.miit.gov.cn/n1146312/n1146904/n1648372/c7827571/content.html

Mitchell, M., Gottfried, J., Barthel, M., & Shearer, E. (2016). The modern news consumer. *Journalism.* Retrieved from https://www.journalism.org/2016/07/07/the-modern-news-consumer/

Mitchelstein, E., & Boczkowski, P. (2010). Online news consumption: An assessment of past work and an agenda for the future. *New Media & Society, 12*(7), 1085–1102.

Molyneux, L. (2018). Mobile news consumption. *Digital Journalism, 6*(5), 634–650.

Moyal, A. (1992). The gendered use of the telephone: An Australian case study. *Media, Culture and Society, 14*(1), 51–72.

Nel, F., & Westlund, O. (2012). The 4C's of mobile news. *Journalism Practice, 6*(5–6), 744–753.

Newman, N., Fletcher, R., Kalogeropoulos, A., Levy, D., & Nielsen, R. (2017). *Reuters digital news report 2017.* Reuters Institute for the Study of Journalism, University of Oxford. Retrieved November 3, 2018, from https://reutersinstitute.politics.ox.ac.uk/sites/default/files/Digital%20News%20Report%202017%20web_0.pdf

Newman, N., Fletcher, R., Kalogeropoulos, A., Levy, D., & Nielsen, R. (2018). *Reuters digital news report 2018.* Reuters Institute for the Study of Journalism, University of Oxford. Retrieved November 3, 2018, from http://media.digitalnewsreport.org/wp-content/uploads/2018/06/digital-news-report-2018.pdf

Newman, N., Fletcher, R., Kalogeropoulos, A., & Nielsen, R. (2019). *Reuters Institute digital news report, 2019.* Reuters Institute for the Study of Journalism, University of Oxford. Retrieved October 28, 2018, from https://reutersinstitute.politics.ox.ac.uk/sites/default/files/2019-06/DNR_2019_FINAL_0.pdf

Nielson. (2018, April). Take-up of mobile-first. *Nielsen Holdings plc.* Retrieved from https://www.nielsen.com/hk/en/insights/news/2018/nielsen-media-index-take-up-of-mobile-first.html

Oeldorf-Hirsch, A., & Sundar, S. (2015). Posting, commenting, and tagging: Effects of sharing news stories on Facebook. *Computers in Human Behavior, 44*, 240–249.

OFCA. (2019). *Key communications stats.* Retrieved from https://www.ofca.gov.hk/en/data_statistics/data_statistics/key_stat/

Office of the Telecommunications Authority (OFTA). (2005). Data and Statistics. Retrieved from http://www.ofta.gov.hk/en/datastat/key_stat.html

Olmstead, K., Mitchell, A., & Rosenstiel, T. (2011). *Navigating news online: Where people go, how they get there and what lures them away.* Pew Research Center. Retrieved from https://www.journalism.org/2011/05/09/navigating-news-online/

Park, Y., Kim, H., & Lee, J. (2010). An empirical analysis on consumer adoption of mobile phone and mobile content in Korea. *International Journal of Mobile Communication, 8*(6), 667–688.

Pelosi, N. (2020, February 14). *Speaker Pelosi remarks at Munich Security Conference.* Retrieved from https://www.speaker.gov/newsroom/21420-1

Pestin, D. (2011). *News on the go: How mobile devices are changing the world's information ecosystem.* Washington, DC: Center for International Media Assistance and National Endowment for Democracy.

Peters, C. (2012). Journalism to go: The changing spaces of news consumption. *Journalism Studies, 13*(5–6), 695–705.

Pew Research Center. (2012). *The demographics of mobile news.* Retrieved July 30, 2019, from https://www.journalism.org/2012/12/11/demographics-mobile-news/

Pew Research Center. (2014, March 26). *State of the news media: Overview.* Retrieved November 2, 2018, from https://assets.pewresearch.org/wp-content/uploads/sites/13/2017/05/30142556/state-of-the-news-media-report-2014-final.pdf

Pew Research Center. (2017, March 16). *China outpaces India in internet access, smartphone ownership.* Retrieved December 3, 2019, from https://www.pewresearch.org/fact-tank/2017/03/16/china-outpaces-india-in-internet-access-smartphone-ownership/

Poindexter, P. (2016). *News for a mobile-first consumer.* New York: Peter Lang.

Pool, I., de Sola. (1983). *Technologies of freedom.* Cambridge, MA: Harvard University Press.

Poushter, J. (2017, March 16). *China outpaces India in internet access, smartphone ownership.* Pew Research Center. Retrieved from https://www.pewresearch.org/fact-tank/2017/03/16/china-outpaces-india-in-internet-access-smartphone-ownership/

Preacher, K., & Hayes, A. (2004). SPSS and SAS procedures for estimating and comparing indirect effects in simple mediation models. *Behavior Research Methods, Instruments, and Computers, 36,* 717–731.

Prior, M. (2007). *Post-broadcast democracy: How media choice increases inequality in political involvement and polarizes elections.* New York: Cambridge University Press.

Putnam, R. (2000). *Bowling alone: America's declining social capital.* New York: Simon & Shuster.

Rakow, L. (1992). *Gender on the line: Women, the telephone, and community life.* Champion-Urbana, IL: University of Illinois Press.

Rawnsley, G., & Rawnsley, M. (2012). The media in democratic Taiwan. In D. Blundell (Ed.), *Taiwan experience since martial law* (pp. 395–417). Berkeley, CA: University of California Press.

Rayburn, J., & Palmgreen, P. (1984). Merging uses and gratifications and expectancy-value theory. *Communication Research, 11*(4), 537–562.

Repnikova, M. (2017). *Media politics in China: Improvising power under Authoritarianism.* Cambridge, UK: Cambridge University Press.

Reuters Institute Digital News Report. (2019). Reuters Institute for the Study of Journalism, University of Oxford. Retrieved from https://reutersinstitute.politics.ox.ac.uk/sites/default/files/2019-06/DNR_2019_FINAL_0.pdf

Rheigold, H. (2006). *Smart mobs: The next social revolution.* New York: Basic Books.

Rice, R. (1984). *The new media: Communication, research, and technology.* Beverly Hills, CA: Sage Publications.

Rice, R., & Hogan, I. (2007, May 24–28). *Social connectivity, multitasking, and social control: US and Norwegian college students' use of Internet and mobile phones.* Paper presented at the 57th Conference of ICA, San Francisco, CA.

Robinson, J., & Levy, M. (1996). News media use and the informed public: A 1990s update. *Journal of Communication, 46*(2), 129–135.

Ruggiero, T. E. (2000). Uses and gratifications theory in the 21st century. *Mass Communication and Society, 3*(1), 3–37.

Sawhney, H. (2009). Innovations at the edge: The impact of mobile technologies on the character of the Internet. In G. Goggin & L. Hjorth (Eds.), *Mobile technologies: From telecommunications to media* (pp. 120–132). New York: Routledge.

Schrock, A. R. (2015). Communicative affordances of mobile media: Portability, availability, locatability, and multimediality. *International Journal of Communication, 9,* 1229–1246.

Schrøder, K. (2019). What do news readers really want to read about? How relevance works for news audiences. *Reuters Digital New Publications: 2019 Report.* Retrieved from http://www.digitalnewsreport.org/publications/2019/news-readers-really-want-read-relevance-works-news-audiences/

Schudson, M. (1998). *The good citizen.* New York: Free Press.

Schudson, M. (2003). *The sociology of news.* New York: Norton.

Shanghai Gov. (2016). State of the newspapers and periodicals in Shanghai. *Shanghai Yearbooks 2014.* Retrieved from http://www.shanghai.gov.cn/nw2/nw2314/nw24651/nw39559/nw39592/u21aw1139446.html

Shanghai Statistics Bureau. (2010). *Shanghai statistical yearbook.* Retrieved from http://www.stats-sh.gov.cn/2003shtj/tjnj/nj10.htm?d1=2010tjnj/C1317.html

Shao, G. (2009). Understanding the appeal of user-generated media: A uses and gratification perspective. *Internet Research, 19*(1), 7–25.

Shen, F., & Zhang, H. (2014). Predicting media credibility in China: The influence of Weibo use. *Asian Journal for Public Opinion Research, 1,* 234–248.

Shen, F., Lu, Y., Guo, Z., & Zhou, B. (2011). News media use, perceived credibility, and efficacy: An analysis of media participation intention in China. *Chinese Journal of Communication, 4*(4), 475–495.

Shim, H., You, K., Lee, J. K., & Go, E. (2015). Why do people access news with mobile devices? Exploring the role of suitability perception and motives on mobile news use. *Telematics and Informatics, 32*(1), 108–117.

Shoemaker, P. J. (1996). Hardwired for news: Using biological and cultural evolution to explain the surveillance function. *Journal of Communication, 46*(3), 32–47.

Sidlow, F. (2008). *Consumption of news among various age groups: Traditional media versus new media* (MA thesis, California State University). Retrieved from ProQuest Dissertations & Theses Global.

Singapore Statutes Online. (2012). *The Broadcasting Act: Protection from Online Falsehoods and Manipulation Act.* Retrieved from https://sso.agc.gov.sg/Act/BA1994/

Singapore Telecoms. (2010). *Mobile-and-broadband.* Retrieved from http://www.budde.com.au/ Research/2010-Singapore-Telecoms-Mobile-and-Broadband.html

Sirkkunen, E., & Uskali, T. (2019). Virtual reality journalism. In T. P. Vos & F. Hanusch (Eds.), *The international encyclopedia of journalism studies.* New York: Wiley.Skoric, M., & Poor, N. (2013). Youth engagement in Singapore: The interplay of social and traditional media. *Journal of Broadcasting & Electronic Media, 57*(2), 187–204.

Skoric, M. M., Zhu, Q., & Pang, N. (2016). Social media, political expression, and participation in Confucian Asia. *Chinese Journal of Communication, 9*(4), 331–347.

So, Y. (2016, September 8). Further decline in credibility ratings for Hong Kong news media. *Ming Pao*, A32.

Sobel, M. (1982). Asymptotic intervals for indirect effects in structural equation models. In S. Leinhart (Ed.), *Sociological methodology* (pp. 290–312). San Francisco: Jossey-Bass.

Spyridou, L., Matsiola, M., Veglis, A., Kalliris, G., & Dimoulas, C. (2013). Journalism in a state of flux: Journalists as agents of technology innovation and emerging news practices. *International Communication Gazette*, 75(1), 76–98.

Statista. (2016, December 16). *Smartphone penetration rate as share of the population in Taiwan from 2015 to 2020*. Retrieved from https://www.statista.com/statistics/755288/taiwan-number-of-smartphone-users/

Statista. (2019, February 18). *Smartphone penetration rate as share of the population in Singapore from 2017 to 2023*. Retrieved from https://www.statista.com/statistics/625441/smartphone-user-penetration-in-singapore/

Struckmann, S., & Karnowski, V. (2016). News consumption in a changing media ecology: An MESM-study on mobile news. *Telematics and Informatics*, 33(2), 309–319.

Sundar, S., & Limperos, A. (2013). Uses and grats 2.0: New gratifications for new media, *Journal of Broadcasting & Electronic Media*, 57(4), 504–525.

Taiwan Communication Survey. (2017). *The 2017 Taiwan Communication Survey (phase two, year one): The utility and impacts of media use I*. Retrieved from http://140.109.171.222/webview/index/nn/MyServer/English.d.6/Cross-sectional-Surveys.d.186/Taiwan-Communication-Survey-TCS.d.287/The-2017-Taiwan-Communication-Survey-Phase-Two-Year-One-The-Utility-and-Impacts-of-Media-Use-I/fStudy/D00175en

Taiwan Mobile Market. (2010). *Taiwan—mobile market—overview and statistics*. Retrieved from http://www.budde.com.au/Research/Taiwan-Mobile-Market-Overview-Statistics.html

Tandoc, E. (2018). *Singapore. Reuters Institute Digital News Report, U.K.* Reuters Institute for the Study of Journalism, University of Oxford. Retrieved April 12, 2018, from http://www.digitalnewsreport.org/survey/2018/singapore-2018/

Tandoc, E. (2019). Tell me who your sources are: Perceptions of news credibility on social media. *Journalism Practice*, 13(2), 178–190.

Tandoc Jr., E., & Duffy, A. (2016). Keeping up with the audiences: Journalistic role expectations in Singapore. *International Journal of Communication*, 10, 3338–3358.

Tewksbury, D., & Rittenberg, J. (2012). *News on the Internet: Information and citizenship in the 21st century*. New York: Oxford University Press.

Thorson, E., Shoenberger, H., Karaliova, T., Kim, E. A., & Fidler, R. (2015). News use of mobile media: A contingency model. *Mobile Media & Communication*, 3(1), 1–19.

Thorson, K., Vraga, E., & Ekdale, B. (2010). Credibility in context: How uncivil online commentary affects news credibility. *Mass Communication and Society*, 13, 289–313.

Today. (2020, March 23). *Smartphone penetration in Singapore the highest globally: Survey*. Retrieved from https://www.todayonline.com/singapore/smartphone-penetration-singapore-highest-globally-survey

Trilling, D., & Schoenbach, K. (2013). Skipping current affairs: The non-users of online and offline news. *European Journal of Communication*, 28(1), 35–51.

Tsfati, Y. (2010). Online news exposure and trust in the mainstream media: Exploring possible associations. *American Behavioral Scientist, 54*(1), 22–42.

Tsfati, Y., & Cappella, J. N. (2003). Do people watch what they do not trust? Exploring the association between news media skepticism and exposure. *Communication Research, 30*(5), 504–529.

Valeriani, A., & Vaccari, C. (2016). Accidental exposure to politics on social media as online participation equalizer in Germany, Italy, and the United Kingdom. *New Media & Society, 18*(9), 1857–1874.

Van Eimeren, B., & Frees, B. (2006). ARD/ZDF-online-studie 2006: Schnelle zugänge, neue anwendungen, neue nutzer. *Media Perspektiven, 8*, 402–415.

Vásquez, I., & Porčnik, T. (2018). *The Human Freedom Index of 162 countries in 2018.* Washington, DC: Cato Institute. Retrieved from https://www.cato.org/human-freedom-index-new

Verclas, K., & Mechael, P. (2008). *A mobile voice: The use of mobile phones in citizen media.* Retrieved from http://socialbrite.s3.amazonaws.com/A%20Mobile%20Voice-The%20Role%20of%20Mobile%20Phones%20in%20Citizen%20Media.pdf

Verkasalo, H., López-Nicolás, C., Molina-Castillo, F. J., & Bouwman, H. (2010). Analysis of users and non-users of smartphone applications. *Telematics and Informatics, 27*(3), 242–255.

Vishwanath, A. (2016). Mobile device affordance: Explicating how smartphones influence the outcome of phishing attacks. *Computers in Human Behavior, 65*(3), 198–207.

Wallis, C. (2011). New media practices in China: Youth patterns, processes, and politics. *International Journal of Communication, 5*, 406–436.

Wang, Z., Pan, S., & Qiang, Y. (2014). *Annual report on media development in Shanghai.* Shanghai: Social Sciences Press.

Watson, Z. (2017). *VR for news: The new reality?* Retrieved January 5, 2020, from https://reutersinstitute.politics.ox.ac.uk/our-research/vr-news-new-reality

Watten, R. G., Kleiven, J., Fostervold, K. I., Fauske, H., & Volden, F. (2008). Gender profiles of internet and mobile phone use among Norwegian adolescents. *Seminar. net, 4*(3). Retrieved from https://journals.hioa.no/index.php/seminar/article/view/2474

Weaver, D. H. (1980). Audience need for orientation and media effects. *Communication Research, 3*, 361–376.

Webster, J. G. (2011). The duality of media: A structurational theory of public attention. *Communication Theory, 21*(1), 43–66.

Weeks, B., & Holbert, R. (2013). Predicting dissemination of news content in social media: A focus on reception, friending, and partisanship. *Journalism & Mass Communication Quarterly, 90*(2), 212–232.

Wei, C., & Kolko, B. E. (2005, July). Studying mobile phone use in context: Cultural, political, and economic dimensions of mobile phone use. In *Proceedings of International Professional Communication Conference, 2005* (IPCC 2005, pp. 205–212). IEEE.

Wei, R. (2008). Motivations for use of the cell phone for mass communications and entertainment. *Telematics & Informatics, 25*(1), 36–46.

Wei, R. (Ed.). (2016). *Mobile media, political participation, and civic activism in Asia: Private chat to public communication.* Dordrecht: Springer.

Wei, R. (2020). Mobile media and political communication: Connect, communicate, and participate. In R. Ling, L. Fortunati, G. Goggin, & S. Lim (Eds.), *Oxford handbook of mobile communication and society.* New York: Oxford University Press.

Wei, R., Huang, J., & Zheng, P. (2018). Use of mobile social apps for public communication in China: Gratifications as antecedents of posting articles on WeChat public accounts. *Mobile Media & Communication*, 6(1), 108–126.

Wei, R., & Lo, V. (2006). Staying connected while on the move: Cell phone use and social connectedness. *New Media & Society*, 8(1), 53–72.

Wei, R., & Lo, V. (2015). News on the move: Predictors of mobile news consumption and engagement among Chinese mobile phone users. *Electronic News*, 9(3), 177–194.

Wei, R., Lo., V., Chen, Y., Tandoc, E., & Zhang, G. (2020). Press systems, freedom of the press and credibility: A comparative analysis of mobile sews in four Asian cities. *Journalism Studies*, 21(4), 530–546.Wei, R., Lo, V. H., Xu, X., Chen, Y. N. K., & Zhang, G. (2014). Predicting mobile news use among college students: The role of press freedom in four Asian cities. *New Media & Society*, 16(4), 637–654.

Weiss, A. (2013). Exploring news apps and location-based services on the smartphone. *Journalism & Mass Communication Quarterly*, 90(3), 435–456.

Wen, N., & Wei, R. (2018). Examining effects of informational use of social media platforms and social capital on civic engagement regarding genetically modified foods in China. *International Journal of Communication*, 12, 3729–3750.

Wenner, L. (1982). Gratifications sought and obtained in program discrepancy: A study of network evening news programs and "60 Minutes." *Communication Research*, 9, 539–560.

Westlund, O. (2008). From mobile phone to mobile device: News consumption on the go. *Canadian Journal of Communication*, 33(3), 443–463.

Westlund, O. (2010). New(s) functions for the mobile: A cross-cultural study. *New Media & Society*, 12(1), 91–108.

Westlund, O. (2013). Mobile news. *Digital Journalism*, 1(1), 6–26.

Westlund, O. (2015). News consumption in an age of mobile media: Patterns, people, place, and participation. *Mobile Media & Communication*, 3(2), 151–159.

Williams, R., & Edge, D. (1996). The social shaping of technology. *Policy Research*, 25(6), 865–899.

Wolak, J., & McDevitt, M. (2011). The roots of the gender gap in political knowledge in adolescence. *Political Behavior*, 33(3), 505–533.

Wolf, C., & Hohlfeld, R. (2012). Revolution in journalism? Mobile devices as a new means of publishing. In C. Martin & T. von Pape (Eds.), *Images in mobile communication*. Berlin/Hedelberg, Germany: VS Verlag fur Sozialwissenschaften.

Wolf, C., & Schnauber, A. (2015). News consumption in the mobile era: The role of mobile devices and traditional journalism's content within the user's information repertoire. *Digital Journalism*, 3(5), 759–776.

World Internet Stats. (2020). *Asia Internet usage and population statistics*. Retrieved from http://www.internetworldstats.com/stats3.html

Xu, X. (2011, July 13–17). *Comparing mobile news use among college students*. Paper presented at the annual International Association for Media, Communication and Research, Istanbul, Turkey.

Ying, C. (2010). Microblogs reshape news in China. *China Media Project*. Retrieved from http://cmp.hku.hk/2010/10/12/8021/

Yu, H. (2011). Beyond gatekeeping: J-blogging in China. *Journalism*, 12(4), 379–393.

Yu, R. (2019). Motivational or incidental? News and political information use on social media. *Chinese Journal of Communication*, 36(2), 39–79.

Zaller, J. (2003). A new standard of news quality: Burglar alarms for the monitorial citizen. *Political Communication, 20*(2), 109–130.

Zhang, H. (2013). *Media credibility of Chinese media in transition*. Nanjing, China: Nanjing Normal University Press.

Zhang, H. (2018, August 6–9). *Media credibility of Chinese media: A follow-up study*. Paper presented at the 2018 annual conference of AEJMC, Washington, DC.

Zhang, H., Zhou, S., & Shen, B. (2014). Public trust: A comprehensive investigation on perceived media credibility in China. *Asian Journal of Communication, 24*(2), 158–172.

Zhang, L., & Pentina, I. (2012). Motivations and usage patterns of Weibo. *Cyberpsychology, Behavior, and Social Networking, 15*(6), 312–317.

Zhang, X., & Ha, L. (2016). Mobile news consumption and political news interest: A time budget perspective. *Journal of Applied Journalism and Media Studies, 5*(2), 277–295.

Zhang, X., & Zheng, Y. (2009). *China's information and communications technology revolution: Social changes and state responses*. London: Routledge.

Zhao, Y. (1998). *Media, market, and democracy in China: Between the party line and the bottom line*. Champaign, IL: University of Illinois Press.

Zhou, B. (2019). Fear of missing out, feeling of acceleration, and being permanently online: A survey study of university students' use of mobile apps in China. *Chinese Journal of Communication, 12*(1), 66–83.

Zhu, J., Lo, V., Weaver, D., Chen, C., & Wu, W. (1997). Individual, organizational and societal influences on media role perceptions: A comparative study of journalists in China, Taiwan and the United States. *Journalism and Mass Communication Quarterly, 74*(1), 84–96.

INDEX